Organizational Culture *in* Action

A Cultural Analysis Workbook

Gerald W. Driskill
University of Arkansas, Little Rock

Angela Laird Brenton
University of Arkansas, Little Rock

SAGE Publications
Thousand Oaks ■ London ■ New Delhi

For information:

Sage Publications, Inc.
2455 Teller Road
Thousand Oaks, California 91320
E-mail: order@sagepub.com

Sage Publications Ltd.
1 Oliver's Yard
55 City Road
London EC1Y 1SP
United Kingdom

Sage Publications India Pvt. Ltd.
B-42, Panchsheel Enclave
Post Box 4109
New Delhi 110 017 India

Printed in the United States of America.

Library of Congress Cataloging-in-Publication Data

Driskill, Gerald W.
Organizational culture in action: a cultural analysis workbook /
Gerald W. Driskill, Angela Laird Brenton.
    p. cm.
Includes bibliographical references and index.
    ISBN 1-4129-0560-5 (pbk.)
1. Organizational behavior. I. Brenton, Angela Laird. II. Title.
HD58.7.D77 2005
302.3'5—dc22

                                                        2004019618

This book is printed on acid-free paper.

05   06   07   08   09   10   9   8   7   6   5   4   3   2   1

Senior Acquisitions Editor:	Todd R. Armstrong
Editorial Assistant:	Deya Saoud
Production Editor:	Tracy Alpern
Copy Editor:	Kristin Bergstad
Typesetter:	C&M Digitals (P) Ltd.
Indexer:	Gloria Tierney
Cover Designer:	Glenn Vogel

Contents

Preface   ix

Acknowledgments   xi

Part I: Cultural Analysis Planning   1

1. **Introduction: Setting the Stage**   3
   Objective: Understand the pervasiveness
   of organizations in our lives, the goal of
   cultural analysis, and how to select an
   organization for analysis.
   Rehearsal 1.1 Determining Your
        Purposes for a Cultural Analysis   9
   Rehearsal 1.2 Identifying an Organization   10
   Rehearsal 1.3 Method Acting and Getting Real   13

2. **The Significance of the Stage**   15
   Objective: Understand the value of a cultural
   analysis and the major steps in the process.
   Rehearsal 2.1 Creativity and Constraint   18
   Rehearsal 2.2 The Value of a Cultural Analysis   20
   Rehearsal 2.3 The Value of Writing a Culture Article   22

Part II: Cultural Analysis Basics   25

3. **Step One: Understanding the**
   Concept of Culture: Constructing the Set   27
   Objective: Understand the concept of culture and
   the significance of different images and metaphors
   for organizations.
   Rehearsal 3.1 How Do You Define Culture?   32
   Rehearsal 3.2 Playing With Metaphors   33
   Rehearsal 3.3 Writing a Cultural Analysis Proposal   36

4. **Step Two: Identifying**
   Cultural Elements: Understanding Roles   37
   Objective: Understand the major cultural
   elements as a template for identifying a
   variety of types of cultural data.
   Rehearsal 4.1 Exploring Web Sites   55

Rehearsal 4.2 Getting More From Our Stories   57
Rehearsal 4.3 A Game of Metaphors   60

Part III: Cultural Data Collection and Interpretation   **63**

An Introduction to Step Three:
Use Multiple Methods for Gathering
Cultural Information: Method Acting   **64**
Objective: Learn the importance of using multiple
data collection methods.
Rehearsal III.1 Introduction to Method
Acting: The Last Time I Was Wrong   68
Rehearsal III.2 Sample Informed Consent Form   71

5. **Method Acting: Observation**   **73**
Objective: Understand the basics
of improving the way we observe culture.
Rehearsal 5.1 A Potpourri of
Things to Observe in Cultural Analysis   82
Rehearsal 5.2 Alien Culture Observation   84
Rehearsal 5.3 Note-Taking Guidelines   86

6. **Method Acting: Interviews and Surveys**   **88**
Objective: Learn to use interviews to gathering
cultural data.
Rehearsal 6.1 Sample Interview
Questions for "Reading" a Culture   97
Rehearsal 6.2 Alien Culture Interviews/Surveys   101

7. **Method Acting: Textual Analysis**   **103**
Objective: Understand the basics of conducting an
analysis of cultural artifacts.
Rehearsal 7.1 Selecting Texts for Analysis   105
Rehearsal 7.2 Content Analysis   110
Rehearsal 7.3 Critical Linguistic Analysis   110

8. **Step Four: Synthesizing and Interpreting**
Cultural Data: Getting Inside the Character   **113**
Objective: Develop your interpretation of the
culture through data synthesis and interpretation.
Rehearsal 8.1 Finding a Theme   118
Rehearsal 8.2 A Practice Stage   121
Rehearsal 8.3 Reliability/Validity Check   123
Rehearsal 8.4 Cultural Analysis Write-Up Guides   124

Part IV: Cultural Analysis Application   **127**

An Introduction to Step Five:
Identifying Applications for Cultural Analysis   **128**

9. **Casting Against Type: Diversity**   **131**
Objective: Tie the larger framework of national and
organizational cultures to the issues of managing
diverse organizations.

Rehearsal 9.1 Are You a Privileged
    Member of Your Organizational Culture? 136
Rehearsal 9.2 Diversity Survey 140

10. Improvisation: Managing Change **144**
Objective: Introduce a model
for managing cultural change.
    Rehearsal 10.1 Forces Driving Change 145
    Rehearsal 10.2 Cultural Approach to Change 149
    Rehearsal 10.3 Adapting
       Change Messages to the Culture 155
    Rehearsal 10.4 A Change Plan 157
    Rehearsal 10.5 A Change Case 157

11. An Honest Portrayal: Ethics **160**
Objective: Provide a framework
for understanding and addressing
the ethical challenges organizations face.
    Rehearsal 11.1 Applying the
       Economizing Value Tension 164
    Rehearsal 11.2 Applying the
       Power Aggrandizement Value Tension 165
    Rehearsal 11.3 Applying the
       Ecologizing Value Tension 166
    Rehearsal 11.4 Other Value Tensions 168
    Rehearsal 11.5 Ethics and
       Communication Leadership 169

12. The Director's Chair: Symbolic Leadership **170**
Objective: Understand the role of
the manager in meaning management.
    Rehearsal 12.1 Assessing Yourself as a Leader 182
    Rehearsal 12.2 Case Study of Cultural Leadership 184

13. Reading Reviews: Organizational Effectiveness **186**
Objective: Connect Chapter 1 discussions on the
significance of culture to issues of effectiveness.
    Rehearsal 13.1 How Do
       You Measure Effectiveness? 188
    Rehearsal 13.2 Finding the
       Drawbacks of the Best Fit 190
    Rehearsal 13.3 Gauging Effectiveness 193

14. Opening Night: Conclusion **194**
Objective: Provide an application
template for interpreting and applying
the data collected in the process.
    Rehearsal 14.1 Action Plan for
       Professional Communication Development 196
    Rehearsal 14.2 Organizational
       Development Action Plan 200

Appendix: Example Student Analysis   207

References   219

Index   224

About the Authors   228

Preface

In 1984, Angi Brenton, PhD, introduced a course on Organizational Culture to the graduate students in the Masters of Interpersonal and Organizational Communication at the University of Arkansas at Little Rock. Her students came from a wide array of organizations (high tech to medical to industry) and positions in those organizations (management to HRD to entry-level employees). This same array of students continued to participate in the Organizational Culture course when Gerald Driskill, PhD, began to teach the course in 1994. Over time, our approach to working with these students resulted in this application-focused workbook.

The workbook is a hands-on approach to learning to "read" organizational cultures and using that cultural knowledge in symbolic management, training, organizational change, building effective teams, supporting diversity, and unleashing creativity. It also serves as an introduction to qualitative research methods, introducing students to field observation, interviewing, qualitative surveys, content analysis, and other methods of textual analysis.

Students have consistently commented on the practical and powerful nature of the approach outlined in this workbook for their professional lives. We have developed this text as an applied workbook to supplement and apply organizational theory. It answers the two central questions we always hear from our students: "How can I understand the intangible culture that is so important to working in an organization?" and "How can I use this cultural information once I understand it?"

We are convinced that the application of this text could help new managers shorten their learning curves and avoid costly mistakes, while understanding the power of strategic symbolic managerial performances in creating identification and values. It could help the new MBA to choose a company consistent with her values rather than realizing after 6 months she "just doesn't fit here." It will reinforce to the training and development director the importance of storytelling in organizational socialization. It will equip those seeking organizational change to understand ways in which change must happen through the culture to be effective.

We believe the value of this workbook can be seen by viewing life in organizations as analogous to a theater company. For actors to truly appreciate their roles and have maximum effectiveness, they need to "go backstage" or get behind the performances observed onstage. Just having a script is not enough. To create an effective performance, actors must determine appropriate and effective ways to perform their roles. To craft an effective performance, the actor must explore within himself as well as exploring the script and the character through various means. The "organizational drama" may leave a new organization member with many questions about why certain things are done, what certain actions mean, or why certain actors gain power while others do not. The answers to these questions are often found "backstage" in unarticulated organizational values and norms. The study of organizational culture provides the backstage experience needed to understand appropriate and effective organizational performances.

In a similar vein, to become a director, you must go beyond an understanding of a given actor's role or script. To produce an effective performance, not only must directors bring the troupe together as a team, but they must also be aware of previous performances and various options for interpreting the play. Organizational leaders face the same challenges of understanding the role of history and heroes in shaping the current organization, of understanding how members interpret actions and statements, and of understanding the interpretations of the same event drawn by members of organizational subcultures. Understanding culture is critical for the organizational leader.

We each participate in multiple organizations, and that participation demands the art and skill of interpretation and presentation, of making sense of what is going on around us and then determining what messages we need to construct in response. We want you to complete this workbook with an increased awareness of the value of cultural concepts. Yet we also want you to be able to transform theories into practice. To reach these goals, we have integrated a variety of activities for application. Neither of us uses all of the suggested activities; we encourage you to select activities based on your needs and interests.

Acknowledgments

Those who made this workbook a reality easily come to mind. For any names we omitted, we accept the blame and ask your forgiveness.

- Our students, who have journeyed with us in learning about culture, refining methods for teaching it, and sharing with us ways they have applied what they learned in their organizations
- Alumni of our course, Lyle Steward, Amy Amy, Pat Sweeden, and Patricia Hawkins-Sweeden for their frequent guest appearances in the course; and thanks to Amy Amy and Lara Keck-Schock for allowing us to use their cultural analysis paper
- Applause to graduate program alumni who provided rich feedback via a survey that further shaped this workbook: Debbie West, Robert Mock, Michelle Young, Pat Sweeden, Patricia Hawkins-Sweeden, Jane Martin, Sherrie Sandor, Cheryl Johnston, Elaine Wooten, Martha Lowry, Tracy Pleasants, Wanda Culbreath, Hope Coleman, Brenda Winston, Lisa Rawn, and Michael Strobel
- Current faculty in the Speech Communication Department who motivate us to aim for excellence in the scholarship of teaching: Mike Hemphill, Linda Pledger, Carol Thompson, Rob Ulmer, Yong-Jin Song, Alex Lyon, and Avinash Thombre; and faculty emeritus who passed on a legacy of passion for students: Alan Ward, Jerry Butler, John Gray, and Ralph Eubanks
- Reviewers of various drafts who encouraged us to develop this project: John Gribas, Phil Clampitt, John Meyer, and Linda Putnam
- Writers and colleagues who have shaped and enriched our thinking with their contributions to the study of interpretive approaches to organizational communication: Chuck Bantz, Lee Bolman, George Cheney, Charles Conrad, Terry Deal, Stan Deetz, Eric Eisenberg, Buddy Goodall, Allan Kennedy, Bob McPhee, Nick O'Donnell-Trujillo, Mike Pacanowsky, Linda Putnam, M. Scott Poole, Patti Riley, Linda Smircich, and Karl Weick
- To our common mentor, colleague, and friend for his support during our KU days and beyond, Cal Downs
- To you, the colleague, student, and/or practitioner, for what you will contribute to your organizations and to the dialogue over improving life in organizations

PART I

Cultural
Analysis Planning

1

Introduction

Setting the Stage

All the world's a stage,
And all the men and women merely players:
They have their exits and their entrances;
And one man in his time plays many parts. . . .

Shakespeare, 1564–1616,
As You Like It, Burchell (Ed.), 1954, p. 42

Objectives:

- Understand the pervasiveness of organizations in our lives
- Learn the goal of cultural analysis
- Apply guides for selecting an organization for analysis

Stage Terms:

- Organizational culture
- Cultural analysis
- Organization
- Organizational performance

Cradle to Grave

Our first experiences in organizations were like many of yours: Bright lights and masked strangers welcomed us into a hospital birthing room. Since that time, we have lived, breathed, laughed and cried, worked or consulted with, and dreamed and been bored in a wide array of organizations from business offices, advertising agencies, nonprofits, universities, prisons, and day cares. Beyond the myriad examples of tragic and comic tales we could each tell from our experiences as employees, we also have countless stories from our experiences as customers, volunteers, and patients. The point is clear—we cannot escape an inextricable connection with organizations. Yet we easily take for granted the impact of organizations, the very stages on which we live out our lives. We know when to show up, we know when something goes wrong with a piece of equipment or a relationship, but we rarely see the big picture of how all the various aspects of the stage impact us. The purpose of this workbook is to equip us to create more competent organizational performance by understanding the impact of organizational culture.

> *Organizations are places that carry us from cradle to grave by shaping our sense of identity, role, and meaning in life.*

In the years that have passed since the startling birth experience, we have come to believe that organizations are no more and no less than a significant stage for human drama. Our research on cultures in hospitals, engineering firms, churches, banks, airlines, phone companies, schools, and day care centers and our service experiences in hospitals, multinationals, and nursing homes have all underscored our conviction that organizations are far more than the places where we work and make money. They are places that carry us from "the cradle to the grave" by shaping our sense of identity, role, and meaning in life.

Thus, while our motivation to study organizations began with a pragmatic sense that our livelihoods depended on being able to work in organizations, a deeper, more fundamental concern has emerged. We want to improve our ability to shape and direct organizations in ways that are more humane. We believe such an effort to be fundamental to practitioners, scholars, teachers, and students, but more importantly as participants in the human drama. The goal of this workbook, therefore, is not simply to teach you how to conduct a cultural analysis, but it has implications for your role as a change agent within an organization and within your community. One goal is a heightened awareness of what we all have done for many years in an unconscious way. In short, the workbook is designed to help you do better what you do almost everyday—make decisions about the best ways to lead and communicate in your organization(s). The quality of such decisions is enhanced through understanding the heart of this workbook—conducting a cultural analysis.

FAQs on Cultural Analysis

Stage setting involves paying attention to the scenery and props used to identify the location of a dramatic production. This chapter sets the stage by clarifying the approach we take in this workbook. While the remaining chapters provide greater depth on the "how to" of understanding and improving organizational performances, our goal here is to respond to six common questions about the major approach and features of this workbook. As you review our responses to these questions you should gain a clearer sense of the process of cultural analysis, as well as criteria to consider in selecting an organization.

1. What Do You Mean by Organizational Culture?

We provide a more thorough definition in Chapter 3; however, each organization has a unique way of doing things. Just as each national culture or civilization has its own unique language, artifacts, values, celebrations, heroes, history, and norms, each organization is unique in these same ways. At a deeper level, [organization members create and/or are indoctrinated into unique beliefs and assumptions that form the basis for acting together.] These beliefs and assumptions may operate at a conscious level. Basic assumptions such as those about human nature and human relations are more likely to operate at the unconscious level. For example, I might just assume that supervisors make decisions and employees carry them out without ever consciously questioning that assumption.

When actors understand the history, norms, and values of a group, they can become a true ensemble cast by coordinating their actions more effectively with others'. They can also understand the symbolic significance of events and actions in a more thorough way and identify the many subcultures that together form and shape the overall organizational culture.

2. Just What Do You Mean by a Cultural Analysis?

Just as anthropologists immerse themselves in a foreign culture to understand it, [students of organizational culture use many of the same methods to understand an organization's culture.] For example, they systematically observe artifacts and interactions, analyze written documents, participate in rites and rituals, and interview culture members about the meanings they attach to organizational objects and events. Interestingly, actors use many of the same techniques of observation, interviewing, and analyzing scripts in the process of crafting a credible and compelling performance on the stage or in film.

One way to gain clarity about the organizational cultural analysis process is to use analogies: to make connections between the familiar and the unfamiliar, the known to the unknown. One organizational culture class participant said that the cultural analysis process was like the *Wheel of Fortune* television game. In that game, participants have to fill in the missing letters of a phrase based on a clue from the moderator. If participants guess too early and get it wrong, they are penalized by losing a turn. And of course, if they guess too late, they risk losing to other contestants willing to take a risk. The challenge is to have enough information about the word puzzle to make a credible interpretation. In the same way, if you attempt a definitive interpretation of a culture too early in the process, you may pay the price of misunderstanding the culture. We also recognize that, at some point, you have enough data for a realistic (although not perfect) cultural interpretation, and you need to move ahead to application. We agree with the need to balance thoroughness with timely application, and you will learn in this workbook a process of cultural analysis that emphasizes careful reflection on cultural data combined with application. We have identified two different analogies as a way to clarify the process and to encourage you to move systematically through the five cultural analysis steps outlined in this workbook.

Gerald's Analogy: The Atom. This analysis process appears to be like an atom. The main point of this analogy is that through the cultural analysis process we focus on communication behaviors that give rise to culture and shape culture. Three major parallels between the atom and cultural analysis are worth mentioning. First, the important elements of this cultural analysis process, like an atom, are invisible. We are dealing with constructs like culture and therefore we will be introducing images, models, along the way to help us understand a dynamic force. It will be critical to ground our ideas and discussions in visible aspects of reality while at the same time recognizing that we will never fully see subatomic realities or the forces that hold atoms together. In short, culture is elusive.

Second, like an atom, the invisible nature of such constructs as culture does not take away from their power or influence. We know that if we do not understand the forces that shape and influence our behavior, we are unlikely to have as much influence in making changes we see as needed. For example, as we will explore further in Chapter 10, certain cultural values can have a restrictive force on minorities or anyone not aware of the subtleties of culture. In short, what we are unaware of can hurt us. The process of writing and speaking about our own organizational cultures is a powerful one. In a sense, as we tell and retell and reframe our cultural stories, we will be splitting the nucleus of the atom in that we will be examining the core, central defining element of human existence, our use of symbol.

Third, an atom is defined by its components (the relative weight of protons, electrons, etc.). The process of cultural analysis will also take shape as we define cultural elements. While we will not assign atomic weights to cultural protons and electrons, we will take time to examine a finite set of components (e.g., rules, rituals, values) that influence our organizational communication. We will also examine the powerful forces binding these elements together in a whole that is more than a sum of its parts. Chapter 4 provides a discussion of each of these elements of culture and encourages you to identify them in your organization. In all, the atomic analogy mirrors communication theories like structuration that stress the role of culture as a communicative process and our role as participating in shaping culture (Giddens, 1979).

Angi's Analogy: The Jigsaw Puzzle. The cultural analysis is similar to putting together a complex jigsaw puzzle without having a picture on the box to guide your efforts. The point of this analogy is to understand the tensions between seeing parts versus the whole and to appreciate the impact the process has on the person doing the analysis. This metaphor applies in several ways:

First, it is often difficult to get a sense of the big picture when you are looking at individual pieces. Only after you have assembled a number of segments can you start to get an idea of the picture the puzzle will create.

Second, it takes both dark and bright pieces in most cases to assemble a complete puzzle. I recently read a story of a young girl who secretly stole pieces of a puzzle her family was assembling and hid them under the sofa cushion because they were so ugly. In frustration, her family began to despair of ever being able to put the puzzle together because so many pieces were missing. Only when the girl provided the dark pieces could the entire picture be revealed. Sometimes in our cultural analysis it is tempting to linger on the positive stories and upbeat images. They rarely form the complete picture. Sometimes you must provide the dark elements to understand the complete culture. Critical theorists such as Mumby (1993); Deetz (1991); and Deetz, Tracy, and Simpson (2000) have encouraged this phase of analysis.

Finally, the process of putting together the puzzle is often as important as the finished product. The mental exercise of seeing connections, of developing creativity, and of growing in patience and discipline will develop the puzzle builder even if the particular puzzle is not a particularly useful one. Chapter 8 guides you through this process of interpretation of cultural data.

Unlike puzzles, which have a set order and only one way for all of the parts to fit together, cultural analysis is a complex and interpretive pursuit. Four different people sitting around a table would see the picture from different perspectives and develop similar but varying pictures, and each of those constructions would have degrees of validity and usefulness for understanding the organization.

3. What Is an Organization?

Okay, you may not be asking this, but maybe you should. The boundaries and membership of organizations are not always as cut and dried as they may appear. For example, who counts as a member of a professional sports team? Only the athletes, cheerleaders, and coaches? Team physicians who may be members of a medical practice but travel with the team on weekends? What about the die-hard fans who come to every game and may have a 50-year history of following a team? A significant decision you will face is who "counts" as an organization member and where you want to draw your boundaries of the organization. There are no single correct answers for all the questions posed above. For some purposes, a researcher might want to define an organization more narrowly by focusing primarily on employees, while for other purposes an expanded view that includes organizational stakeholders might be more appropriate.

4. What Is the End Goal of the Process?

Comments from practitioners who have applied this cultural analysis process provide examples of how they have used the cultural insights.

- I now have the ability to see situations from different frames.
- I got my last job because the interviewer was intrigued by my answers about organizational culture and how quickly I could "read" the organization.
- I have improved my ability to apply theory to the real world.
- I saved myself a lot of time and energy by deciding during an interview process that I didn't fit the culture. Even though the salary was great, I would have become frustrated quickly.
- I have gained a better understanding of my organization and the steps involved in a cultural analysis.

- Seeing how I impact an organization. It was a little upsetting to see how I could have made more of a positive difference. I wish I had known last fall what I know now.
- I have learned that in any organization, change must start with me.

While you may not make one of these statements, we are confident that anyone completing this process will learn how to conduct a cultural analysis. You will also be taken through an application section that allows you to develop links between your analysis and organizational effectiveness, diversity, change management, symbolic leadership, and ethics. We included these application chapters because many students question how culture relates to organizational effectiveness. We are convinced that culture gives a new and distinct lens through which to view organizational processes such as change, leadership, and the encouragement of diversity. We are confident that as a result of this workbook, you can become a more competent and assured actor in your organization, better able to understand and question basic organizational assumptions and practices.

5. What Is in This Workbook?

The workbook is organized around *five major steps* for the conduct of a cultural analysis. These steps are reviewed in the next chapter and provide the skeleton for this text. You will be taken through background material on the concept of culture before covering the basics of data collection, interpretation, and application. The major chapters share in common the following features:

- *Stage Terms:* At the start of each chapter we list important terms and concepts covered in the chapter. The reader may want to pay special attention to definitions and explanations of these terms contained in the chapter.

- *Connections:* In sections labeled "Connections" we assist the reader in making connections between theories and constructs and organizational practice by extended examples.

- *Rehearsals:* A variety of case studies and other activities are designed for hands-on experience with concepts. We incorporated activities that we have found enriching for workshop participants and students. You will find these activities in Rehearsal boxes in the workbook as well at the ends of most chapters.

Each of the chapters builds toward a final project of analyzing an organizational culture in depth. You may want to analyze your own organization to understand its culture more fully, or you may want to practice your skills by choosing an organization of which you are not a member, or only a tangential part. Each choice has advantages and disadvantages.

6. How Do I Select an Organization for a Cultural Analysis?

There are a variety of factors to consider in selecting an organization. First and foremost, much depends on your goals for a cultural analysis. Use the following Rehearsal to determine your goals:

Rehearsal 1.1 Determining Your Purposes for a Cultural Analysis

Check any of the following purposes that describe your reasons for conducting an organizational cultural analysis:

_____ Learn cultural analysis skills for work as a consultant

_____ Gain insight into another type of organization for career development

_____ Develop insight as a new employee to move up in your organization

_____ Learn to use cultural data to be a more effective leader in your own organization

_____ Identify ways to serve community organizations through knowledge of their respective cultures

_____ Learn about a different culture in an organization similar to your own to compare and contrast

_____ Other reason: _____

Your answers to these questions should influence your decision to do an analysis or audit as an "insider," a person who works for the organization you analyze, or as an "outsider," one who comes to the organization as a stranger. To facilitate your decision, we have outlined the pros and cons associated with each role.

As you reflect on your goals in light of the relative advantages and disadvantages of insider/outsider roles, realize that that these options may be viewed more as a continuum. Your relative knowledge and experience with an organization should be weighed. For example, in your own workplace, you may be new to the organization and/or industry, thus your knowledge of the culture and ability to work with the culture are far different from someone with extensive knowledge or experience. On the other hand, outside of the workplace, you may be a relative insider as a volunteer for the Arthritis Foundation or a church organization. You may also be somewhat of an insider due to weekly visits to a favorite restaurant or health club. Farther down the continuum toward being an outsider, you may have never worked for GM, but you have worked for another major auto company, and thus know something of the basic aspects of this industry. You may have read widely about a given industry, but have yet to visit an actual site. And then there are organizations that are completely alien to your world—you have heard of high-tech companies but have not read about, visited, or studied one.

The key in examining the pros and cons of the "insider" versus "outsider" perspective is more complex, and perhaps your decision ultimately comes down to your immediate and/or long-range goals for developing this skill set. We have found value, as have our students and workshop participants, in engaging in a cultural analysis with goals ranging from "becoming a consultant," to "learning the ropes as a newcomer," to "enhancing the way one serves in the community." Regardless of your decision, the steps we outline will guide you in gaining valuable experience in conducting an analysis.

Rehearsal 1.2 Identifying an Organization

Purpose: Identify organizations that you might make the focus of an analysis.

Steps:

1. Review the pluses and minuses of being an insider versus an outsider in the cultural analysis process in Table 1.1.

2. Consider an organization you might serve as an outsider/consultant and then list the top three reasons it would be advantageous to the organization for you to serve in this role.

Organization: _____

_____

_____

_____

3. Consider an organization you might serve as an insider and then list the top three reasons it would be advantageous to the organization for you to serve in this role.

Organization: _____

_____

_____

_____

Table 1.1

As an Insider in the Organization	
Advantages	*Disadvantages*
Ease of access	Lack of perceived freedom for analysis
Personal communication insights	Bias due to being enmeshed in the culture; start with hidden assumptions
Potential value to your own organization	Too familiar, thus "see less," ask fewer questions
Time—ease of data collection	People don't explain things to you the same way they would to an outsider

As an Outsider to the Organization	
Advantages	*Disadvantages*
Insights for career development	May misinterpret some cultural data
Skills for "newcomer" socialization	Access to the organization
Less familiar, thus "see more"	Time outside of job to collect data
See the more obvious layers of the culture	

The Value of Reflection and Critical Insight

This workbook will have the greatest value to readers willing to shift from going through the motions of acting on stage without reflection and critical cultural insight to full engagement in the production. Competent leadership in organizations involves going backstage; that is, active reflection on the cultural forces that shape communication practices. The steps previewed in the next chapter reflect a process that we all participate in each day. For instance, we decide what and how and when to communicate in our organizations; we decide what changes in organizational practices we can and/or should encourage or discourage; and we determine what changes we believe we are empowered or powerless to introduce. Perhaps most critical of all, we make decisions whether to reflect on our communication or remain somewhat unconscious of our influence in an organization. In all, we share in common the fact that our communication behavior is based on interpretive processes that we take for granted.

These day-in and day-out taken-for-granted interpretive processes are based on our informal "data collection" about our organizations (e.g., norms, what is allowed, what is expected, how to communicate, whom to communicate with). Based on our interpretations of these data, we act and react. Before reading this workbook, you may never have considered yourself someone who collected and used cultural data, or thought of yourself as an actor on an organizational stage. However, you may have heard a story about a recent firing and wondered if all the details were true. You may have read a staff development workbook and been left wondering why no one seemed to follow the suggestions on career paths in the organization.

Or you may have heard during a performance evaluation that no one else was having trouble with clients like "you are," and found yourself wondering about the norm: "Am I really that bad?" When faced with the mysteries or uncertainties embedded in these types of questions, we may become more aware of unspoken or unwritten rules and values in an organization.

This workbook assumes that we can always improve the quality of the data we collect and the accuracy of our interpretations, as well as our organizational communication performances in response to these data. As you move through this workbook, we hope you will be reminded of what we observe each time we cover this material in the classroom, in a training, or consultation—how and why we communicate in our organizations matters. To follow Shakespeare's well-worn analogy, our challenge is to be on the stage not merely as players or actors, but also as co-directors and producers of the communication practices in our organizations.

> *We can always improve both the quality of the data we collect as well as our communication performances in response to these data.*

Summary

1. An organizational culture involves the unique ways of doing things in an organization that are best captured by such elements of culture as the history, norms, and values of a group.

2. A cultural analysis involves improving on methods we use each day in our organizations—we observe, ask questions for understanding, and read various documents such as newsletters. In the process of analysis we not only gain insight about the organization, but may also improve our ability for effective communication.

3. How we define an organization is based on the boundaries of the membership. You will need to make a decision in the organization you analyze about who is considered a member, which may entail a narrow (employees, management) or a broad (customers, stakeholders, etc.) definition.

4. The end goal of the process is to learn how to conduct a cultural analysis and make application of this analysis to critical aspects of organizational life such as ethics, change, and diversity.

5. This workbook will help you understand the concept of culture as well as the basics of data collection, interpretation, and application. Pay attention to the key organizing features of the book: *Stage Terms*, to introduce relevant theories and concepts; *Connections*, to aid your understanding of concepts; and *Rehearsals*, both within the chapters and at the end of chapters to aid you in application.

6. You should have a clear sense of how to select an organization for a cultural analysis based on the pros and cons of being an insider versus an outsider.

Rehearsal 1.3 Method Acting and Getting Real

Purpose: To reflect on your expectations concerning the process of conducting a cultural analysis in order to identify beliefs that may help or hinder your progress.

Overview: Method acting is a term that captures a major approach to training actors (Vineberg, 1991). At the core of this method is active observation of the real and genuine emotion (or mining the real experiences of the actor or actress). Strasberg (1987), the major proponent of this method in the United States, notes that the procedures for developing an actor's capacity are "equally, if not more, necessary for the layman" (p. 201). This activity is designed to apply method acting concepts to your own work in the cultural analysis process. In short, the more you are real with your own reactions and emotions concerning the process, the more you will be able to overcome hurdles to making it a valuable experience.

Steps:

1. Briefly list two or three of your own initial reactions to this first chapter. What was clear? Unclear? What appeared promising for your own application? What emotions, if any, did this chapter evoke in you?

   _____

   _____

   _____

   _____

   _____

   _____

2. Have you had a previous positive experience with cultural analysis? What happened? What was your reaction?

   _____

   _____

(Continued)

(Continued)

_____

_____

_____

_____

2. Have you had a previous negative experience with
   cultural analysis? What happened? What was your
   reaction?

   _____

   _____

   _____

   _____

   _____

3. What will need to happen for you to have a positive, ful-
   filling experience in learning about conducting a cultural
   analysis? In particular, what concerns do you have?
   Questions?

   _____

   _____

   _____

   _____

   _____

   _____

2

The Significance of the Stage

Most anyone entering an unfamiliar work setting knows the feeling of being an outsider. . . . Real wisdom in such situations means recognizing that the unspoken is more powerful than what can be conveyed through speaking. One gradually gains a sense of the feel, the smell, the personality of a workplace, a way of working, or a kind of work—though it may be difficult to translate all of this into words that an outsider could grasp.

—Louis, "Perspectives on Organizational Culture," 1985, p. 27

Objectives:

- Appreciate the value of a cultural analysis
- Learn the five major steps in the process

Stage Terms:

- Construct
- Culture
- Structuration

The Tales We Could Tell

We all have stories about a wide array of experiences in organizations. These tales reveal the good, the bad, and the ugly about life in organizations. These stories prompt laughter and tears, meaning and confusion, love and hate, hope and fear. We have all been told and listened to stories mirroring these ranges of experiences. From mundane frustrations over time schedules, to anguish in dealing with a difficult boss, coworker, employee, and/or customer, to fears over a change being introduced, one theme common in organizational stories relates to the challenges placed on our communication abilities.

In order to gain a new perspective on our experiences in organizations, to shed light on the good, bad, and ugly found in our stories, we developed this workbook. In this chapter we introduce our personal hopes for you in this process, some background history on the study of organizational culture, the value of cultural analysis, and the major steps in the process.

Any Hope of Change?

Unfortunately, theory is not always translated in a way that will assist us with the range of difficulties listed above. It is not uncommon to hear the following complaint against theory: *I don't see how this theory helps my life now!* In the midst of reading, reflecting, and theorizing about organizational communication, we have been asked fair and challenging questions like the following:

- Is all of this work of analysis really worth it?
- How can I apply the cultural information I'm learning?
- Can a cultural analysis really help me bring change to my organization?
- Given the ingrained nature of communication habits, is it realistic to expect change in myself or in the organization?

Our reply to such questions continues to be the same: If we were to say no, then we would see the need to give up not only on the teaching enterprise, but on the human experience as well. As educators and as human beings, we hold an optimistic view of the human condition, that we are all capable of change and growth. As far as personal changes go, we have had the good fortune and blessing of witnessing changes not only in our communication behavior, but also in others as a result of courses and workshops that use the learning approach presented here. However, for this workbook to work, for any development in our communication abilities to happen, we have to be willing to play 100%. Organizational change is also possible. Many change efforts fail because they are undertaken without sufficient knowledge of the nature or importance of organizational culture. We note throughout the text that knowledge of culture is essential for significant organizational change.

While we *affirm that change is possible*, it is often difficult and uncomfortable. We have developed habitual ways of acting and reacting. Changing ingrained habits in any area, whether it is nail biting, reactions in conflict, a golf slice or tennis serve, is not easy. Often in the change process we get worse before we get better because the new behavior seems unnatural. Our old response was unconscious, and in contrast we must think constantly about the new behavior. Only in time does the new behavior fade into the comfortable, taken-for-granted. Strasberg (1987) comments on the basic premise of method acting—that to create a performance that seems natural and unpracticed takes many hours of practice and preparation. He writes, "The preparation of every art must be conscious—you know how and what you are going to do. Don't trust your inspiration. . . . Then being trained in the method do it to the best of your ability. Conscious preparation, unconscious result" (p. 79). So while this workbook will provide the tools for change, ultimately we realize that it takes a longer period for the new behaviors and habits of interpreting and developing messages, and organizational change strategies to take root. The significance of the construct called "organizational culture" is that it can aid in this change process.

We also provide a number of other applications of cultural knowledge in addition to change—symbolic leadership, diversity, ethics, and organizational effectiveness. We believe that cultural knowledge can help you choose the right job, can help you become socialized in an organization, and can help you as a leader in understanding the motivations and values of your employees.

A Bit of History

We recognize that culture is a *construct*—a term or concept used to explain events or various phenomena. A construct is "a theoretical creation that is based on observation, but cannot be observed directly or indirectly" (Babbie, 2001, p. 21). Culture, like other constructs (e.g., personality, intelligence, motivation, climate, attitude), has value if it helps us make sense of our world. Thus, as we discuss this construct, it is important to understand that the term has its own story to tell.

Culture became a buzzword in the late 1970s and the 1980s and continues to appear in the popular and research literature (Deal & Kennedy, 2000; Eisenberg & Riley, 2001; Frost, Moore, Louis, Lundberg, & Martin, 1985; Kotter & Heskett, 1992; Pacanowsky & O'Donnell-Trujillo, 1982; Schein, 1992; Stohl, 2001). The continued use of this construct suggests that it is not merely a fad but that its explanatory value is likely to continue. Culture appears to be something almost every organizational member recognizes as important. Our goal is to refine our understanding of this construct and reconstruct it so that we can best use it in the actual conduct of an organizational cultural analysis.

Pacanowsky and O'Donnell-Trujillo (1982) introduced communication scholars to the concept of organizational culture, although the notion of interpretive studies emerged in the social sciences in the 1970s. Their basic premise was that organizations needed to be studied as cultures of interest for their own sake: as places where we "gossip, joke, knife one another, initiate romantic involvements, cue new employees to ways of doing the least amount of work that still avoids hassles from a supervisor, talk sports, arrange picnics" (p. 116). Pacanowsky and O'Donnell-Trujillo (1983) recognized the explicit link between cultural competence and the metaphor of acting in their article, "Organizational Communication as Cultural Performance."

Although few managers would welcome the study of their organization as simply an interesting phenomenon, the pragmatic value of interpreting the culture of an organization has caused a tide of interest in the concept. Descriptive studies of organizations capture insights into communication practices that might otherwise go unnoticed. For example, Mary Helen Brown (1990) described a typology of stories told by employees to socialize new employees in a nursing home. That typology might be used in future studies to determine the effectiveness of various narrative techniques in socialization. More recently Meares, Oetzel, Torres, Derkacs, and Ginossar (2004) examined employee stories of mistreatment in the workplace. Although the study was descriptive, it has clear implications for organizational strategies to treat all employees with respect and dignity. In addition, the researchers suggest strategies for employees to "gain voice" to resist unjust treatment.

Furthermore, a cultural analysis may provide insight into communication patterns that have proved frustrating. Most of us, for example, could tell stories of dealing with a management dictate that makes little sense. We may feel trapped by a culture and constrained in our communication choices. As Scott Adams (1996), the creator of the *Dilbert* cartoon, illustrates, a business plan has two steps: (a) "gather information" and (b) "ignore it" (p. 162). While we may find humor in frustrated *Dilbert* characters dealing with meaningless business plans, none of us likes to be in those roles. The power of analyzing a culture is that new options might emerge that had not been seen. For instance, employees might find that a cultural ritual had been so engrained and unconscious that it had blinded them to more effective ways to interact.

Rehearsal 2.1 Creativity and Constraint

1. Describe a "taken-for-granted" practice in your organization.

2. How was/is this practice created through interaction?

3. How does it constrain future interaction?

Example: In most classrooms, teachers are in an authoritarian role. They direct interaction in the classroom setting, and the students (for the most part) sit passively in attention and obey directions given by the instructor. This pattern of authority is created through interaction. Each class that the teacher and students have enacted over their educational careers has reinforced the authoritarian role of the teacher and the submissive role of students to the point that most students wouldn't think of violating the expectations or enacting a different kind of role. This pattern constrains more egalitarian roles in the classroom. Many students would resist behavior by a teacher asking them to take a more active role in setting their own educational goals and taking responsibility for their own learning. Certain questions or more assertive student behavior is often constrained by patterns of teacher authority.

A theory called "structuration" helps explain the grassroots nature of culture, how members shape culture, but also how culture constrains their actions (Giddens, 1979). *Structuration* is a term that was coined to describe the philosophical paradox of choice versus constraint. Structuration assumes that both choice and constraint are simultaneously true. A review of this notion of structuration should clarify this effort to deal with the paradox (Poole, Seibold, & McPhee, 1986).

The term *structuration* implies that we are constrained by structures (i.e., social norms, organizational decision-making hierarchies) but that we participate in maintaining, changing, and defending these structures in an ongoing process (Poole, 1992; Poole et al., 1986). For example, according to this theory, each time I decide to follow a management directive, while I may feel constrained by the directive, my willing submission to the directive adds to the power of such directives in the future. We also have the choice to disobey the directive, which may result in a revolution within the system (or being fired!). Structures are reproduced through our collective action because their constraint on our actions is often not at the level of our consciousness.

For another example, consider a church organization. Do members continually question how to celebrate a ritual, such as communion, or how to select leaders or conduct worship? If you are like most of us, you simply take such structures for granted as the way things are done. In some denominations, however, these very processes are challenged at some point, such as when ordination of women was first proposed in some churches. This point of change is the time when the unconscious structure moves to conscious questioning, and a time when a new structuration process, over the years, may create a new taken-for-granted reality. In other words, as humans, we actively participate in creating and re-creating the determinative power of our communication structures.

The process of structuration is part of what we seek to understand in the study of culture. We study how organization members create values, norms, and metaphors, as well as the binding force or power of culture once it is developed. We also consider the process of cultural change at periods in which members challenge existing ideas.

In a related way, this process of structuration involves management of meaning. For example, you may have faced situations in which you felt that an organizational culture and relationship with management dictated your decisions. Such constraint may be a problem if you believe the decisions might be unethical or in someway harmful to the company. A recent example is the abuse of Iraqi prisoners by American soldiers. Some of these soldiers claimed that they acted on their own but believed that their actions served military intelligence. Others seemed to indicate that they were acting under direct orders. What was the nature of the military culture that prompted them to justify abusive behaviors? What was the nature of the authority structure that made them feel constrained to obey orders they may have known to be wrong? How might the culture be changed to clarify the boundaries for humane treatment of prisoners? What changes would be needed to support independent judgments while maintaining military discipline? The analysis process can provide insights in response to such fundamental questions, and answers to these questions underscore the benefits of studying culture.

Connections: Benefits of Studying Organization Culture

The structuration process implies the importance of paying closer attention to culture. The study of culture focuses on symbolic processes that facilitate shared meaning (Morgan, 1986). Because "cultures are communicative creations, they emerge and are sustained by the communicative acts of all employees, not just the conscious persuasive strategies of upper management" (Conrad & Poole, 1998, p. 116). This relationship between communication and culture suggests four specific benefits of a cultural analysis. A cultural analysis can

- provide a picture of major beliefs and values in the organization that influence communication practices and therefore help determine the kinds of communication skills needed in the organization;
- help organizational members see various communication practices that often go unnoticed, such as important rituals and routines or ways power is exercised for ethical/unethical purposes;
- provide insight for new job orientation and job promotion practices;
- assist the change management process by uncovering cultural strengths and potential problem areas.

 Rehearsal 2.2 The Value of a Cultural Analysis

Purpose: Identify what you believe would be the primary value of an analysis for your organization.

Steps:

1. Review again the four bulleted points above.

2. Write down the language you would use to capture *two potential values* of an analysis of your own organization or of the organization you are considering as a focus for an analysis.

3. You might consider possible problems you currently perceive in the organization and describe how a cultural analysis would help you better identify solutions to these problems. Or you might reflect on current changes being considered or implemented and ways a cultural analysis would help in the process of change management.

_____

_____

_____

_____

_____

_____

_____

_____

_____

_____

Cultural Analysis in Practice

This workbook introduces a five-step process for conducting a cultural analysis. When you complete the process, you will have a set of tools for understanding the communication norms, the resources and obstacles for introducing change, as well as insights for developing your own leadership communication practices. The five major steps are as follows:

1. *Understand the concept of culture.* The concept of culture needs to be understood beyond the popular business literature on improving corporate culture. Understanding the richness of this concept will help us clearly articulate the value of a cultural analysis for organizations and for ourselves.

2. *Identify major cultural elements.* We review research on and examples of elements such as stories, rules, and heroes. The importance of being aware of these elements is that each one provides a different vantage point on the often hidden aspects of organizational life. Too often an analysis will focus on one element to the exclusion of others.

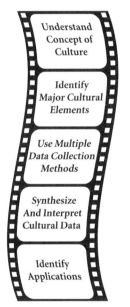

3. *Use multiple data collection methods to understand the elements of culture.* We demonstrate the importance of using multiple methods as we focus on observations and systematic analysis of organizational texts to gain a rich data set. Surveys and interviews will also be introduced as alternative, but more obtrusive methods, for both insiders and outsiders. "Obtrusive" means how obvious the research method is to organizational members, thus how likely to alter their behavior.

4. *Synthesize and interpret cultural data.* You will be challenged to draft an interpretation of an organization. The notion of an interpretation is important in that a culture analysis does not claim to be an objective and neutral video recording. Instead, the analogy we use is that of a dramatic performance, like a play. Two directors may take the same play and stage two very different productions based on different interpretations of the written word. Indeed, the assumption with a cultural analysis is that an objective and neutral cultural recording is impossible. Instead, the individual (or team) works to provide a meaningful, valuable, and valid interpretation.

5. *Identify applications.* Like any good dramatic interpretation and presentation, an effective cultural analysis should inspire new insights. Again, since this process is not linear, these insights may occur before you have worded your final interpretation. In the final section of the text, you will be challenged to reflect on various application arenas including organizational effectiveness, diversity, change management, symbolic leadership, and ethics.

Summary

The following key ideas were introduced:

1. Change in our own as well as organizational communication behaviors is enhanced by knowledge of culture.

2. A *construct* is a term or a concept used to explain events or various phenomena—as a construct, culture was popularized in the 1970s and early 1980s.

3. The term *structuration* refers to the idea that we are constrained by structures (i.e., social norms, decision-making hierarchies, etc.) and that we participate in maintaining, changing, and defining these structures in an ongoing process.

4. Four major benefits of studying organizational culture include the following:

- Provide a picture of major beliefs and values in the organization that influence communication practices and therefore help determine the kinds of communication skills needed in the organization
- Help organizational members see various communication practices that often go unnoticed, such as important rituals and routines or ways power is exercised for ethical/unethical purposes
- Provide insight for new job orientation and job promotion practices
- Assist the change management process by uncovering cultural strengths and potential problem areas

5. The five analysis steps follow:
   a. Understand the concept of culture
   b. Gain an awareness of major cultural elements
   c. Use multiple data collection methods
   d. Develop your interpretation of the culture
   e. Identify applications

Rehearsal 2.3 The Value of Writing a Culture Article

Overview: Depending on your role as an insider or an outsider as well as on your relationship with the organization you analyze, you might find it helpful to take a step beyond the brainstorming activity on describing the value of a cultural analysis. We encourage you to take initiative and actually write an article that would argue for the merits of a cultural analysis. Such an article would have the pragmatic benefit of introducing your organization to the concept of cultural analysis.

Whether you propose to study your own organization, or you make a request to study a different organization, you will need to provide an explanation and rationale for the cultural analysis process. Why should a company want to do it? What benefits could they expect? This Rehearsal might yield information surprising to you. Furthermore it might yield information of value for publication in a company newsletter.

Purpose: (a) translate academic language on organizational culture into popular, organizationally relevant language; (b) summarize specific benefits or values of analyzing the culture of an organization; and (c) write a brief newsletter-style article communicating these benefits to an organization.

Steps:

1. Read a research article (i.e., it should include methods, results, etc.) on the topic of organizational culture. As a research article it should be in an academic journal as opposed to a popular press magazine. A research journal, if recent, will sometimes contain information about organizational culture studies that have not been picked up in the popular press.

2. Determine from the article two or three specific benefits of understanding the culture of an organization. You may want to add additional benefits discussed in Chapter 2 or that you identified in your brainstorming activity.

3. Summarize these values of the cultural analysis process in a one- to two-page (length will ultimately be determined by the publication source) article that uses language that would be welcomed by members of your organization.

4. Use a format that would be appealing, like a newsletter style (i.e., catchy title, headers, bulleted points, relevant examples from your organization and the article, etc.).

PART II

Cultural Analysis Basics

3

Step One: Understanding the Concept of Culture

Constructing the Set

Man is an animal suspended in webs of significance he himself has spun, I take culture to be those webs.

—Geertz, *The Interpretation of Cultures*, 1973, p. 5

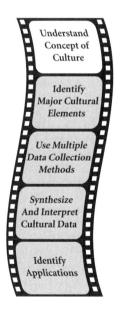

Objectives:

- Understand the concept of culture
- Realize the significance of different images and metaphors in understanding organizations
- Understand three "levels" of organizational culture
- Realize that most organizations do not have a single commonly understood "culture"
- Learn the approach to defining culture used in this workbook

Stage Terms:

- Culture as a variable
- Levels of culture
- Culture as a root metaphor
- Metaphor

Good News, Bad News

To enhance our performances on the stage, we have to be clear about what play we are performing. The set construction will be determined not only by the play but also by the director's interpretation of the work. In short, in order to construct the set, we need to define the term *culture*. The good news is that culture can be defined. The bad news is that different ways of defining the term can sometimes lead to confusion. The examples below are just a few of these differing takes on the term *culture*.

- Culture is the way things are done in the organization (Deal & Kennedy, 1982, 2000).
- Culture is "a basic pattern of assumptions . . . that has worked well enough to be considered valid, therefore, to be taught to new members as the correct way to perceive, think, and feel in relation to these problems" (Schein, 1992, p. 9).
- "Culture is a system of shared symbols" (Geertz, 1973).

The differences in definitions betray important assumptions about what to study when analyzing culture. Each definition may produce different but useful views of organizational culture. Popular literature on organizational culture may not make the differences clear, and consultants and managers may not realize the importance of these differences. For example, if culture is just one more facet of an organization, then it may be changed as easily as a strategic plan or office layout. If culture is something an organization is, then it may be harder to change and should be considered in all other decision making within the organization.

The Concept of Culture

Smircich (1983) provides a good beginning place for defining culture by raising the key question concerning organizations and culture: Does the organization have a culture or is it a culture? According to Smircich, there are two major ways culture has been studied in organizations: as a variable and as a root metaphor. Most current research and consultation on cultures take one of these approaches or a combination of both. These two approaches indicate the richness and diversity of ways to study culture. Understanding these approaches will aid you when you pick up other books or articles on the topic of organizational culture in that you will better understand their focus. Furthermore, these differing approaches provide a backdrop for the approach we take in this workbook.

Culture as a Variable

The culture-as-a-variable approach focuses on causality. Culture is thought to be able to predict and thus cause certain outcomes. You might view culture as variable "X" (values, norms, etc.) that is influencing variable "Y" (productivity, for example). This relationship, as you might imagine, is complex due to the fact that culture is not an easily defined variable. For example, try to answer the question, *What make a culture "good" or "strong"?* and you will find that the answers are not easily placed in a formula. Based on the variable approach, a manager who does not have a clear understanding of the complexity of the culture variable might say something like: "If we could just get our culture stronger, our productivity would go up." The challenge or potential problems arise when this same manager attempts to strengthen the culture without a clear sense of what is to be strengthened and how culture influences productivity. Are values to be strengthened? Rules? Norms?

In the above example, the complexity of the variable of culture is evident. Within the variable approach, however, there are two lines of inquiry: internal variable and external variable. The variable approach may focus on internal variables thought to influence culture. In this instance, organizations are viewed as producing culture as evidenced in such cultural artifacts as rituals, heroes, and norms. Consultants and researchers are therefore interested in exploring aspects of culture (e.g., leadership values, norms, structures) that predict organizational survival and effectiveness (Collins, 2001; Deal & Kennedy, 1982; Peters & Waterman, 1982).

The variable approach is also evidenced in comparative or cross-cultural management research that takes into account culture as an external variable. As an external variable, culture is seen as a map for navigating differences across organizations and differences in national cultures. For example, Mexican organizations have been compared with U.S.-based organizations in their orientation to time and relationships (Condon, 1997). In this example, the values of the larger national culture influence the organization in connection with communication surrounding time and relationships. This approach focuses on ways to tap into national cultural differences to win out over the competition (Harris & Moran, 2000; Ouchi, 1981). Hofstede (2003) has done extensive research on the underlying value assumptions that help to differentiate workers in one national culture from another. Thus, for instance, U.S. culture shares common assumptions about the value of individualism in contrast to Japanese or Hispanic cultures that tend to be more collectivistic. Given the widespread recognition of international economic interdependence, the importance of understanding national cultural influences will only increase.

Understanding the influence of national culture on organizational culture is an important, and often overlooked, aspect of organizational culture analysis. Many of the deepest unconscious assumptions we bring to our work life are often rooted in our cultural socialization. As Figure 3.1 indicates, some researchers have focused on cross-cultural organizational studies. The approach to cultural analysis that we take in this text, however, involves delving into the unique patterns of an organization. In organizational cultural analysis we seek to describe the patterns of assumptions, beliefs, practices, and artifacts that make an organization unique.

Root Metaphor

This second major approach to the study of culture focuses on understanding how organizational members create cultures and how the culture affects the members who are a part of it. It is more about culture as process than as product or variable. The core idea of this approach is that culture is something an organization "is" versus culture as something an organization "has." Thus, for example, if someone were researching or consulting with Enron, consultants using the variable approach would explore links between the culture and the problems Enron faced. They might say, "To solve the problems at Enron we must change the core values of the culture." In contrast, consultants using a root metaphor approach would attempt to describe various aspects of the culture, including the resultant outcomes. They would seek to describe as fully as possible the entire Enron organization since they

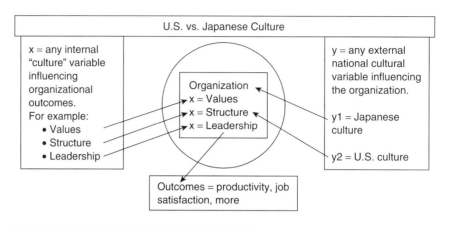

Figure 3.1   The Variable Approach to Culture

assume that the terms *organization* and *culture* are interchangeable. Their end product would be a description, rather than a set of cause-effect variables. Yet as you might infer from the Enron example, both see the pragmatic value of understanding culture.

There are three major research traditions within the root metaphor approach. Researchers in these traditions formulate or focus on different aspects of culture.

1. *Culture as shared cognition.* In this tradition, the beliefs or assumptions of the members of the culture are the focus on the inquiry (Harris, 1979; Schall, 1983). Researchers examine how employees think and what patterns of logic are shared among organization members. Researchers, for example, might describe assumptive differences between members of the same organizations who come from different national cultures (Driskill & Downs, 1995).

2. *Culture as systems of shared symbols.* This research places a focus on the actual language, nonverbals, and other organizational symbols (Geertz, 1973; Smircich, 1983). A consultant or researcher using this approach might observe and record interaction patterns to understand and describe the way members use language to manage conflicts or build friendships (Driskill & Meyer, 1994).

3. *Culture as the expression of unconscious processes.* This focus involves an exploration of the way symbols reflect underlying beliefs and assumptions of the members. Such research might explore the deeper unconscious meaning of a common metaphor used in the organization or on the underlying archetype that predominates the lives of the members (Jung, 1964; Levi-Strauss, 1967).

A visual depiction of these approaches captures the contrast (Figures 3.1 and 3.2). The internal variable approach assumes that culture is one element of an organization that can be studied and used to make predictions about organizational effectiveness. In the same vein, the external variable approach addresses culture as a force outside the organization, such as the norms of the larger national culture (e.g., Japanese vs. U.S. culture). In contrast, the root metaphor approach assumes that the organization is the

Figure 3.2   The Root Metaphor Approach to Culture

culture and therefore, depending on how culture is defined, various aspects of the culture may be explored. ⌐

Connections: Definitions, Metaphors, and Our Approach

These contrasting approaches or definitions to the study of culture suggest the three particular connections. *First, definitions matter.* Definitions guide analysis. Definitions determine what we pay attention to and ignore. Therefore, it is important to keep several questions in mind before you embark on an analysis. You need to determine the following:

1. How will you define culture? *For example:*
   - As a variable? Internal? External?
   - Root metaphor?
   - Shared beliefs? Shared symbols? Unconscious processes?
2. How will the results be used? For example:
   - Change the culture?
   - Adapt to the current culture?
   - Assist multinationals via cross-cultural comparisons?
   - Describe good and bad communication action/patterns?
   - Make unconscious processes part of our conscious?

These basic questions, if bypassed, can lead to trouble. For example, if you operate with a definition of culture that is limited to one aspect of culture, such as values, you may fail to capture and understand other dynamics at work, such as the rituals or norms. Furthermore, if you are not clear about the use of your cultural analysis results, you may find employees slow to get on board with change efforts you hoped would flow from your analysis. For instance, employees typically resent efforts by management to manipulate their behaviors. If they sense your study is directed at them to gain information that will be used to make a change that is management driven without employee involvement, they may work to sabotage the effort. In summary, if a cultural analysis begins with an overly simplistic definition of culture and the relationship of culture to productivity, then other key aspects of culture may be missed, such as a better understanding of how employees are socialized.

Rehearsal 3.1 How Do You Define Culture?

Purpose: Identify commonly held definitions of culture as well as your own definition.

One way to keep theoretic and definitional discussions from being meaningless is to engage in writing your own definition. Based on the review of perspectives above, answer the following questions:

1. What definition of *culture* do you believe to be most commonly held in your own organization?

_____

_____

_____

_____

2. How do you define the term *culture*?

_____

_____

_____

_____

To understand culture, the reader should understand that not only are there varying definitions of culture, but also that culture can be understood as having different levels. Schein (1992) describes organizational culture as consisting of three levels:

- Artifacts and creations such as technology, art, and behavior patterns (what we describe in this text as elements of culture)
- Values held collectively by the group
- Basic assumptions held by group members concerning relationship to the environment; the nature of reality, time, and space; the nature of human nature and activity; and the nature of human relationships

Schein explains that the deepest levels of culture, basic assumptions, operate at the preconscious level and affect our behavior without our critical awareness. We are more aware of our values, and can observe our artifacts and process, but often we do not understand their connections to our values and assumptions.

To illustrate Schein's levels, you might observe an organizational ritual in a factory of workers clocking in and out as they begin and end their workday. To fully understand the cultural meaning of that behavior, it would be necessary to dig deeper into values and assumptions. The time accountability might be based on assumptions about time, the inability to trust the honesty of workers, and accountability of employees to supervisors.

A second way to understand cultures, in addition to definitions and levels, is through metaphors. Morgan (1986) presents a multitude of images as a way to understand and capture our experience in organizations. These images range from common metaphors such as systems or cultures to less common images, such as prisons. Bolman and Deal (1998) take a similar approach but focus on four specific metaphors or frames for viewing organizations. Each frame (structural, political, human resource, and symbolic) represents a way of viewing organizations. For example, the structural frame focuses on organizational charts, work processes, and role definitions. Managers operating within this frame will tend more readily to see organizational problems and possible solutions in terms of role uncertainty versus role clarity. The political frame focuses on the use of power in the organizations and how interactions are structured to maintain or challenge power. The human resource frame directs attention to the training and motivation of employees. The symbolic frame is similar to what we present in this workbook as culture and views the organization as enactment of theater through symbols, stories, and performances that create meaning for employees.

REHEARSAL

Rehearsal 3.2 Playing With Metaphors

1. What is a metaphor you would use to describe your organization?

   _____

   _____

   _____

   _____

2. What are implications, both positive and negative, of this metaphor?

   _____

   _____

   _____

   _____

The value of reflecting on images or metaphors should be clear: Metaphors capture the assumptions we hold about ways to think and communicate about problems and solutions in organizations. Metaphors correspondingly provide clues to alternative ways to think about how we manage our communication behavior. For example, an image of an organization as a prison captures the reality of certain political restraints in an organization. Members of an organization or unit in such an organization might say things like, "I feel trapped here" or, "We don't hear much besides where to move next, never why." Such comments reflect the constraints members of this culture see in their organization. Leaders seeking to work with employees operating with this image of the organization may run into difficulty if they try to deny these perceptions. Saying, "You have no reason to feel trapped" would do little to change things. Instead, the challenge for leaders and employees in this situation would be to explore the aspects of the culture that are influencing these perceptions (e.g., history, norms, rituals). The core challenge is to remember that we live by the images we hold; thus, we are both constrained and enabled by what we view as possible or impossible in our communication behavior.

The cultural analysis process can serve to make us aware of the dominant images held in an organization as well as the images we hold: These images or metaphors influence our communication behavior every day. Cultural analysis can be used to learn how our images of organizations can be obstacles as well as how we can use insights from cultural analysis to become better problem solvers and leaders. For example, if managers became aware of their excessive focus on the structure of an organization (e.g., roles and routines), they might be more likely to explore other metaphors or ways of thinking about their organization. If they were to include reflection on the political frame or power issues (a political metaphor), they might be more likely to reflect on structures in terms of how communication roles need to be clarified as well as communication norms about why and how decisions are being made.

Metaphors matter, and a cultural analysis can help reveal the implicit metaphors influencing the way we communicate and coordinate our behaviors. Part of the power and value of a cultural analysis comes from the fact that organizational members not only create, but also maintain and transform organizational meanings and expectations. Thus, the challenge for individual members is how to use insights from an analysis to improve their own use of messages as resources for growth and change for themselves and their organization, rather than focusing on only the constraints embedded in the messages. Such a shift from constraints is made more likely if we understand and reflect on the metaphors operating under the surface. Chapter 4 further explores metaphors as one of the elements of a cultural analysis.

Third, this discussion of definitions of culture sets the stage for the approach taken in this workbook. Are we left with the choice of variable versus root metaphor approaches? We do not see the two approaches as incompatible. We draw from both perspectives in examining the implications of organizational culture, while developing a comprehensive and complex interpretation of culture. Managers and consultants using a variable approach make claims indicative of a desire to introduce changes in organizational outcomes via culture. Given that managers are most often concerned with how knowledge of organizational culture can help their bottom line, the variable approach makes sense. However, the descriptive/root metaphor approach does not preclude the use of cultural information relevant to important organizational outcomes. For example, it is not hard to conceive of the value of thorough descriptions of a culture. An insider or outsider with such descriptive data would be able to understand the assets and liabilities of various cultural patterns.

Our focus is on using qualitative research skills to capture cultural elements, themes, and definitions that have practical significance for the organization you study. In Chapter 4 we introduce cultural elements that are foundational to the study of a culture. We believe that studying multiple elements encourages a valid and credible analysis as opposed to an exploration of a single feature of the culture. The focus on qualitative research skills (i.e., observation, systematic analysis of organizational texts such as newsletters, and in-depth interviews and open surveys) does not preclude you from using other types of quantitative data (e.g., a standardized survey on job satisfaction). It does suggest that culture is not a concept that can be easily captured through brief or easily constructed surveys. Beginning in Chapter 5 we review various qualitative research skills aimed to sharpen what you do throughout your day—observe, read, talk to others, ask questions.

Our approach has a bottom line of enhancing your performance as well as that of your organization. We will do this by enhancing your awareness of various cultural elements (Chapter 4), sharpening your ability to collect data about these elements (Chapters 5–8), and then guiding your application of insights from the cultural analysis (Chapters 9–14). Our experience and that of our students and clients has proven valuable for improving our understanding of organizations and our ability to lead and serve these organizations. Our hope is that the cultural analysis process will assist us in our efforts to be better observers, interpreters, and thus leaders and managers who not only survive, but thrive in the organizations that greet us at birth and carry us to the grave.

Summary

We can easily get tangled in the web of culture if we do not pause to understand it. A failure to pay attention to how the set is constructed, how the construct culture is defined, can lead to problems. A practitioner, for example, might pick up a cultural survey, measure the culture, and then assume changes suggested by survey results will result in a payoff for the company. Although well intended, such efforts may fail from a lack of understanding of what is being measured. Several major ideas were introduced in this chapter to head off such problems and to lay the foundation for the rest of this workbook:

1. The "culture as a variable" approach focuses on internal (values, rules, etc.) or external (national culture) variables that are thought to predict important organizational outcomes (productivity, employee satisfaction).

2. Cultures should be understood as having multiple levels or dimensions. Some levels exert influence on organization members at an unconscious level.

3. The "culture as a root metaphor" approach focuses on describing the organization. These descriptions differ depending on the way culture is perceived (shared beliefs? shared symbols? shared unconscious processes?).

4. The dominant images or metaphors (prisons, structures, etc.) that are held by members of the organization influence their communication behaviors, for example, the way problems and solutions are identified.

5. Culture is often complex and thus not easily captured through brief or easily constructed surveys. Therefore we will rely on a combination of qualitative research methods to improve the validity of the process of cultural analysis.

6. Our goal is to guide you in the "how to" of conducting an analysis as well as the "how to" of applying insights for improving such important aspects of organizational life as managing change and ethics.

Rehearsal 3.3 Writing a Cultural
Analysis Proposal

Purpose: Develop a formal proposal for conducting a cultural analysis in an organization.

Steps:

1. Identify the person (CEO, HRD manager, etc.) whom you know to be the person to contact concerning the analysis. It might be useful to have some informal visits first, before sending the formal proposal.

2. Develop a 1- to 2-page proposal in which you:
   - Identify who you are and your relationship to the organization
   - Review the basic goal of a cultural analysis
   - Discuss the advantages or value of the analysis—be specific and when possible connect it with relevant issues within the organization (i.e., if you know turnover has been high, you could discuss the way an analysis often uncovers socialization practices)
   - Gain agreement on confidentiality of individual responses or identifying data collected during the cultural analysis

3. Have a trusted colleague critique or review your proposal before sending it.

4. Schedule an interview to discuss your proposal.

Note: A formal letter of permission is required for your project, even if you are studying your own organization.

4

Step Two: Identifying Cultural Elements

Understanding Roles

*T*he burglars came in the back door about midnight. They knew the layout of the restaurant and went right to the office and demanded money from the safe. When I first saw them I was with the store manager by the dishwasher some 30 feet from the office. They wore ski masks and each held something like a pipe. I still recall the command: "Everybody get down and stay where you are." I hit the floor as fast as I could and my manager was right there on the floor with me. We waited and in a few minutes we heard laughter and then a scuffle. I craned my neck and saw the district manager, who happened to be in town to evaluate our restaurant, picking up one of the burglars while trying to pull off his mask. I did not hear what was said next, but in a few minutes both burglars were running for the back door and all that we heard was the district manager's laughter. I do not recall the district manager's name, but I do recall the look on his face when we let him know that it had not been a joke and that he had just thwarted a burglary.

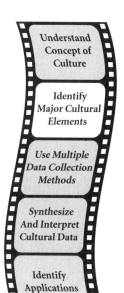

Objectives:

- Gain an awareness of major cultural elements
- Learn ways to identify a variety of types of cultural data

Stage Terms:

- Elements of culture
- Values
- Symbols
- Stories
- Language
- Metaphors

- Artifacts
- Heroes
- Outlaws
- Rituals
- Rules
- Organizational communication style
- History
- Place

The Making of a Legend?

What stories stand out in your mind from past experiences in organizations? The story above grew from an event in 1978 when Gerald worked as a restaurant manager. The story was repeated often in the coming weeks, and no doubt the legend of the brave manager spread beyond to other restaurants in the chain. This legend illustrates the fact that stories are one of the most common means of transmitting organization culture. They are rich with information about informal and unstated rules and about roles such as heroes and villains.

Most of us seek clarity about our own roles in an organization. Yet it is useful to examine what method acting, a widely accepted approach to actor training, teaches actors about roles (Strasberg, 1987). An effective performance grows from becoming a true ensemble, an acting troupe that has such intimate communication with one another and with the set (props, etc.) that where one scene begins and another ends, where one player's lines end and another's begin are almost indistinguishable. In short, the audience gets the sense that the actors are part of a whole (Vineberg, 1991). What does this analogy say about our roles in an organization? Effective organizational members learn to pay attention to more than their own individual role. This chapter will introduce you to various cultural elements that help shape and serve as resources for effective individual, team, and organizational culture performances.

The term *elements of culture* may be defined as various facets or windows that reveal the culture(s) of an organization. We understand from structuration theory, however, that symbolic elements create the culture as well as reveal it. Studies of organizational culture may rely on one element, such as stories (Brown, 1990; Meyer, 1992) or rules (Schall, 1983). Yet to rely on only one element provides a less comprehensive view of an organizational culture. For example, imagine hearing the above story as a new employee. The story may be told to emphasize a safety error in making a joke of the situation, even if the district manager suspected it was a friend playing a prank. Imagine the problems in validity or credibility if you drew conclusions about what was considered acceptable in the culture based on this one story. It may be that the culture really gives limited attention to safety issues, but you would not learn this from a single story. It may be that the whole point of the story was not about safety at all, but was told as a "hero narrative," to emphasize to the listener the importance of bravery or protecting the home front.

Indeed, reliance on one element of culture to draw inferences about effective or appropriate communication behaviors is a source of communication problems for organizations. Furthermore, limiting your analysis can result in overlooking variations in a message found in one element in comparison to another message. Conquergood (1991), for example, found that various organizational performances (gestures, food, ritual, etc.) express attitudes and issues that are political in nature and often contain multiple meanings and purposes. Thus simple rituals like a coffee break may reveal information about who is allowed to take breaks and for how long as well as something as basic as what is appropriate talk during a break. The bottom line of this chapter is that an awareness and analysis of multiple elements is central to improving our ability to gain a credible understanding of a culture.

> . . . reliance on one element of culture to draw interferences about effective or appropriate communication behaviors is a source of communication problems for organizations

Understanding Elements of Culture

Researchers define and discuss different elements of culture (Bolman & Deal, 1998; Dodd, 1998; Pacanowsky & O'Donnell-Trujillo, 1983). The elements discussed in this chapter are not intended to provide an exhaustive treatment but should provide sufficient direction to explore culture. Several guides should be kept in mind as we discuss these elements. *First, various elements tend to be embedded in one another.* The opening story, as already indicated, contains potential information about organizational heroes, rules, and values. A full description of a ritual, such as a holiday party, will often contain information about organizational language, rules, heroes, and other cultural elements. Or, in the same vein, communication rules may be inferred from an interview designed to gain information about metaphors or stories.

Second, the common definitions of these elements will be implied in this text. Specialized definitions of an element may be used in certain texts and articles. For example, a study of stories may focus on various types of stories, such as legends, sagas, myths, or fairy tales. However, for our purpose, the more general terms and definitions will suffice.

Third, to stress a point already made, conclusions drawn about a culture should be based on more than one element. Defining a value, for example, based on a single ritual can be misleading. It is best to determine what contradictory or complementary conclusions can be drawn by looking at several elements.

Fourth, there is usually a difference between the picture of culture drawn from officially sanctioned organizational sources and the picture drawn from the rank-and-file members of an organization. For example, learning about culture from looking at only the official mission statement, reading an annual report, or listening to the CEO's state-of-the-company address gives only part of the picture. It is often enlightening to ask the employees of an organization what the mission statement is to see if anyone knows it or if their recasting is anything close to the official version. The values of top management are not necessarily the values of the members of the organization.

Fifth, the clarity and patterns of the elements you identify may depend on whether the organization you study has a strong or weak culture. Just as there are different definitions of culture, there are different ways to define a "strong" culture. Peters and Waterman (1982), taking a culture-as-variable approach, might describe a strong culture as an appropriate and clear management strategy to align values and symbolism with the competitive environment. The judgment on the culture would come in organizational profitability. Schein (1992) might define a strong culture by the depth and integration of levels of culture. One might ask if cultural practices were grounded in shared values and assumptions among organizational members.

Louis (1985) in evaluating the strength of subcultures uses a concept of "penetration" that might be helpful to the assessment of strength of organization culture as well. She offers three types of cultural penetration: psychological penetration, the extent to which individuals hold similar cultural meanings; sociological penetration, the pervasiveness of cultural understandings among employees; and historical penetration, the stability of cultural values and meanings over time.

[In strong cultures, values permeate all levels of the organization and all aspects of its functioning. The elements are consistent in their support of overall values and guiding root metaphors. This consistency indicates a strong base of assumptions and values creating the regularities across employees. In weak cultures, however, you may be pressed to identify even common values. Organization members may know little about the organization's history, for example, or have no clear cultural heroes. Symbols are multiple and inconsistent and there are no clear norms to create unity or predictability. Having a strong culture doesn't necessarily mean that the culture is positive. Enron had a strong organizational culture, and yet it was one in which engrained values encouraged employees to take risks and skirt legalities, and the strong culture was eventually part of the downfall that lost many investors millions of dollars as the company collapsed. Table 4.1 distinguishes between strong and weak cultures.]

Sixth, you may at times find multiple, instead of unitary, organizational cultures. As you collect data on various elements and develop preliminary interpretations, it is important to remember the complexity of culture. Martin (1992) argues that three major perspectives should be considered in viewing the elements or manifestations of culture. An "integration" perspective suggests a cultural unity that is relatively free of uncertainty, one in which values are held consistently from the leader on down. The "differentiation" perspective suggests that the notion of unity is only on the surface. The reality is that subcultures exist that may be in conflict with one another. The "fragmentation" perspective suggests that ambiguity is the norm or "the essence of culture" (Martin, 1992, p. 118). The implications of these perspectives for transitions and change in an organization will be developed in Chapter 8. At this point, however, it is critical to realize that at any point in time, all three perspectives may hold true in an organization. In other words, avoid the tendency to search for a "unitary" set of stories, values, or other elements.

Table 4.1   Comparison of Strong and Weak Organizational Cultures

Strong Culture	Weak Culture
Values permeate entire organization	Values limited to top management
Elements of culture send consistent messages	Elements send contradictory messages
Most employees can tell stories about history and heroes	Little knowledge about history or heroes among average employees
Strong identification with culture among all employees	Employees identify more with subcultures than with overall organizational culture
Surface cultural elements tied to employee beliefs and assumptions	Little connection between cultural elements and employee beliefs and assumptions
Culture has historical penetration— has existed over a long period	Culture is recent and not well established

For example, sometimes different geographical or product divisions of a large company may develop their own unique subcultures. Rosenfeld, Richman, and May (2004) studied a large dispersed network culture and found that without strong communication systems, branch offices of a large organization can develop a fragmented culture or one that is differentiated from the overall organization. This can cause lack of trust and interdependence and can impact employees' personal growth. At times even departments such as creative services and account services within a large advertising agency may have distinctly different subcultures. At these times, it is important to probe whether the subcultures share certain uniting elements in their diversity, and what might constitute the cultural core that holds together and unites the subculture. You might also analyze whether the subcultures serve useful purposes for the organization—such as promoting diversity and creativity, matching culture to function of different units, or promoting healthy competition. You may also, however, find that a fragmented organizational culture with competing subcultures is unhealthy and may be a sign of cultural revolution or transition.

Major Elements of Culture

We provide a list of major elements in Table 4.2, and definitions and examples follow the table. We include suggestions for identifying each element; however, we reserve in-depth discussion of element identification for the section on methods. The identification of cultural elements is made easier because we grow up being exposed to them: we hear stories, we participate in rituals, and we learn specialized terms or language. After each element you can jot down your own examples in order to see how familiar you already are with each of the elements. We include a Rehearsal at the end of the section to provide further practice in identifying these elements. Becoming adept at identifying each of these elements will give you a framework for your formal data collection, discussed in the next section.

Table 4.2   Categories of Elements of Culture

Values	(Master Element)
Symbolic Elements	Symbols
	Stories
	Language
	Metaphors
Role Elements	Heroes
	Outlaws
Interactive Elements	Rituals
	Informal rules
	Organizational communication style
Context Elements	History
	Place

We have divided 12 elements into five categories for discussion: values (the master cultural element); symbolic elements (symbols, stories, language, and metaphors); role elements (heroes, outlaws); interactive elements (rituals, rules, organizational communication style); and context variables (history, place).

Values

Definition: the common beliefs and priorities of a group of people. Values are qualities that define a group to its members. They may be the most central cultural construct, on which all other cultural elements rest. In Schein's (1992) model of levels of culture described in the Chapter 3, values are the second level of culture, underlying all observable manifestations of culture. Values tell organization members what is most important, what to pay attention to, and how to interpret meanings. Other elements such as heroes or language gain significance as they provide a clue to a key organizational value. When organization members share values, they form a strong force for motivating the performance of employees. Tompkins and Cheney (1985) refer to this motivating force of values as "unobtrusive control." Employees don't need close supervision or an elaborate set of rules to regulate their behavior if they have strongly internalized the values of the organization.

Examples: Enron at its zenith held collective values of boldness, risk taking, and innovation. These values became embedded in its rituals and defined the heroes of the organization (Seeger & Ulmer, 2003). On the other hand, we have both been in churches that defined themselves as a "healing community" that valued the broken, the discouraged, and scarred individuals. You can imagine that the second value leads to a very different web of culture than Enron's.

Identification: You may find value statements written in conjunction with a mission statement. However, as you collect formal value statements, be sure also to learn about values that are seen, not just heard (practiced vs. merely espoused). You can draw inferences about values from what the organization rewards formally or informally, by the types of indi... who are drawn to the organization, from everyday rituals, and from stories. You may infer values from almost any of the other elements. For instance, values are easily inferred from stories and rituals. Once you determine values, you have the key for interpreting all other cultural elements (Meyer, 1992, 1994, 1995).

An example of a value shared by members of your organization:

_____

_____

Symbolic Elements

The four cultural elements we categorize as "symbolic elements" have in common their focus on language, nonverbal symbols, and meaning. They are all significant in interpreting organizational culture because they represent an important value or meaning in the culture. The cultural elements include symbols, stories, language, and metaphors.

Symbols

Definition: physical objects or icons that represent the organization. Most organizations develop logos to represent themselves to their public. Often great thought and expense goes into choosing a logo, which conveys exactly how the organization wishes to be portrayed. Other symbols can be analyzed as well, such as corporate newsletters, executive speeches, an annual report, building architecture, Web pages, and even individuals who come to symbolize an organization.

Examples: One former client of Angi's started out with values of equality and lack of corporate hierarchy. These values led to a corporate headquarters in which it was impossible to distinguish the office of the CEO from the office of a mid-level computer programmer. The indistinguishable offices served as an important icon representing a key value of equality within the company. As the company became increasingly successful and competed for business worldwide with major banks and organizations, the small and unassuming office of the CEO sent a different and less positive message to visitors from potential clients. The CEO and members of the organization were forced to manage the impression of their symbols both internally and externally.

Physical facilities are another example of significant symbols and are especially interesting to analyze. They can include the building(s), layout of rooms, furniture, parking lots, vehicles, and artifacts such as pictures, signs, plaques, visitor reading material in the lobby, and clothing (official and unofficial uniforms). These features of settings can be viewed as significant symbols (Eblen & Eblen, 1987).

Finally, the organizational Web site is a rich, modern artifact that can yield a wealth of organizational symbolism. It has become the contemporary version of the corporate handbook or newsletter. Not only the content of the Web site, but also the visual layout, the navigation logic, and the security or lack thereof, yields information about organizational culture.

Identification: Some researchers have developed elaborate classification systems to study symbols (Axley, 1984; Holmes, 1988). As with other elements of culture, it is important to probe the meaning and importance of a symbol to members of the organization. Often a symbol that might be interpreted in one way by outsiders has a very different meaning internally. It is also important to distinguish between "official" and "unofficial" organizational symbols.

Symbols in your organization:

_____

_____

_____

Stories

Definition: narratives that organization members tell and newcomers hear. They are often a primary form of socialization for new organization members. When you hear the same story or type of story from many different individuals in an organization, it likely has cultural significance. Stories may be told that feature the storyteller or some other organizational member as a main character. Stories are often disseminated organization-wide to encourage members to accept a certain value or rule. Some stories contain explicit "morals" or lessons, while other stories are more subtle and allow the listener to draw conclusions. Stories may take on fantasy or mythic qualities if they begin to deal with larger-than-life characters and do not seem to be situated in time (like fairy tales, sagas, or legends).

Examples: Stories may be prompted when something goes wrong. As an employee in a retail store, Gerald recalls a story being told after a minor accident. The occasion of the minor accident prompted telling the story of a major accident as a cautionary tale. The manager used the occasion to tell about a major accident that cost the company thousands of dollars. Employees, both recent hires and old-timers, were thus exposed to a company value on following procedure. As a consultant in one hospital setting, Angi heard a wide variety of stories about status differences. All the stories had different main characters and different inferences drawn. One story might be about racial differences. Another might be about insensitive doctors being unresponsive to needs of staff. Yet the story type of status differences was strong in the culture.

Identification: Stories may be elicited in a direct fashion: "Tell me about the stories a newcomer is likely to hear around this place." However, as will be discussed in Part III on data collection, the indirect approach is often the most valid way to gain cultural information. Thus, you may simply hear statements during an informal discussion or narratives presented during a formal interview. Stories in these settings may begin with statements like, "Let me tell you what happened when . . ." or "That reminds me of a time . . . " or "The boss often repeats . . . ." At times you can elicit stories by asking for an example when interviewees discuss a value or characteristic of the organization. You should be aware that conclusions you draw from a story as an outsider might be quite different from the implications of the story for an insider. Especially interesting are "story types" that you begin to discover in an organization. Because stories often have multiple elements embedded in them (heroes, values, etc.), we have provided a Rehearsal at the end of the section to explore further your own organizational stories (Brown, 1990; Meyer, 1992; Rauschenberg, 1989).

Give a story you have heard in your organization that has symbolic significance:

_____

_____

_____

_____

_____

Language/Nonverbal

Definition: the particular vocabulary or terms (argot, jargon, etc.) used by members of the organization as well as the specialized nonverbal gestures, signs, and so on, that provide clues to important aspects of the culture (Brenton, 1993). Language distinguishes insiders from outsiders and thus helps define cultural boundaries. The specific terms used by a group, as well as grammar and message construction, are also a means for drawing inferences about a group's metaphors and values.

Examples: A university that stresses its "business plan" or "margin" or talks about its students as "customers" may have adopted a business metaphor. This may be a sign of "mission drift," where economics has taken more centrality than education as the mission of the institution.

Identification: Smith and Eisenberg (1987) analyzed a shift in culture at Disneyland from a "theatrical performance" culture to a "family" culture. They discussed this change by analyzing language patterns in employee interviews and official documents. This shift in metaphor had serious implications for rituals, employee expectations, and values. Not only specific vocabulary but also language patterns can reveal an enlightening view of a culture. Brenton (1993) used critical linguistic analysis to analyze a cultural conflict in a church, looking at language features such as passive or active sentence construction, specificity versus abstraction, pronoun references, and how often certain word types appeared in a text.

Give an example of language that is significant in conveying organizational values or in differentiating an insider from an outsider in your organization:

_____

_____

_____

_____

_____

Metaphors

Definition: figures of speech in which one thing is seen through the lens of another; in which two objects, individuals, or events are implicitly or explicitly compared to one another.

Examples: A small company may describe itself as a family because of close relationships among organization members. The metaphor is consistent with the values of caring, nurturing, and permanent commitments. The values embedded in the metaphor are also found in patterns of rituals, informal rules, heroes, and communication networks that profoundly affect how the company does business. While the metaphor may have great utility, it will pose limits for the company during financial stress. How do you lay off a family member? Why should the bottom line take precedence over the best health care insurance possible when providing for family? It also may be challenged during times of corporate growth and change. While the family metaphor may work well in a small to medium-sized organization, it quickly becomes unwieldy when the company grows larger.

One of our students studied a temporary employment agency that characterized itself as a "pride of lions." All the managers were male, and the agents who processed orders and served employees were female. For some of the employees the metaphor captured role division and gender status differences within the agency, as well as values of interdependence and competitiveness of the environment.

Identification: Naturally occurring metaphors, which emerge from language patterns, are generally more valid in cultural analysis than artificially generated ones (Smith & Eisenberg, 1987). An artificially generated metaphor might be elicited by a question such as, "If this company were an animal, what would it be?" One can infer metaphors from language patterns, heroes, rituals, or other culture elements. For example, if employees use terms such as "battle plan," "chain of command," "search and destroy," and "war games," it would be fair to assume that the culture is influenced by a military metaphor. Metaphors offer insight into rules and values. In the military metaphor example, you would expect to find values and norms of loyalty, obedience to orders, and respect for hierarchical positions within the organization.

What metaphor symbolizes your organizational culture?

_____

_____

_____

_____

_____

Role Elements

Although some authors, such as Deal and Kennedy (1982), identify a large number of cultural roles such as high priest, storyteller, and cabal member, we have found two roles especially helpful in understanding cultures. These two roles are hero and outlaw, and they are described below.

Heroes

√ *Definition:* individuals or groups who are respected by a large number of individuals within the organization because they embody group values.

Examples: [Stories, rituals, and an examination of history reveal the continuing influence of founder-heroes such as Sam Walton and Walt Disney.] Stories about Sam Walton still abound among Wal-Mart employees—from his driving a beat-up pickup truck to leading cheers with associates at Wal-Mart stores. A hero may also be someone other than a founder or a CEO though. For example, in one church organization, an 85-year-old church secretary named Helen was widely cited by members as "the heart of the church," and "the custodian of all church stories, history, and procedures." Church leaders had come and gone over the years, while Helen had remained. Her mentoring of new members, her structuring of church services, and her much-sought approval demonstrated her influence over church practices. One member told a story of a minister who didn't stay long once he earned Helen's ire. A critical time in any organization is the transition after the death or retirement of a hero. [In most cases, the hero's influence remains through prominently displayed pictures and symbols, much-repeated stories, and influence on leadership succession processes. If new heroes fail to emerge over time, however, the organization may drift from its values and history.]

Identification: The "hero" may or may not have high formal status within the organization. It is surprising how often you find quick consensus, however, when you begin asking individuals questions such as, "Who is a hero here?" "Who is an organization member you most respect?" "Who embodies this organization at its best?" Within most organizational stories, heroes are easily found. Heroes reveal a great deal about communication rules and cultural values.

Who is a hero in your organization and why?

_____

_____

_____

_____

Outlaws

√ *Definition:* individuals who seem to be paradoxes in the organization, who defy organizational practices or values yet remain as valued members of the organization because they exemplify countercultural values that the organization wishes to cultivate.

Examples: Angi belongs to one of the largest Rotary clubs in the United States, with more than 500 members. Most Tuesdays at lunch one can look over a sea of sameness of American button-down business leaders. The shade of tie may vary here or there, and the color of suit may range from charcoal to navy, but the homogeneity is obvious—as are the informal rules of inter-action: polite conversation. No rocking the boat with political conversation, raised voices, or divisive topics. That is, until you see Rollie—usually dressed in a Ducks Unlimited sweatshirt and always carrying one of his trademark hand-carved walking sticks. Any time he gets the microphone, which is frequently, he may "Call the Hogs" (an Arkansas football cheer), or call the ducks, or tell everyone about his latest political protégé. Why has he gained almost legendary status when he follows almost none of the rules typical of the culture? Maybe because he embodies the spontaneity, fun, honesty, and bravado that many of the business leaders would like to emulate.

Identification: In interviews you can usually ask a question like, "Who is someone in this organization who is different, who doesn't follow all the rules but is still valued?" You can also simply observe organizational inter-action. Outlaws are usually easy to spot because they are dressed differently and interact with others in noticeably different ways than most organization members. Like heroes, outlaws reveal a great deal about communication rules and cultural values. They may embody subtle subordinate values missed in other elements. Outlaws are particularly interesting to identify and study. If they are expelled from the organization, the reasons for their expul-sion tell a great deal about organizational norms and values. If they are allowed to remain in the organization, it may be because they embody impor-tant counterculture values (such as creativity in a traditional culture) that the organization wants to support. It is also interesting to discover times of cul-tural change when a former outlaw becomes a hero, or when an outlaw who was previously tolerated in an organization is expelled or disciplined.

Who is someone who seems to break all the rules in your organization, yet is allowed to remain as a valued member? Why?

_____

_____

_____

_____

Interactive Cultural Elements

The three cultural elements we have identified as "interactive" exist only in interactions between members of the organization and cannot be observed in a single member. They are a clear example of the theory of structuration explained in Chapter 2. They are created through interaction, yet also can constrain the improvisation of actors within the culture. These elements are rituals, rules, and organizational communication style and are explained below.

Rituals

Definition: planned and unplanned events that are carried out through social interaction with explicit or implicit purposes and that have multiple social consequences (see Trice & Beyer, 1984). Rituals are often the "acting out of values" and form a rich source of data from which to mine inferences about other elements of culture such as values, rules, cultural roles and networks, and heroes.

Examples: informal office gatherings, award ceremonies, organizational practices and procedures, coffee room talk. A specific type of ritual is corporate humor or play. What members count as humor and play, often in contrast to work, serve critically important functions in the organization. For instance, humor may function to save face, socialize, convey membership, and gain perspective on negative or tragic organizational events (Bolman & Deal, 1998; Meyer, 1997, 2000). In a similar way, play may encourage flexibility and adaptation.

Identification: One way to identify formal and informal rituals is to ask about the events that characterize the organization. For instance, are family picnics or Friday afternoon happy hours common? Or are members rewarded, either formally or informally? Does the organization have rites for recognizing stakeholders outside of the organization (community members, volunteers)? Once you have identified rituals, you can probe for values, rules, roles, networks, and heroes. For example, you might ask questions like: What signs of status are apparent from interactions? How do employees do their work? How do they greet strangers/customers/visitors? How do they interact in meetings?

What is a ritual in your organization? What does it tell you about the culture?

_____

_____

_____

_____

Informal Cultural Rules

Definition: "the organization and logic that provide for behavior production" (Sigman, 1980). Informal organizational norms tell what behavior is preferred, permitted, required, or prohibited in organizational life.

Examples: When Angi began as an assistant professor years ago, several colleagues took care to share a story about an assistant professor who, as legend had it, was denied tenure the year after he refused a request by the dean to chair the college United Way effort. She was left to deduce her own conclusions about organizational norms from the story. Was it expected that all employees are active in United Way because of a strong community engagement? Was it prohibited for a junior faculty member to deny a request from the dean?

Identification: Uncovering the complex, often unconscious ways of thinking in an organization that make some actions obligatory, some permissible, some discouraged, and some prohibited is challenging. You may find rules for behavior listed in an employee handbook (no smoking, etc.). However, informal cultural rules, like values, are rarely explicitly stated or written. Because rules operate in the unconscious taken-for-granted realm, some organizational members cannot identify rules if they are asked a direct question about them. In a story about a hero or an outlaw, you may learn what types of behaviors are encouraged or discouraged. You also can uncover rules in field observations of interactions among culture members. When you observe regularities of behavior over time and across actors, the regularity is generally produced by informal cultural rules. Who calls whom by first names or formal titles? Do people arrive early or late for meetings? Who is exempt from the "corporate uniform" and why? What distinguishes those who get promotion and honors from those who do not? What are common threads among those who are fired or voluntarily choose to leave the organization? It is important, once you identify the regularity, to ask organizational members to explain it. Their underlying logic is the key element in identifying the cultural norm or rule. Informal cultural rules are embodiments of organizational values and a direct outgrowth of organizational metaphors (Schall, 1983).

What are informal norms at your organization that may not be written down but still have a strong effect on how actors behave?

_____

_____

_____

_____

Organizational Communication Style

Definition: a collective preference by organization members for certain channels of communication. Usually organizations fall into three "styles": oral/interpersonal, written/formal documentation, and electronic.

Examples: As we have consulted with organizations, we have found one major aspect of culture involves the collective communication patterns and preferences of the group. Some prefer face-to-face communication in an oral tradition. They value the personal contact, and may not "count" that they have received a message until someone has talked to them about it. A typical comment might be, "I saw some memo about that, but no one has actually talked to me about it yet." Cultural socialization and history are conveyed through stories and interactions. A fatal flaw in such a culture would be offering feedback or praise to a group through a memo versus a more personal contact. Change must be achieved by face-to-face appeals and coalition building.

A written culture, on the other hand, places emphasis on standardization of procedure and formal documentary evidence. This communication culture is most prevalent in bureaucratic organizations or in organizations with a high proclivity toward legal actions or grievances. In this culture, oral communication does not "count." A comment in a meeting must be followed by a formal written proposal. A request is not considered effective until it is put into writing. An affirmation would seem incomplete unless it is formalized in writing with copies to all affected parties.

A hybrid of the written culture is the electronic communication culture. In this culture speed and ease of communication are highly valued, perhaps because the pace of change is intensified in highly competitive and fast-moving fields. Organization members are expected to be accessible through e-mail, pager, voice mail, or cell phone at any given time. In this culture, a faux pas might be sending a message by mail instead of by a more rapid channel, insisting on a paper copy instead of an electronic communication, or failing to check messages frequently. Challenges within this culture include information overload, improperly targeted messages, and "flaming" in which anger is more easily expressed in impersonal channels.

negative example

Angi recently consulted with a company in the midst of cultural change. Along with changes in organizational structure (eliminating a layer of middle management), growth, changes in corporate ownership that had added more bureaucratic procedures, and changes in personnel, a change in communication culture had gone almost unnoticed, even though it had created major repercussions. The organization before the round of changes had a strong oral/interpersonal communication culture. Employees got things done by knowing the right person at corporate headquarters to call, and cultivating personal relationships across branches took the place of formal communication channels and mechanisms. As part of the corporate change, the company had adopted an electronic communication style. Oral briefings declined. Employees were expected to keep up with policies by e-mail updates and Web page postings. As faces were shuffled in and out, employees no longer knew who was in charge of what and whom to call when emergencies arose. Complaints abounded about the difficulty of navigation, impersonality, and competition among branches. Most of these arose out of grief over losing a comfortable and efficient culture of communication without it being replaced by a clear strategy for how electronic means could serve the same functions as the previous communication culture.

Identification: You can ask organization members in interviews how most people communicate with one another. You can also observe face-to-face interactions, meeting schedules, the inbox (how many paper transactions), and the average number of e-mails per day.

What is the communication style of your organization? How do you know?

_____

_____

_____

_____

Context Elements

The two elements we classify as context elements, history and place, recognize that an organizational culture is substantially shaped by its placement in space and time. An organization located in India will develop different values and norms from one located in France. An organization located in New York City will have a different climate from one formed in

Plains, Georgia. Organizations also do not exist in a time vacuum. Their history is vital for understanding how the organization was founded and how it has changed. It is hard to understand present organizational patterns without grounding cultural understanding in the organization's history.

History

Definition: history involves knowledge of the purposes of its founding, and how it has evolved over the years; it also involves knowing information about the founders of the organization. Learning the history of an organization—the time period at which it was formed, the purposes for which it was formed, the personality of the individual(s) who founded it—can offer great insight into persisting organizational patterns or resistance to change. The insights gleaned from the history are valuable even when organizations have changed dramatically from their initial beginnings.

Examples: One of Angi's clients is a large university hospital with roots as a charity hospital for indigent patients. Even though it has now grown into an internationally recognized medical center, the value of offering universal access to health care remains. Understanding the historic value of access to care explains tensions that result from serving different patient populations.

History reveals the continuing influence of a founder such as Sam Walton or Walt Disney. It is enlightening to determine how much the average organizational member knows or understands about organizational history. In strong cultures, the history is often told and retold. One of our cultural audits was performed in a publishing group that started on a shoe-string. Each employee we interviewed and even recent hires could tell about the early days when writers signed on with no salary and just a promise of future profit sharing. Most could tell about the first winter in a warehouse so cold that writers draped a stray cat across their shoulders for warmth as they sat before a typewriter. The history was a vibrant part of the culture because the publishing group did not want to leave behind the value of passionate dedication to creativity. In organizations drifting away from founding values, members often know little about history. In contrast, a founder's values guide the response of an organization facing a crisis (Ulmer, 2001).

Identification: History, like the other elements, is often embedded in stories of heroes or the founding of the organization. Rituals that capture certain common organizational memories are also important places to gain a sense of the history of a place. Artifacts, such as pictures of the founder or pictures of earlier corporate headquarters, also show that an organization consciously tries to build on its history.

What do you know about your organization's history? How does your knowledge affect your present behavior in the organization?

_____

_____

_____

_____

Place

Definition: the complex environment in which an organization resides, whether it be a community, a state, a nation, or a multinational context.

Example: Organizations are products of their environments, as well as entities that shape their environments—the same duality of creativity and constraint discussed earlier in structuration theory. Authors such as Florida (2002) discuss the increasingly important role of place in the new creative economy. Creative employees such as university professors, software developers, medical researchers, information engineers, and others have highly portable careers. They can choose to live and work where they want. Florida points out that the days when employees moved to where the jobs are have passed. Now the creative class chooses to live in environments characterized by technology infrastructure, diversity, and a rich cultural life, and the companies follow. Florida has developed a "creativity index" on which cities such as San Francisco, Austin, Minneapolis, Santa Fe, and Washington, DC, score high. He posits that companies such as Dell Computers have flourished precisely because they were developed in such rich environments that nourished creativity and innovation.

Identification: This element challenges the researcher to move beyond observation of the internal environment to consider the impact of "place." What are characteristics of the external environment? Big city or small? Homogenous or diverse? Traditional or cutting edge? Prosperous or struggling? How does the environment contribute to the organization's culture? How does the organization contribute to its environment?

How does the physical environment in which your organization is located affect the organizational culture?

_____

_____

_____

_____

Connections: What About Ambiguity?

Elements of culture may be viewed as the primary roles in the organizational culture drama. From your reading of the different elements and reflection on your experiences in organizations, did you notice instances when a rule or story or ritual was complex, multifaceted, layered, or ambiguous in its meaning? For instance, in the burglar story at the beginning of the chapter, the moral of the story might be that even a great manager can make a nearly deadly mistake. Or conversely it might be that the moral is about bravery in that this manager saved the day by recognizing that these burglars were a joke and not to be taken seriously. The meaning of the tale and the significance to the company depends on who retells it and for what purposes. Is it, for instance, told at an orientation on safety or is it told at a picnic in which the virtues of brave managers are extolled?

Part of its value and richness in embodying and shaping the culture is because of this very ambiguity.

The notion of ambiguity in meaning is critical to interpreting and applying cultural data. Smith and Eisenberg (1987) and others (Meyerson & Martin, 1987; Morgan, 1986) have drawn attention to the role of strategic ambiguity in organizational communication. Strategic ambiguity is being deliberately unclear or nonspecific for a strategic purpose. Common assumptions about organizational communication often deal with clarity and certainty about messages and meanings. This is especially true in popular literature about organizational culture. Leaders are encouraged to send clear and specific messages about values and expectations.

However, the importance and existence of ambiguity should not be overlooked. Another way to think about ambiguity is to consider the value of being able to look at something a different way. If all communication were clear and certain, there would be no room for adjustments, change, and alternative perspectives. In fact, the ability to interpret and then translate the meaning of a cultural element in different ways (as allowed by the degree of ambiguity present) is a skill relevant to managing organizational change. In addition, Eisenberg (1984) points out that strategic ambiguity allows for "unified diversity" in which different groups within an organization can feel a common commitment to an abstract value into which each can read its own connotations. Such unity would break down with more specifically drawn goals.

Strategic ambiguity may also be exploited by those wishing to use organizational rituals to initiate change. For instance, Brenton (1993) studied the ritual of going forward at the end of a church service as a way to introduce changes in a church organization. Brenton noted how one church member, in conflict with the leadership, utilized this ritual to confess his problems and sins in dealing with a particular issue in the church. His use of the ritual for confession was clearly within the communication rules of this ritual, but his use of the confession to implicate current problems with leadership behavior was part of the ambiguity in the ritual—an ambiguity that allowed him to introduce new ideas and changes.

The concept of ambiguity as related to the elements of culture connects with the notion of culture as a resource. We would want you to see that ambiguity about cultural elements may not be all bad. Yes, there may be times when ambiguity creates a source of confusion or "action paralysis," yet it can also provide an opportunity to be innovative (Martin, 1992, p. 134). The competent leader or communicator seeks to tap into culture, its ambiguity, and how to exploit it to advance ethical performance goals. As in the study by Brenton, the church member recognized the need to work within the culture and did so by utilizing the ambiguity in an existing ritual to effectively introduce a change. We therefore are not merely caught in the web of culture if we are aware of the influence of culture. Consistent with the example above, we can learn to tap into the resource of culture to develop and enact meanings that we view as important.

Summary

This overview of the major elements of culture suggests just how commonplace most of the elements are in our everyday experience. Although we observe them every day, until now you may not have recognized their value to studying culture. While we may not formally reflect on implied rules or see a coffee break routine as an important ritual, we nevertheless learn, respond to, and enact cultures in a variety of ways. Specifically you should have learned from this chapter:

1. Elements often are a "window" on organizational culture.

2. Comprehensive organizational analysis should be based on conclusions drawn from multiple cultural elements.

3. We should consider both "official" management information and "unofficial" information from rank-and-file organizational actors when we draw conclusions since culture must pervade the entire organization to be influential.

4. Elements are often "nested" within one another. One can learn about values from stories, history, or heroes, for example.

5. Part of the richness of cultural elements is their ambiguity and their ability to convey multiple meanings simultaneously.

With an awareness of the elements gained, the next task is to refine our ability to gather in-depth information about each of these elements before interpreting and applying their meaning. Two activities at the end of this section provide ways to take a closer look at stories and metaphors. When you have completed the first two steps of the analysis process, "Defining culture," and "Becoming aware of elements," you should be in a position to discuss the value of the cultural analysis process.

If all communication were clear and certain, then there would be no room for change and alternative perspectives.

Rehearsal 4.1 Exploring Web Sites

Purpose: Identify and evaluate cultural elements that can be assessed from a company Web site.

Steps:

1. Identify two different company or organization Web sites. We encourage you to select organizations of interest to you in terms of consulting, career development, or benchmarking.

2. Identify as many different elements of culture as possible based on the summary list provided below:

   Values—the common beliefs and priorities of a group of people; they are qualities that define a group to its members

---

(Continued)

(Continued)

Rituals—include planned (rites) and unplanned events that are carried out through social interaction with explicit or implicit purposes and have multiple social consequences (see Trice & Beyer, 1984); rituals are often the "acting out of values"

Stories—narratives that organization members tell and newcomers hear

Heroes—individuals or a group within the organization that is respected by a large number of individuals within the organization because they embody organizational values

Outlaw—someone who seems at the fringe, someone who bucks the rules or challenges the system, yet is tolerated and even valued because he or she embodies countercultural values that the group wishes to retain

Language/Nonverbal—the particular vocabulary or terms (argot, jargon, etc.) used by members of the organization as well as the specialized nonverbal gestures, signs, and so on that provide clues to important aspects of the culture

Symbols—one of a variety of a ways that an organization represents itself to the public, for example, logos, corporate newsletters, representative photographs or graphics, Web sites, executive speeches, annual reports, building architecture, even individuals who come to symbolize an organization

Metaphors—figures of speech in which one thing is seen through the lens of another, in which two objects, individuals, or events are implicitly or explicitly compared to one another

History—the time period at which the organization was formed, the purposes for which it was formed, the personality of the individual(s) who founded it

Informal Cultural Rules—the organization and logic that provide for behavior production

References to Place—the environment of which the organization is a part, and the ways in which the external environment influences the organization

Indication of Organizational Communication Style—oral, written, or electronic

Rehearsal 4.2 Getting More From Our Stories

The role of narratives or stories in understanding our organizational communication experiences is common both in and outside academia (Fisher, 1987; Kirkwood, 1983, 1985, 1992). In fact, in consultation with a day care organization, Gerald used stories to improve communication practices (Driskill & Meyer, 1994, 1996), and Angi helped leaders gain insights into their culture by analyzing stories told in employee interviews. The leaders first examined the balance of positive and negative stories, and then analyzed story themes to identify values and problems within the culture.

Reviewing a story is to participate in the ancient rite of storytelling. We are always amazed at the range of events that come to our minds when we review our organizational stories with others engaged in the same review process. The stories range from mundane first job memories, to ethical dilemmas, to examples of the way a change in management practice can reshape an entire work environment. Interactions with mentors or heroes, and the values and informal norms taught by positive and negative experiences, have shaped all our lives in powerful ways. While each of the individual stories has significance in defining aspects of each individual organizational culture, the stories as a whole form a narrative or script of our own organizational drama. Each of the early scenes shapes the action and events of later scenes. A positive experience with an employer will influence how you interpret behavior and evaluate later bosses. For instance, a nurturing boss and mentor might prompt you to take growth-producing risks on another job. Conversely, a negative experience may prompt you to enact your own set of informal rules that limits your willingness to take many risks. An early successful or unsuccessful experience with a group will shape your reactions to teamwork.

Such storytelling demonstrates four important roles of organizational stories. *First, stories function as a type of life review or life construction.* The recalling of past events, this habit of reminiscing, is something we often associate with the elderly. Gerald still hears stories from his Dad of working in Alaska and in China during the 1940s. He has mental and actual pictures of a frozen winter land and of bombed-out buildings. Angi has

(Continued)

(Continued)

a prized possession of an audiotape of her grandfather telling stories of his early days as a circuit-riding preacher in Arkansas and Tennessee and being paid in chickens and produce.

Yet the elderly are not the only ones who engage in this review process. In fact, as soon as we are able to create symbols, we tell stories, we make sense out of the world and do our best to create stories that others will find interesting. The standard question, "So, what did you do at school today?" is an invitation to create a story—to piece together events in a way that will make sense to us and to others. Such a process plays a critical role in our social development and in our sense of well-being. For example, imagine having no stories to tell. Or imagine if all of your stories about organizational life were dark? To be human is to be a storyteller.

Second, stories function as a means of passing on values and norms. Although we may recall past events simply in order to reminisce or to recount an event, these same stories and others often become both an explicit and implicit way to hand on norms, values, and expectations. Rather than simply say, "That is not how we do things around here," a member might socialize a new member by telling about the fate of someone who did things right (or wrong). Gerald can still recall hearing a story 15 years ago about a company's loss of thousands of dollars due to a mistake in a paint-mixing procedure. Of course, he was being taught the correct procedure as the boss told the story.

Third, stories create a virtual shared reality for actors with little common experience. Bormann (1969) writes about narrative functioning to create community among strangers. As we enter into the details of a vivid story, we have a virtual experience of overlapping reality. That is why narrative is such a potent medium for transmitting and creating cultural identity.

Fourth, in these stories, you have illustrated *one route for exploring your own communication practices.* If written in detail, each story would reveal something of the cultural constraints and resources you perceived in each situation (see Eisenberg & Goodall, 1997). We could determine the implicit theories you held during the interaction, the extent to which you considered options for your response to the situation, and so on. Furthermore, we would learn something of how you frame the story in light of your current values and communication practices. What does the story tell, for example, about your values and ethics? What does it reveal about your reaction to authority? What does it have to say about your relationships with coworkers? What might we learn about your response to change?

Fifth, and finally, organizational stories can be *used to analyze the culture of an organization.* This point will be discussed in greater detail later, but suffice it to say that details from your stories do more than reveal your own practices; they also say something about the context of the stories. That context includes both the broader national culture as well as the immediate organizational culture. For instance, Gerald's research on a multinational firm revealed the employees were aware of the influence of national culture differences but not always clear on how they influenced such things as decision making and perceptions of effective supervisor behavior (Driskill, 1995; Driskill & Downs, 1995).

As a way to review the pervasive influence of organizations in our lives, consider completing the following exercise.

1. **Make a list** of 10 organizations that you have belonged to and/or currently belong to.

2. **Review this list and then, based on your memories of events in the above organizations, write down four organizational experiences** (stories of any type) that come to your mind. Do not take time to analyze or write details. Instead, jot down a phrase in two lines or less that captures the event. If you draw blanks before you reach four experiences, review your list of 10 organizations and ask: "Now, what experiences first come to my mind when I think about my time with organization 'X'?" Put down the first stories that come to mind.

3. **Reflect on the following questions concerning the stories you recalled:**
   - What themes predominated in your organizational stories?
   - Do you have stories of success as well as failure?
   - Do you have stories that you would still rather not talk about?
   - Are there situations that still perplex you?
   - Do you have stories that still excite and motivate you?

Rehearsal 4.3 A Game of Metaphors

Though usually unconsciously, we act out "cultural" scripts of what we view as appropriate and effective communication (Fairhurst & Sarr, 1996). Even in an era of film and videotape, it is hard to see our own performances, our ways of responding to organizational structures. We have neither the eyes nor the objectivity of an outsider for viewing our own actions. A metaphor game can help gain some perspective. Let us illustrate.

If someone were to ask Gerald what it is like to work at the university, one answer would be that it is like being on a "team of circus clowns." The metaphor refers to a department that maintains a sense of humor amid the constant coordination needed to adjust to continuous changes. Faculty sometimes wear faces to diffuse a conflict and are engaged in improvisational acting as they juggle competing demands and schedules.

Angi, in a past role as an administrator at a Christian university, might use the metaphor of a Japanese Kabuki theater—thick masks often concealing personal identities and feelings, with a high degree of drama and traditional ritual.

Now it is your turn. Identify a metaphor or analogy that comes to mind that best captures one of your own organizations. Perhaps you can think of more than one metaphor. These metaphors, as we will see, provide a rich source of insight. For example, Gerald's circus metaphor suggests the expectation of being able to take a joke and other roles of humor associated with workload pressures. The circus clown metaphor also suggests that if you cannot laugh at yourself, your own mistakes and limits, as others laugh with you, then you will not be viewed as an effective member of the organization. Furthermore, you should not spend time complaining about changes, workloads, and so on. Faculty must juggle many duties (advising, writing, teaching, consulting, committee work, etc.). A clown with a sad face is not viewed in a positive light. In action, then, the metaphor does more than provide a simple view of life in the department—it suggests a great deal about our communication behavior and how we define effective or competent communication.

Angi's theater metaphor implies the value of learning tradition so you can perform your role in a way that will be accepted. In a similar vein, Angi's theater metaphor implies that members need to stay in character and not let the mask slip.

There is also an implication that improvisation is less valued than scripted organizational rehearsal. Put differently, even if you are not familiar with a Kabuki theater, you are likely to recall situations when someone (or perhaps everyone) in your organization values certainty and predictability over spontaneous and less predictable behavior.

Although a single metaphor is far from a complete cultural analysis, the exercise demonstrates one way to begin the process of cultural analysis. If such an exercise were repeated across a representative sample of organizational members, patterns would likely emerge that would capture important elements of the culture, such as heroes and values. Combined with other cultural analysis methods, the identification of metaphors becomes a potent way to portray culture.

After you identify one or more metaphors, reflect on the following questions:

- What does the metaphor reveal about what is permitted in the organization?
- What does the metaphor reveal about what is prohibited in the organization?
- How widely held is the metaphor (i.e., across departments, roles, etc.)?
- What does the metaphor suggest about organizational values?

PART III

Cultural Data Collection and Interpretation

An Introduction to Step Three

Use Multiple Methods for Gathering Cultural Information: Method Acting

The Meeting

You walk into a meeting and before you sit down, you notice that all the seats are taken except the one next to the boss. Everyone stops talking as you quickly, but quietly, sit down. You place your folder in front of you and look at your watch, finding that you were only 2 minutes late. The boss is talking about second-quarter earnings, and as she talks you glance around the room. You see one of your colleagues, hired just months before you, gazing out the window, apparently paying little attention. You shuffle a few papers in front of you to prepare for any questions you might be asked and then notice that several other partners in the firm are engaged in writing notes and are not paying attention. "No one seems to respect the boss" is the first thought that comes to mind.

The boss finishes what appears to be a tirade against poor time management on everyone's part and then asks for comments and questions. You think it strange that she says nothing about the rude behavior of her subordinates. Silence ensues, and while you want to ask a question about discrepancies you observed in the earnings statements, you see most everyone glancing at their watches and thus you decide to be silent. The boss calls the meeting to an end about 15 minutes after it started.

Understand Concept of Culture

Identify Major Cultural Elements

Use Multiple Data Collection Methods

Synthesize And Interpret Cultural Data

Identify Applications

Objectives:

- Learn the importance of using multiple data collection methods.
- Understand the value of different methods for identifying the cultural elements.
- Gain insight into the rationale for the methods introduced in this workbook.
- Understand the process of protecting human subjects in a research study.

Stage Terms:

- Ethnography
- Triangulation
- Institutional Review Board

An Introduction to Cultural Analysis Methods

If you were the organizational actor in the story at the start of this section, you would be drawing inferences from the meeting you observed. Is it usual for employees to be early for meetings? Why is no one paying attention or asking questions? Why is the meeting so short? While we all observe interactions around us and try to make sense of what we see, we often are not equipped with specific methods for observing interactions and analyzing them in a systematic way.

Method actors use a variety of tactics to provide a credible interpretation of their roles and the script of the play. They have as their "essential task the reproduction of recognizable reality—on stage (or screen), based on an acute observation of the world" (Vineberg, 1991, p. 6). In a similar vein, anthropologists who immerse themselves in a foreign culture rely on three primary methods of data gathering and analysis: systematic observation, conversational interviews, and systematic analysis of various oral and written texts. Such qualitative techniques are often grouped under the heading of "ethnomethodology" or "ethnography." Goodall (1989) defines ethnography as "representing in words what you have lived through as a person when your stated purpose was to study a culture" (p. xxiii). A professional ethnographer might spend years attempting to integrate herself into the culture to fully understand it. During those years, she would repeat many iterations of observing regularities, asking natives of the culture for their interpretations of the regularities or their tacit knowledge of the culture, and analyzing field notes, interview transcripts, and cultural artifacts. The results of one layer of analysis would lead to a new round of interviews and conversations.

The cultural analysis described in this text is a shorter and shallower exploration of organizational culture. We ask you to penetrate the culture for only a few months of part-time exploration, using the same methods an anthropologist or method actor might use. Rather than dozens of repeated observations and interviews, you might conduct only a few. Yet you will find the same methods useful and productive, and you will come to understand the relationships among observation, interviews, and systematic analysis of texts, and how one often leads back into the other.

We suggest you start your process with observation, to gain a feel for the organization and its players and to notice regularities or paradoxes that will form the ground for interviews and qualitative surveys. Interviews will form the second step of the investigation. These interviews, almost conversations with organization members, will help you understand how they interpret the events you have observed. Surveys with open-ended questions that invite narrative responses can also be an effective way to gain interpretive data from a larger sample of organization members. Systematic analysis of organizational texts is the third technique for understanding culture. You will use it with your field notes of observations and with your

Table III.1   Overview of Data Collection Methods

Method	Focus	Cultural Elements Revealed
Observation	Artifacts	Rules Heroes History Values Communication style
	Interactions	Rules Heroes, villains, and outlaws Rituals Communication style
	Language	Metaphors Stories
	Symbols	Heroes Values Metaphors
Interviews/ Qualitative Surveys	Place Representative texts Heroes and villains Stories Rules History Metaphors Communication style	Values Root metaphors Cultural themes

Analysis
of Texts
	Field notes of observations
	Interview summaries or
	    transcripts
	Representative organizational
	    texts, drawn from
	    organizational communication
	    style (narratives or speeches,
	    documents, electronic
	    communication artifacts)
		Values
		Root metaphors
		Cultural themes

interview transcripts or summaries. You may also uncover important organizational texts during the process of observation and interviews. You should not automatically assume that mission statements, annual reports, employee manuals, or corporate newsletters are the most significant organizational texts to analyze. Organization members might suggest that internal memos, employee e-mails, or even coffee room bulletin boards are truer reflections of organizational culture. We suggest a variety of systematic methods for analyzing organizational texts. Table III.1 suggests a focus for each method and the cultural elements revealed.

For example, in observation you might choose to focus on artifacts such as office arrangement, objects hanging on the walls, corporate dress style, and public meeting spaces such as conference rooms or break rooms. In this analysis you might especially look for signs of history—pictures of the founders prominently displayed or historical pictures. You might also look for regularities that would suggest formal rules or informal norms, such as a lack of personal items in offices or conformity in style of dress. You might also find suggestions of heroes—pictures hanging on the wall, prominent office locations, employees who are frequently mentioned with high regard. You can subtly infer values from the artifacts you observe. How does the organization present itself to insiders and outsiders?

In interviews or qualitative surveys you would follow up on the things you have observed, to ask their meaning from an inside perspective. You'd also ask about things it is difficult to observe—things such as stories, representative texts, the influence of place, metaphors, and communication style.

As you do your analysis of organizational texts, you will analyze your observation field notes and interview summaries or transcripts in systematic ways. You will also perform a series of analyses of representative texts to tease out a sense of history, language, symbols, metaphors, and other clues that will ultimately lead you to conclusions about organizational values, root metaphors, and other cultural themes.

Table III.1 merely suggests a place to start with each method; it is not a prescription of what information necessarily is paired with each method. Indeed, you can usually find any of the 12 elements of culture revealed in any of the methods we cover in Chapter 5.

Each of us has used the data collection methods outlined in this unit. We may not have consciously walked backstage and taken on the role of anthropologist or method actor. Whether or not we viewed them as "methods" per se, we have been observers of organizational behavior, we have read documents in our organizations to gain knowledge or insight, and in most cases we have participated in informal interviews and possibly in formal surveys. Thus, the process of collecting data about culture, like the notion of cultural elements, is not foreign ground. Put differently, to be a member of an organization is to be a "sense-maker," someone who is trying to make sense of his or her environment (Weick, 1995). This process of sense making is important not only during the first weeks as a new member of an organization, but also during organizational changes and job promotions (Kramer & Noland, 1999). The only ways to gain information, to make sense of an organization is to observe, ask questions, and/or ask someone else to observe or ask questions for us.

These naïve approaches to understanding culture can have great practical significance for the organization member. Angi conducted one cultural analysis in which there was one employee in an insurance company that no one could stand. The cultural analysis team had probed to understand why this woman was so disliked and rejected by the majority of other employees. All agreed she was competent and hard working. When pressed for details, many of the employees gave the same answer about her failure to fit in. "She brings crackers to the office potluck," several explained, assuming that we would understand immediately the significance of this culinary contribution.

Only in analyzing the culture further did they understand the significance. The monthly office potluck embodied several of the organization's defining values and a sense of community and sharing, nurturing, and generosity. All the employees put great effort into bringing creative and tasty dishes. The fact that this employee brought crackers signified to the others that she did not care about the group and that she was cheap. It, of course, signified that she did not share other important group values. The employee probably never grasped the seriousness of her offense or understood why she was disliked by coworkers. She had not picked up on cultural cues about values or the significance of the potluck ritual within the company.

Two "safe" assumptions about our everyday data collection habits prove the value of this approach. *First, we tend to draw conclusions about culture based on sporadic, biased, and incomplete information.* In short, we can improve the thoroughness and validity of our efforts. And *second, incomplete data lead to interpretations that can harm the effectiveness of our communication and thus adversely influence the ethicality and credibility of our leadership efforts.* The hypothetical meeting presented at the start of this chapter is an example of one person's observations. Notice how the story contains a mix of descriptive data ("2 minutes late") and interpretive data ("they must not respect the boss"). The newcomer made a decision not to ask a question based on everyone else's behavior. It is clear, however, that he has much to learn about the function of these meetings and when, if ever, questions can be asked at meetings. In short, the newcomer's observations, his experience of this meeting, form an important aspect of information that will guide his future behavior. The question, then, is how can he improve his abilities as an observer? As a participant in the confusing, often ambiguous world of organizations, how can he move forward from this meeting to contribute to an organizational culture that is more effective and ethical?

Just as consultants and researchers can be critiqued based on their methods used for data collection and interpretation, so can and should we be. If, for example, from the above meeting experience, I fail to ask questions of colleagues even after they present incomplete or inaccurate information at a meeting, then my behavior is no longer simply that of "fitting in"; it can be challenged on ethical grounds.

Rehearsal III.1 Introduction to
Method Acting: The Last Time I Was Wrong

Purpose: Identify the types of informal data you collect and the consequences of relying on these data.

Steps:

1. Recall a time when you drew an inaccurate conclusion about a work relationship, a company policy, or perhaps a change introduced in your organization.

2. What types of cultural data did you use to infer your mistaken conclusion?

3. What other types of data might have helped? What other cultural elements might have helped improve the accuracy of your inference?

Miller and Jablin (1991) point out an inverse relationship between risk and information accuracy when seeking information in organizational entry. The less obtrusive ways of gathering information, such as observing the behaviors of others and drawing inferences, may be perceived as "safer" by the average employee because there is less risk of offending someone or appearing stupid. Yet this less direct way of gathering information can lead the employee to draw the wrong conclusions about the behaviors observed. The more direct information-gaining strategy of asking specific questions produces more reliable data but may be seen as more risky by the employee because of fear of loss of face or being perceived as incapable.

Connections: Getting the Best Data

The basic rationale for using multiple methods is that the validity of our cultural interpretations can be improved. The idea of multiple methods is called method "triangulation" and suggests that rather than relying on perceptions from a single method, such as surveys, the effective cultural analyst uses additional methods, such as observations, to enrich the data set (Miles & Huberman, 1984). For example, informal "interviews" in the organization may prompt you to take note of a metaphor used by an employee who says, "Working here is like visiting cyberspace." Observations of work teams or the physical setting may be used to determine the pervasiveness and salience of the metaphor (e.g., is it found in company logos, newsletters, or in language used during meetings?). For instance, if space was devoted each week in the newsletter to applications of the latest and best of technology, then support exists for the metaphor beyond the one-time mention by a single employee. Surveys use triangulation to find a point by identifying two vectors that intersect. Triangulation provides the basis for drawing more credible conclusions about a culture.

Will Multiple Methods Result in Objectivity?

A common misconception is that that you can somehow create an objective interpretation if you get the right data. We would point out that even triangulated data do not produce an objective view of organizational culture. A researcher always develops subjective conclusions from a point of view. Triangulation produces data drawn from multiple points of reference but still contains elements of subjectivity. You will need to accept at the outset that your conclusions about the organizational culture may be different from those another individual might draw. This does not mean that either is invalid. It does mean that you need to be explicit about supporting your conclusions with data and explaining why you drew the conclusions you did from the data you analyzed. This transparency of logic would allow your readers or listeners to compare the ways in which they might draw different conclusions from the same data set.

What About Examples of Cultural Analysis That Have a Single Method or Single Cultural Element Focus?

Researchers sometimes use multiple methods to obtain information about one or at times two cultural elements. In some cases, however, a more specialized approach (e.g., root metaphor, linguistics, rules) may focus on a particular "element as a method" for interpreting culture. For example, an analysis of stories may be the method used to decipher organizational values (e.g., Meyer, 1995). The goal of this workbook is to help you perform a more comprehensive cultural analysis in order to produce competent individual and organizational performances. The key is to allow these researchers to spark your imagination regarding the various methods that can be used to interpret culture. Furthermore, the examples gleaned from these articles are of focused efforts designed to "impress" you with the value or importance of a given element. Our goal is to go beyond the study of one element to gaining a richer description of the culture than can be obtained from a focus on a single method or element.

In the following four chapters we explore each method in more depth and offer practical suggestions for how you can use each to gain insight into your organizational culture. We begin with the most basic tool for actors seeking to be more effective at directing and leading the communication practices on the stage-observation.

One other general caution should be stressed in formal studies of organizational culture, such as the one you are undertaking through this text. Most universities require researchers using human subjects to seek approval from an institutional research board (IRB). This requirement applies to student projects as well. Your instructor can guide you with the particular requirements and processes at your university.

In general, protection of human subjects is based on three principles contained in the Belmont Report of Ethical Principles and Guidelines for the Protection of Human Subjects of Research, which was issued by the National Commission for the Protection of Human Subjects of Biomedical and Behavioral Research (previously the Office for Protection of Research Risks) in 1979. These three principles include (a) that the study will pose no undue risks to the life, health, or integrity of research subjects; (b) that any risks to subjects are outweighed by the potential significance of the study; and (c) that subjects have the opportunity to give informed consent about their participation in the study.

An informed consent form must contain information about the purpose and procedures of the study, any risk involved, the voluntary nature of participation and ability to withdraw at any stage of the study, and contact information for questions or concerns. It also must inform subjects of the nature of confidentiality and how their privacy will be protected in the study. It will also inform them about what will be done with the information obtained in the study. An example of an informed consent form is included in Rehearsal III.2.

Summary

Before diving into your analysis, you should understand several key ideas in the overview of methods:

1. The cultural analysis you will conduct seeks to gather valid and credible data without engaging in the years of data collection that might be involved in an ethnography of an organization.

2. We suggest that you use the methods introduced in the coming chapters in the following order: observation, then interviews and surveys, followed by systematic analysis of organizational texts.

3. You have used the data collection methods outlined in this unit, yet your everyday data collection process tends to provide incomplete and biased information that can decrease effective leadership.

4. Less direct or obtrusive methods of data collection, such as observations, are safer in terms of influencing participants but may lead to wrong conclusions. Conversely, more direct information-gaining strategies such as formal interviews are less safe but may provide more reliable data because of your ability to gain insider perspectives.

5. Triangulation or using multiple methods will result in more credible conclusions about a culture.

6. One person's conclusions about the organizational culture may be different from those another individual might draw.

7. You should seek to collect information about all of the major cultural elements.

8. You may need to seek approval from a university institutional review board before beginning your study.

Rehearsal III.2 Sample Informed Consent Form

Adapt the following informed consent form for use in your cultural analysis.

This consent form applies to:

Name: _____

The following information is provided to inform you about the research on _____. Please feel free to ask any questions you may have about this study and the information given below. You will be given an opportunity to ask questions and to have your questions answered. In addition, you will be given a copy of this consent form.

1. **Purpose of the study.** This study is being conducted by [researcher's name and faculty/student status] of the Department/School/College of [subject] at the University of [university name] in order to better understand [research topic]. This research will help [who?] better understand how [process of issue being investigated]. Your responses in the interview are confidential and available only to the [interviewer/researcher/faculty supervisor].

(Continued)

(Continued)

2. **Description of the procedures to be followed and approximate duration of the study.** Participants in the research will participate in [describe data collection process], which will focus on [research topic]. This [data collection process] will last approximately [length of time].

3. **Description of the discomforts, inconveniences, and/or risks that can reasonably be expected as a result of participation in this study.** Discussing [research topic] may be uncomfortable, and [care services] will [or will not] be available to you as a result of your participation.

4. **Description of how confidentiality will be assured and the limits to these assurances, if any.**

5. **Anticipated benefits resulting from this study.**
   A. The potential benefits to you from participating in the study are [describe benefits]. The study may be helpful to increase your understanding of [issue being investigated].
   B. The potential benefits to science and humanity that may result from this study are [describe benefits]. This study will provide information to [intended audience of research results] to help them [intended outcomes of the research results].

6. **Alternative procedures.** If alternative procedures exist, please describe them here. Otherwise, include a statement that says: There are no alternative procedures to participation in the interview.

7. **Contact information.** If you have any questions about this study, you can contact the person(s) below:

Name of Principal Investigator _____

Department/School _____

Name of Supervisor (if PI is a student) _____

Department/School _____

Include name, address, telephone number, and e-mail addresses

If you have any questions about your rights as a research subject, please contact the Chair of the Institutional Review Board at [telephone number].

5

Method Acting

Observation

Step Three: Use Multiple Data Collection Methods to Understand the Elements of Culture

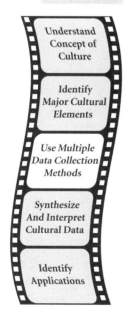

Understand
Concept of
Culture

Identify
Major Cultural
Elements

*Use Multiple
Data Collection
Methods*

*Synthesize
And Interpret
Cultural Data*

*Identify
Applications*

Observation

To concentrate, one must have an object of concentration; one cannot concentrate abstractly. The simple presence of an object will not induce concentration. If you look at a chair and try to concentrate, nothing will happen. If you start asking yourself simple questions—How wide is the chair? How tall is it? and so on—simple concentration will take place.

—Strasberg, *A Dream of Passion*, 1987, p. 131

Objectives:

- Learn four major observation roles
- Understand ways to enhance the validity and reliability of observation data

Stage Terms:

- Obtrusive and unobtrusive observation
- Complete observer
- Observer participant
- Participant observer
- Complete participant
- Field notes
- Bracketing

Imagine an actor (or a director) who never took the time to go behind the scenes, research a script or character, or learn the basic methods of acting. We would quickly judge such an actor to be incompetent. However, we all have moments when we realize that our observations can be skewed or biased; yet even with such awareness it is often easier and more comfortable to maintain our roles and avoid change. This awareness of bias in our perception can and should motivate us to sharpen our observation skills. Given this need, the goal in this chapter is to improve our understanding of and our ability to enact effective observer roles—the core or foundation of method acting and cultural analysis.

Observation is critical to method actors, as expressed by Lee Strasberg (1987). He describes training actors to concentrate on the particulars of a process that has become automatic, such as drinking a beverage. Only in concentrating on each element of the habitual behavior can the actor master the subtleties of re-creating a common behavior on stage. The actor must spend many hours in analyzing and practicing a behavior in order for it to appear natural and compelling on stage. Strasberg writes, "The ability to interrupt the automatic functioning of the nerves and muscles in order to create an object's presence for oneself . . . is part of the process of creating reality rather than imitating it" (p. 133).

Observer roles can be categorized by examining the degree of "obtrusiveness" or degree of influence the observer has on the members of organizations. "Obtrusive" behavior is that which calls attention to the observer, affecting the flow of behavior being observed. Different behavior may be seen as obtrusive depending on the organization. For example, extensive note taking during a meeting may be the norm in certain organizations, thus taking notes during a meeting would be unlikely to influence the flow of the meeting. Conversely, such note taking during a ritual morning coffee break would be likely to trigger responses from other members of the organization. Reviews of four observation roles followed by observation guidelines are presented as ways to consider the implication of each type of observer role.

Selecting a Method of Observation

There are four major observer roles. Each role involves trade-offs based on such factors as objectivity, insight into interactions, and ethics. As you review these, realize that it is not uncommon to move between different roles. In other words, entering into one type of observation role does not preclude your engaging in another type of role at some other point in time. For example, we have had students begin observation of a given nonprofit as a complete observer and switch to a participant observer as they began to identify with the mission of the nonprofit and get to know the staff and volunteers.

1. Complete Observer

In this role, you observe the culture with or without the organization's knowledge and without direct interaction with members. (Please note, however, that your instructor may require you to gain permission from the organization, even if you are studying your own organization.) To use the drama metaphor, you would be an actor doing research for a role, observing behavior of people similar to the character you are to portray. Assuming this role carries several implications:

- In traditional research terms, the researcher may have increased objectivity due to the lack of involvement with organization members that might bias his or her judgment.

- On the other hand, qualitative researchers would argue that the researcher would possibly also have fewer and less valid insights due to the distance from experience of members.

- The role of complete observer can raise possible ethical problems if you observe individuals without their permission, depending on the purposes of the research. If the organization studied is a professional football team, for instance, and performances are public, then the ethical concerns are less of an issue. In all instances, ethical guidelines must be observed.

- The complete observer role may be best when you do not have full access to the organization, when you have organizational permission to observe the organization, and/or when members' knowledge of your presence would be likely to harm research objectives. For example, individuals considering a career move who are trying to learn more about a particular type of organization may find this method appropriate. If, for instance, they want to learn more about the automotive industry, they may find it useful to show up at a public event or simply to walk through public areas of the organization to learn what they can from the setting and artifacts on display.

2. Observer-Participant

In this role, you would let members know they are being observed, and you would participate partially with them in the organization. This role carries different implications:

- This role somewhat reduces objectivity due to involvement, yet possibly increases validity by interacting with organization members and gaining their insights.

- Some would question validity when members are aware of your involvement.

- You may find adopting the observer-participant role places you on more solid ethical ground due to member knowledge of your involvement.

- This role is best when you have access to the organization and/or when member knowledge of your presence would be unlikely to harm research objectives; for example, observation of meetings to understand norms and interaction patterns for the purpose of enriching the current employee handbook.

3. Participant-Observer

In this role, you let members know they are being studied, and you become fully involved in the organization. The implications of this role include the following:

- According to a traditional research perspective, it produces reduced objectivity due to high involvement in the organization.

• This role produces increased access to the views and insights of organization members, and the researcher herself begins to understand the organization from both internal and external perspectives.

• This role places similar constraints on you as an observer-participant in relation to member awareness of your involvement, yet the more organizational members accept you as a participant, the less they are aware of you as an observer.

• Since organization members are aware of your dual role (researcher and participant), you are on fairly solid ethical ground.

• This role is best when you have longer-term access to the organization and/or when member knowledge of your presence would be unlikely to harm research objectives; for example, observation of day-to-day communication to understand positive and negative patterns that would affect training interventions.

4. Complete Participant

In this final role, you become fully involved without letting members know of your observation efforts. The implications include the following:

• You have reduced objectivity due to high involvement, and have a high level of insight due to identification with members.

• Possible ethical problems would ensue because of lack of notification of research subjects, depending on purposes of the observations. For example, if you dropped in on meetings without informing those present that you were also there to evaluate and report their behaviors, then your efforts would be judged unethical because of the potential harm that could result to those present. This approach might also be inconsistent with protection of human subjects if you did not allow informed consent of your observation.

• This role is best when you have access to the organization and/or when members' lack of knowledge of your presence would not influence the ethicality of your research purpose. For example, as a human resources department (HRD) manager you could serve and lead more effectively if you gleaned insights about norms and rules through observation of meetings and rituals.

Standards of protection of human subjects, presented in the overview to this section, are critical in cultural research, as well. If you present a cultural study to the CEO of an organization, and your study inadvertently reveals rule breaking or violation of cultural norms, it could have serious career implications for individuals you study.

One of the observation role options, "complete participant," should stand out as the form of observation we engage in every day. Unless you decide to inform others in the workplace of your analysis efforts, you are a complete participant. As a complete participant you are doing something external analysts and researchers are challenged to justify—"clandestine data collection." The ethical justification for an insider is based on the reality that your observation is doing what all members of organizations do, but simply doing it in a more systematic and planned manner. Nonetheless, realize that, for some, it will be appropriate to seek the permission of a manager or to inform employees of your analysis plans. For example, you may be a trainer in your organization or work in a role that has made you aware of the need for a cultural analysis. After reviewing the value of the study with those you decide to inform, you may want to move ahead with a formal analysis that would involve a participant observer role. Regardless of the role you select, the key is to be aware of the specific issues related to objectivity, validity, and ethics.

Conducting Observations

Once you have decided on the most appropriate role, review the following guides for help in the process of conducting the observation and taking notes. Approach the observation with some theoretical framework or purpose in mind. You cannot observe and record everything. You need to have a rationale for what you notice and record. The elements of culture provide such a framework. Try to notice those things you think might be tied to history, a value, a norm, or a cultural hero. We suggested in the introduction to the section on methods (see Table III.1) that your cultural observation could focus on artifacts, interactions, language, and symbols. We also suggested cultural elements most closely tied to each of these observable organizational representations. Look for things that have cultural significance as you follow these guidelines:

1. Make like an alien by making use of various techniques to become a "stranger."

a. *Write notes on the mundane*, seemingly unimportant events. Improving the quality of our observations, especially if you have been with an organization for much time, involves seeing things with new eyes. The first step in this process is taking notes that record information that you have grown to take for granted. For example, if you were an "old-timer" in the case study that began this unit, you would record the setting, the sitting arrangement, and when and how the meeting began and ended. Such detailed notes force you to see situations with new eyes.

b. *Mutate metaphors* by drawing comparisons or making analogies between things that you normally do not compare (Weick, 1979). Mutating metaphors involves merging or synthesizing two metaphors to capture conflicting values or rules. For example, imagine if you frequently heard two metaphors in your organization: "fast track" and "outer space." As you listened you got the sense that "good" employees were expected to be on the fast track. However, you also heard sarcastic statements about working in outer space with the implication being that there was not a clear sense of what was up or down, since in outer space "up and down" and "north and south" are arbitrary. To capture these two metaphors you might mutate them to create a new metaphor like "working at Organization Z is like being on a corporate ladder without ever knowing which direction is up or down." This mutated metaphor captures what members may be aware of but have not clearly articulated—"We hear about the expectation to move up the ladder but we do not know which way is up!" Such comparisons may clarify or serve to identify a problem in the organization.

Smith and Eisenberg (1987) in their article on Disneyland, for example, indicated that the root problem in employee relations might have begun when employees began seeing their work through the family rather than the drama metaphor. Rules and actions that might have been easily accepted through the drama metaphor became inappropriate when viewed through the lens of family. For example, you might replace a cast member who is incompetent in a role, but you do not fire family. If you were consulting with an organization that had operated primarily through a family metaphor, what implications would a change in that metaphor have for employees? Customers? Helping the organization manage change might involve a metaphor mutation—if employees were able to mutate metaphors they could envision the change in a new way. For example, the mutation might involve both metaphors, "an acting family" that has to determine who is best for what role.

c. *Ask "why" and "what function" questions of everything.* Though you will have to decide the appropriateness of asking others these types of questions, you should at the minimum reflect on them yourself. For example, you might observe an organization's annual retirement banquet and assume that it indicated a culture in which employee contributions were valued. However, if you asked a member of the organization about it, she might say that there is great pressure for older employees to take early retirement so that less expensive younger employees can be hired. Or she might note that it is a sign that the company values seniority more than excellent performance since the only significant award banquet in the organization is to honor retirees rather than high performers. Once you have made your own possible interpretations, you can make notes to ask organizational insiders how they would interpret the regularities you have observed.

2. If you do not or cannot take notes while observing, reserve time immediately after observation to jot down notes.

Note taking has the potential advantage of improving the quality of the information you collect on the organization. For those who rarely take notes or keep journals, the process will be awkward and feel like a waste of time. Still, the key is to make time for this process of describing what you see. You may think you will remember details later, but chances are you will forget many important details. Doing a thorough cultural analysis requires noting fine details of language, artifacts, and interaction. These are best captured in detailed field notes. Another value of the process of writing involves not just putting words on paper, but taking the time to capture events, reflect on them, and in time make sense of them. An enhanced or improved cultural analysis depends on your seeing all the possible "dots" in a connect-the-dots worksheet. Sometimes you draw conclusions—connect dots—without adequate attention to details that could change the shape of the picture. To use the drama analogy, note taking may force you to see a way to interpret the language being used in the play in a different light. For example, a review of notes might reveal a pattern you had not seen concerning the way certain types of conflicts were not discussed. This newly emerged pattern might then shed light on other practices, such as premature closure on decisions to avoid conflict. As shown in this example of conflict, your notes should reflect your observation of things that did *not* happen that one might have expected. For example, why did no one ask questions? Why did no one talk about anything not on the formal agenda? Why don't employees have any personal items in their offices?

3. Attempt to include observations of meetings, rituals, and so on as well as observations of less formal interactions, events, and the like.

The tendency, for example, may be to take notes of a ribbon cutting ceremony or a company picnic, but fail to record observations of communication at the coffeepot. Culture, as previously noted, reflects how members experience daily life in the organization. A weekly office meeting or daily coffeepot ritual provides just as much insight into organizational culture as an annual awards banquet. It may be that those coffeepot interactions include significant relationship development rituals that an insider may not see immediately. Such insights may help current employees do more to engage new employees to ensure the latter are not forced to catch on to the importance of the ritual on their own.

4. Use brackets [ ] to help you focus on descriptions instead of interpretations.

"Bracketing" refers to the idea of putting your first impressions, initial definitions of the culture, and inferences or insights inside of brackets. For example, your first weeks spent in observation might surface the way the lounge area has unique rituals with language you did not hear in other places in the building. These observations might prompt you to draw a conclusion about the overall culture. Strong personalities in interviews or meetings can also prompt a researcher to draw conclusions early in the process. Indeed, our own ambiguity or uncertainty in a new organization will often prompt us to develop premature conclusions. *The key is to bracket these conclusions until you have used other methods and explored all of the elements.* These premature conclusions, if not set aside, can prompt you to slant your future data collection toward supporting these conclusions. They help you separate description from your tentative interpretations as you process your observation. For example, in research on an organization that is involved in community building, Gerald is regularly challenged to place his own biases in brackets. The leaders that he participates with in this organization have differing political and theological positions. It's important for him to bracket reactions to these differences so other information about actual interactions remains in the foreground.

Using the above example, here are four different types of bracketed information that might occur while taking notes during participant observation of a leadership meeting in an organization.

a. *Questions to ask (other) insiders:* There were several new faces today, including two guests. [How would you compare and contrast what happens in a meeting when visitors or newcomers are present versus those times when just the old-timers are there?]

b. *Possible paradoxes, contradictions, root metaphor:* The meeting facilitator briefly introduced the guests who spoke about a recent statewide political initiative. [In past interviews I recall hearing discussions about being cautious about inviting guests to make presentations. I am not clear on the criteria being used . . . .]

c. *Later comparisons—see how your perceptions change:* The meeting ended with a ritual prayer and then with an additional prayer over a leader who was moving to another state to take on an international role in the unity movement. [The special send-off made me think about other meetings that included a special send-off. This particular send-off makes me want to compare the differences in that a value emerged that I had not heard before—a global vision of cooperation among faith leaders. The member seems to be in position to be a hero for this movement.]

d. *Personal reactions/differences:* The guest speakers talked about positive and negative reactions to their political initiative. [I was not fully comfortable with the presentation. I am not sure why, perhaps it was that I did not get to hear the full story, the rationale of their opponents. Has this group ever considered inviting those with divergent views to their meetings? This insight makes me consider business organizations that end up with groupthink because they do not have someone or charge someone to voice divergent views.]

5. If a newcomer or an outsider, make use of insiders to check your understanding of jargon and your inferences about cultural elements.

Use informal interviews to check if your understanding is accurate. We will discuss the role of interviews in greater depth; this guide is a reminder that observation alone is not sufficient.

Often your own interpretation of an artifact or event may be quite different from the way an insider (or a different insider) might interpret the same event. For example, in one study, conclusions were drawn about an organization's culture from its newsletter, only to discover later that no one read the newsletter, thus it had little impact on culture at the grassroots level. Another cultural analysis included a conclusion based on the many positive memos that the CEO sent to employees. They inferred that the culture was positive and supportive. When checking this conclusion with employees, they found that the memos from the CEO had become a joke because they were sent so frequently and so indiscriminately.

6. Review your notes to determine if they allow you to draw reasonable inferences about most of the cultural elements from your notes.

For example, do the notes of a meeting provide enough detail for you to make relatively valid inferences about communication rules? For instance, take a minute to read an edited version of the notes used in one of the previous guidelines:

> There were several new faces at the meeting today, including two guests. The meeting facilitator briefly introduced the guests, who spoke about a recent statewide political initiative. The guest speakers talked about positive and negative reactions to their political initiative. [I was not comfortable with the presentation because I did not get to hear the rationale of their opponents]. The meeting ended with a ritual prayer and with an additional prayer over a leader who was moving to another state to take on an eventual international role in the unity movement.

What inferences could you draw from just this brief section of notes? Notice how even a brief section reveals elements of the culture (e.g., meeting-ending rituals). However, if the above were the entire entry, what questions would you have? What would you have missed? A lack of detail about how the speakers were introduced, as well as participant interactions or reactions to the speaker, is also evident. Also, notice how we excluded brackets that were introduced in the earlier example. The lack of brackets around information means that a later review of these notes would be unlikely to resurface the same questions and observations. If you review notes a week or two later and see a lack of detail, begin to make adjustments. And, again, remember that the goal is to spend a season being a more careful, note-taking observer. This process will pay off in the form of new insights.

7. Categorize notes by elements.

We reviewed elements of culture in Chapter 4. At this point in your data collection, you should take a first step in analysis by entering relevant data from your notes based on these categories (e.g., rules, heroes, history). We provide a Rehearsal activity at the end of this chapter to move you down the road of "performing culture." In particular, as you classify data into elements, you should be aware of two pragmatic goals. First, classifying data into cultural element categories will serve to guide additional data collection by helping you see gaps. For instance, if you have 2 weeks of notes and have been unable to identify a hero or communication rule, you should let this gap prompt closer and more varied (more times, situations) observations. Second, classifying data into element categories will aid you in the creation of an interview guide or survey. We will cover interviews and surveys in the next chapter. A good set of notes categorized by elements will aid you in gaining the most from these additional data collection practices by helping you identify areas where you need greater clarity or confirmation. For instance, you may have identified what you believe to be a major cultural hero from reading a history of the organization. However, the name of this hero never surfaces in informal discussions or formal meetings. Interviews or surveys may help you determine the relevance of the hero's values and vision for the present.

Connections: Getting More From Rites and Rituals

The elements of culture can be either directly observed (for instance, language and rituals) or inferred from observations (for example, rules and values). A frequent and rich object of observation is the organizational rite or ritual—either a special event in the organization or a daily routine with cultural significance. As you stand backstage, you may find it helpful to understand that something as commonplace and easily observed as a ritual may have more to it than you first realize. A study by Trice and Beyer (1984) illustrated the amount of cultural information that can be gleaned from an observation of rites and ceremonies (forms of rituals). They found numerous types of rites, each of which is listed below. Consider noting examples from your own organization as a way to gain insight to the significance of observing these various types of rites.

Types of Rites:

- Passage: facilitates transition into new social roles and status (e.g., Army basic training)
- Degradation: dissolve social identities and power (e.g., firing and replacing)

- Enhancement: enhance social identities and power (e.g., training certification program)
- Renewal: refurbish social structures and improve their functioning (e.g., a retreat for organizational development)
- Conflict reduction: reduce conflict and aggression (e.g., collective bargaining)
- Integration: encourage and revive common feelings that bind members together and build commitment (e.g., office Christmas party)

Observing and analyzing these various types of rites and rituals provides insight into other elements of culture. For example, an analysis of a retreat or a Christmas party may reveal communication rules, heroes, and history. In either of these settings, a speaker (guest or manager) may review past events or honor certain events or employees. As you listen, you will be able to glean something about the espoused values of the organization. However, in your analysis you must be sure to decipher manifest as well as latent meanings of rites. For instance, the manifest or obvious "surface" meaning of a retreat for organizational development might be the value the organization places on personnel training and planning. In contrast, the latent meaning or the hidden, less obvious meaning might relate to the value placed on renewing and reinforcing friendships in the organization. Notice how in this example, based on Trice and Beyer's (1984) categories, one ritual can serve two functions. For example, the retreat may include a time for play and interaction that serves to bind members together—an integration function. During the same ritual, a renewal function may be served if the key speaker recognizes and reaffirms the current structure of the organization by honoring members who have "climbed the ladder."

Yet even the richness of such an analysis should only underscore an earlier point made. If your analysis focuses on a single element, even an element that holds insights for other elements, you are likely to leave the organization with a skewed or inaccurate understanding of the culture.

Rehearsal 5.1 A Potpourri of
Things to Observe in Cultural Analysis

Purpose: Practice observing a variety of organization settings and events that provide insight to elements of culture.

Directions: Review the following list of questions. Select two or three and attempt answers to these based on the organization you are analyzing.

1. What kind of building houses the organization? What impression does it convey to employees? Visitors?

2. What kind of parking is available? Is there any reserved parking? For whom? Is there any pattern of vehicles in the parking lot?

3. What does the entry look like? What kind of security? A receptionist?

4. Is there a waiting area for visitors? Does it have chairs? What kind of furniture? What kind of reading material? What is on the walls?

5. How is office space configured? Are there "premium" offices like corner spaces or windows with a better view? Who has these offices?

6. Are there offices or cubicles? Are office doors open or shut?

7. Is workspace nondescript or are there personal items? What type of personal items do employees have in their spaces?

8. Do people seem to be working alone or in groups?

9. Are there any items on the walls depicting the history? Photographs of founders? Pictures of early physical locations?

10. Are there pictures of anyone in public office spaces? Of whom? Why?

11. What types of common areas are present? Conference rooms? Break rooms or lounges? Does access to these spaces seem to be restricted?

12. What is in the break room? Do people seem to use it?

13. What is on the bulletin boards?

14. What type of technology do members use? Are there computers on every desk? Recent or vintage? Do employees carry PDAs? Pagers? Cell phones?

15. What do people wear? Do there seem to be status differences indicated by dress? Is dress formal or casual?

16. How do people address one another? First names? Level of formality?

17. Observe a meeting. Where do people sit? Who speaks at the meeting and who does not? Do there seem to be cliques supporting different points of view? Is conflict expressed openly? How long do meetings last?

18. Are there awards on the walls? Corporate awards? Individual awards? Team awards?

19. Is there anything in this office to indicate uniqueness based on geographic area, or could this office just as easily be located in Boston as Santa Fe?

20. How much diversity do you observe by race/ethnicity, gender, age, dress?

Summary

Observation as a cultural analysis tool is about taking a step beyond what you do everyday. The key is to be more observant, more aware of what and how you see. Another difference in systematic observation is the formal recording of detailed field notes. At the end of this chapter we provide additional rehearsals aimed at helping you in the observation process in general and the note-taking process in particular. As you engage in these activities and other observation efforts, you should have a better sense of how to apply the major ideas presented in this chapter.

1. There are four observation roles (i.e., complete observer, observer-participant, participant-observer, complete participant). Each has advantages and disadvantages

2. Seven guidelines should aid you in the observation process
   - Make like an alien by making use of various techniques to become a "stranger"
   - Take notes while observing or reserve time immediately after observation
   - Include observations of formal meetings, rituals, and the like, as well as less formal interactions.
   - Use brackets to help you distinguish descriptions and interpretations. Bracket items such as questions, possible paradoxes, later comparisons, and personal reactions/differences.
   - Use insiders to check your understanding of jargon and your inferences about cultural elements.
   - Review your notes to draw inferences about the cultural elements.
   - Categorize notes by elements to guide additional data collection to fill gaps; create interview guides or surveys based on your analysis of data in element categories.

3. Rites and rituals are particularly rich sites for gathering observational cultural data; however, you should remain aware of the need to explore and gather information about all of the elements of culture.

4. As an actor with a renewed commitment to observation, if you enact the various guidelines we have suggested, you should become more adept at competent cultural performance.

Rehearsal 5.2 Alien Culture Observation

Purpose: To develop skills in qualitative data collection and analysis through observing an unfamiliar culture and to become experientially familiar with the concept of seeing a culture through "alien" eyes. The process followed here is a short version of each of the steps of a cultural analysis.

Steps:

1. Identify a culture that
   a. you consider "alien" to your own
   b. you have limited or no existing knowledge about
   c. would not be dangerous to observe (!)
   d. you would most likely not observe if not encouraged to by this Rehearsal

2. Arrange a time to visit the culture
   a. Allow a minimum of 1–2 hours
   b. Be sure to gain permission if needed
   c. Take a friend with you if needed for comfort or "fun"

3. Be as unobtrusive as possible
Remember that unobtrusive behavior depends on the organization. For example, if you visit an open Weight Watcher meeting, unobtrusive might mean keeping things on a first-name basis and not inquiring too much about the background of other participants. In contrast, unobtrusive in an accounting firm might be quietly taking notes during a meeting with the partners.

4. Take field notes during and/or after the observation
   a. Jot down descriptive information related to both verbal and nonverbal communication.
   b. Bracket [ ] information that relates to your own personal reactions, feelings, interpretations.
   c. An example field note entry from an observation of the UK Day Care might look like this:

The corner of the room is blocked off from the rest of the larger room. The children in the area are in the 2-year-old age group. [I find it strange that they spend most of their day away from older and younger kids]. In the morning, all of the children are greeted with a hug, some children stood limply and did not return the hug while others squeezed back tightly. [Why don't they ask if the child wants to be hugged?] A teacher runs from one side of the area to catch a child about to hit another child with a block. He makes it in time and after removing the block takes the little girl's hand and has her softly touch the little boy she was about to hit. The teacher says, "Remember hands are for touching softly, not for hitting and hurting." [Why didn't he say anything about the boy taking the block from the girl!]

5. Develop a summary that
   a. provides example data related to at least three of the elements of culture.

(Continued)

(Continued)

For example:

- **Rules:** Redirect aggression by verbally and nonverbally demonstrating appropriate use of hands. Several teachers were observed telling a child how to touch.

- **Physical Setting:** The setup of the room provides a way for age-specific teaching and interaction to occur.

- **Rituals:** Morning hugs are part of the daily activities.

  b. interprets the data (organized by elements) by stating an overall theme

For example: *Positive use of touch is a mandated and encouraged behavior. Rules and rituals indicate that teachers should initiate touch often during the day as well as encourage children to touch each other in appropriate ways.*

  c. infers an overall definition of the culture based on themes and elements

Examples: A paradox, *The UK Day Care restricts inter-age touching, but mandates adult-child touching.* Or a root metaphor, *The UK Day Care is like. . . .*

6. **Prepare a summary to discuss with a mentor, a colleague, or an instructor.**

Rehearsal 5.3 Note-Taking Guidelines

The best way to sharpen your observation abilities is through practice. A review of note-taking guidelines is provided in a checklist to assist you. Use this checklist to review the field notes you compiled in the "Alien Culture" assignment to be sure you followed all the guidelines about systematic observation.

_____1. Make like an alien by making use of various techniques to become a "stranger":
   a. Write notes on the mundane
   b. Mutate metaphors
   c. Ask "why" and "what function" questions of everything

_____2. If you do not or cannot take notes while observing, reserve time immediately after observation to jot down notes.

_____3. Attempt to include observations of meetings, rituals, and so on, as well as observations of less formal interactions, events, and more.

_____4. Use brackets [ ] to help you focus on descriptions instead of interpretations.
Use brackets for the following:
   a. questions to ask (other) insiders
   b. possible paradoxes, contradictions, root metaphors
   c. later comparisons—see how your perceptions change
   d. personal reactions/differences

_____5. If a newcomer or outsider, make use of insiders to check your understanding of jargon and your inferences about rules and values, and so on.

_____6. Review your notes to determine if you can draw reasonable inferences about most of the cultural elements from your notes.

_____7. Categorize notes by elements to
   a. guide additional data collection to fill gaps
   b. create interview guides or surveys based on your analysis of data in element categories

6

Method Acting

Interviews and Surveys

How employees personally feel, think, and see the company and their work have a significant impact on the character and quality of their work, their relation to management, and their response to innovation and change.

—Deetz, Tracy, and Simpson, *Leading Organizations Through Transition*, 2000, pp. 1–2

Step Three: Use Multiple Data Collection Methods to Understand the Elements of Culture

Objectives:

- Appreciate the challenges involved in interviewing members
- Learn six general interviewing principles
- Understand the different factors to consider when interviewing as a member of the culture versus as an outsider to the culture
- Learn five principles for conducing ethnographic interviews
- Gain a general understanding of qualitative surveys

Stage Terms:

- Ethnographic interviews
- Levels of communication competence
- Open versus closed questions
- Leading questions
- Open souls doctrine
- Rapport

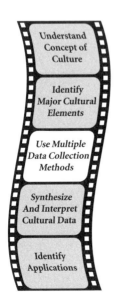

Method actors, like effective observers of culture, become adept at making observations. They also rely on informal interviews as part of survival on stage. Vineberg (1991) reported that Jane Fonda spent weeks interviewing prostitutes in preparation for her role in *Klute*. Similarly, Jon Voight spent hours in a wheel chair each day and spent time talking with Vietnam veterans before he undertook the role of a disabled veteran in *Coming Home*. Communication between actors in a scene, including natural reactions and questions of each other, is at the core of the type of interviewing we introduce in this chapter. We introduce you to ways to sharpen your informal, as well as your more formal, interviewing techniques.

Like observations, interviews can range in their degree of formality and obtrusiveness. "Ethnographic interviews" are by definition best when both participants view them as a "friendly conversation" as opposed to an actual interview. In fact, if an informal interview with a coworker became a series of direct questions, fired one after another, your colleague might shut down at some point by saying, "Hey, what is this, an interview?" To return to the director metaphor, if the actors on stage sense you are "after them," out to put them on the spot, they will be less likely to help you understand what is going on in their world, in the very play you are seeking to guide and direct.

Interviewing organization members about organization culture is grounded in several assumptions:

• Organizational culture is constructed by organization members and woven deeply throughout organizational sense making. It is not the property of organizational leaders. The values and views of leaders are not culturally defining unless members of the organization share the values and interpretations of management.

• Organization members can talk knowledgeably and authoritatively about their own organizational experiences and meanings. Harre and Secord (1973) refer to this as the "open souls doctrine," that one unique attribute of human beings is their ability to reflect and comment on their own behavior.

• However, organization members vary in their degree of consciousness about cultural values and practices. Harris (1979) discussed three levels of "competence," or awareness of communication rules. At a minimal level, culture operates at a subconscious or tacit level. The member may behave in culturally appropriate ways but may not be able to discuss the reasons why certain actions are appropriate. He may not able to communicate effectively with individuals from other national cultures, who don't share the same unconscious cultural background assumptions. At a satisfactory level of competence, the organization member can explain how things are done in the culture but can operate only within the way of thinking and acting in that culture. At an optimal level of competence, the interviewee could explain not only the internal logic but also demonstrate "multiframe" thinking, being able to see the organizational culture from multiple points of view. At this level, the individual is able to adapt or adopt or work toward cultural synergy when interacting with members of another culture. Competence is not synonymous with intelligence or personality. All of us are optimally competent in some cultural aspects and minimal in others.

Before we delve deeply into the particulars of cultural interviews, it would be helpful to discuss general interviewing principles:

Principle 1: Rapport with the interviewee is critical to gaining candid and valid information. The interviewee must understand your purpose, feel some motivation to share information, feel safe, and trust you in order to share sensitive information. It is therefore essential to spend time at the start of the interview building rapport. This initial stage should include a full description of your purpose. If there has been conflict or change in the organization, interviewees may suspect your motives or purpose even when you tell them you are trying to understand the culture. We have both had interviewees tell us they feared the interview because they believed management would use the data as a way to pave the way for further job layoffs or reorganizations, for example.

Motivating the interviewee is also important. This involves sharing the benefits of understanding culture and discussing possible ways that this information can be used to improve working conditions or organizational effectiveness. If interviewees believe that organizational leaders will actually use the information gained for constructive change, they are more motivated to share information. Promising to share results with employees also enhances their motivation. It is important for you to understand, however, that the greatest motivation to participate is intrinsic for the interviewee. Few employees are ever asked about their views or experiences in the organization. Therefore, it is not surprising that being asked to comment as an "expert" on the organization confers a sense of significance and inclusion within the organization. We are continually surprised at how much participants enjoy the process of the cultural interview and how much information they are willing to share.

Rapport is also created through trust and security. Interviewees feel secure as you promise them the interview is confidential and as you create credibility through your communication manner. The promises you make of confidentiality must have a basis in fact. We always negotiate in advance that no raw data from our observation (field notes, surveys, documents) will be available to the organization. We also obtain agreement in advance that we will not reveal the source of interview comments or identity of employees in organizational stories. These assurances are critical to your credibility as a researcher. You must project competence and respect in order to gain this credibility with the interviewee. Box 6.1 captures various stages of rapport building. These stages serve to heighten awareness of normal aspects of the process and factors to keep in mind at each stage. Notice how the higher or more developed the rapport the more the interview is like a partnership in the cultural analysis process. While such levels of rapport are not necessary for an effective cultural analysis, we see the value of making time to develop such relationships.

Box 6.1 Stages of the Rapport Process

Apprehension is a normal first stage experienced by most interviewees. To put interviewees at ease, focus on low-risk descriptive questions such as describing their job or how they came to work at the company. Adapt to each person. The key rule is to keep them talking.

Exploration is the second stage of rapport in which interviewees may test boundaries to ascertain if they can trust you. You can help them in trust building by

- repeated explanations of your role, confidentiality, the analysis process, purpose of questions, and the recording process
- restatement of information in their language; speak as you would to someone in their culture

Cooperation is the third stage of rapport building, in which interviewees begin to see a shared purpose for the interview. You can enhance their motivation to cooperate by describing the constructive uses of the interview and by giving attention and significance to the information they are providing.

Participation is the final stage of rapport building. The interviewee becomes an active participant in helping find ways to assist you in learning about the culture. In this stage the control and direction of the interview are shared, and it becomes more of a conversation.

Principle 2: Select the appropriate wording for your questions. Question wording and construction are critical to eliciting the information you want. You have to ask the right question in the right way to unlock the perception of the interviewee. Question construction and clarity and organizationally appropriate language are all keys to effective cultural interviewing.

Interview questions can range across a continuum from open to closed. *Closed questions* ask for a short, specific answer. They include yes-no answers or questions that ask for a specific piece of information, such as, "What is your title?" "Who is an individual considered a hero in this organization?" "When was this organization founded?" On the other hand, *open questions* such as, "What is it like to work here?" or "Tell me about something that could get you in trouble here" require more expansive answers. Cultural interviewing calls for more open question construction because you are seeking stories, metaphors, explanations, and other rich data to understand organizational logic and values. Some questions, however, are too open to offer sufficient guidance to the interviewee. A question like, "Tell me about this organization" may be open but can also be intimidating to an interviewee who doesn't know where to begin or what you're looking for. Midrange open questions are usually the most effective.

Not only should questions be open, they also must be clear to the interviewee. Using cultural terms you have learned in this text may seem like jargon to the average organization member. For example, instead of asking about recognition rituals you might ask, "How do employees get recognized here? What kinds of honors or awards are given to employees here?" Or instead of asking about symbols, you might say, "Why is the door greeter important to Wal-Mart?" or "What employee is a perfect example of what Company A stands for?" Sometimes a question is just confusing in its wording or hard to answer. As you start your interview process, it is good to "pilot test" your interview questions with a few sample employees who are typical of the subjects who will be interviewed to make sure questions are clear and understandable.

It is also important to use language appropriate in the culture you are studying. As you observe the organization in your first step of data gathering, you need to pay attention to organizational titles, acronyms, and unique terms. Being able to use these terms appropriately in your questions gives you credibility and taps into culture more easily. For example, if sales-people are called associates, that is culturally significant. You should use the term *associate* in your question and ask what it means to them.

Finally, you may need to adapt your questions as you ascertain through your interaction whether your interviewee has minimal, satisfactory, or optimal competence or conscious awareness of organizational logic. If the interviewee has minimal competence, he may respond to many of your questions with, "I don't know why we do it that way. We just do," or "I don't know exactly what that term signifies. That just what we call it." With such an individual you might need to shift your questions to describing how things are done, but not asking that interviewee to interpret or explain. With an interviewee with satisfactory competence, you could expect more explanation and interpretation, but such a person could not offer comparative judgments or explain why one pattern was chosen instead of another value or way of interpreting. An organization member at satisfactory competence is immersed in the current system logic and probably cannot understand the system from multiple points of view or adopt a more objective stance of seeing the organization from an outside point of view. Questions for this type of interviewee might ask for interpretation of what this means within the system or why something is inappropriate, but you could not ask him or her why a certain value was privileged over another potential value to guide the organization. A person with optimal competence, perhaps someone who has experience in several different cultures or someone with a more interdisciplinary background, is a gold mine for an interviewer because he or she can understand the culture from multiple viewpoints and often can provide rich cultural interpretations and explanations.

Principle 3: Use probes or follow-up questions to get the richest and most useful cultural data. For example, stories may emerge after a secondary follow-up question. An interviewee might have said that Mr. Jones is a hero in the organization because he is so compassionate. You ask, "Can you think of an example that illustrates this compassion?" and the response may involve the interviewee sharing a specific story about a time Mr. Jones loaned a car to an employee who had recently lost his car in a wreck. Such stories will tell you more about compassion and how it is defined as a value in this culture. Additional levels of interpretation of the story will tell you other important things about the culture. Follow-up questions require listening carefully for small clues in answers that should be explored further. For example, let's say you hear an answer like, "Mr. Jones would be seen as a hero by some but not others." You need to follow up immediately to ask why he is perceived positively by some and not by others. Probes are different in cultural interviewing from strict research protocols in which every question must be asked in the same manner of each respondent. In a cultural interview, you learn most by following up the particulars of each answer, thus the probes may be quite different in one interview than another, even when the initial interview protocol is the same. Box 6.2 gives examples of probe questions.

Principle 4: It is important to avoid common interviewing errors. *One common error is asking leading questions.* Often interviewers make this

---

Box 6.2 Sample Probe Questions

1. Tell me more about that.
2. Can you help me understand why you see it that way?
3. Can you think of an example of that?
4. Do you think most members of the organization would see it the same way?
5. Why is that important in this culture?
6. Are there differences between leaders and culture members in how that is interpreted?

---

mistake by giving an example when they ask a question, in order to make the question clearer. Unfortunately the example offered tends to direct interviewees' responses in a direction they might not have gone without the example. If you say, "What are values shared in this organization? Like, is responsibility an important value that is expected of all employees?" the interviewee will either agree with you or think of values similar to responsibility or "virtues" rather than talking about diversity, profitability, or other things that might have occurred to him or her without the example.

A second common error in interviewing is rushing into pauses in the interviewee answer. In the United States we are uncomfortable with silence. When there is a gap in conversation, we are tempted to rush in with another question or a summary that puts words in the interviewee's mouth. Good interviewing takes patience. Some interviewees need to take time to think through responses. One of the best interviewing techniques is to remain silent while being nonverbally attentive and connected. This use of silence often encourages the interviewee to say more or to go into an answer more fully, revealing rich cultural information.

A third common error is underestimating the significance of interviewer nonverbal communication. How the interviewer communicates nonverbally has a huge impact on the interviewee. Making eye contact, leaning forward, and using encouraging facial expressions and nodding give the impression of interest and attentiveness. Distracting gestures such as checking your wristwatch or drumming your fingers can quickly shut interviewees down or cause them to shorten their answers. You also need to pay careful attention to the interviewee's nonverbal communication, such as when facial expression or physical tension do not match the interviewee's response to a question.

Principle 5: Consider the implications of the way you record the interview. Choosing to audio-record an interview can have implications for interviewee comfort and for data analysis. You also may need to get interviewees to sign consent forms when you tape record interviews, using forms such as we presented in Chapter 5. Table 6.1 demonstrates advantages and disadvantages of recording interviews.

Another recording issue is whether you choose to transcribe an interview or summarize it with detailed notes about the answers. Transcribing means you write down word for word what was said in the interview. A summary means that you capture the main ideas. A summary might contain a few verbatim quotes of expressions that seemed particularly important,

Table 6.1   Recording Interviews

Advantages	*Disadvantages*
Captures more detail about interviewee answers; allows you to analyze actual language patterns	May inhibit free and open communication and cause mistrust
Frees you from taking notes and allows you to give more attention to the interviewee	Takes more time to listen to interview tapes, to transcribe or summarize
You can focus on the interviewee's nonverbal communication	You may not record impressions gained during the interview; they may be hard to recapture listening to the tape

but it contains mostly conceptual summaries. The advantage of transcripts is that you can do more sophisticated analysis with the exact language that an interviewee used. The disadvantage is that transcripts are extremely time consuming to prepare and analyze.

Principle 6: Consider the advantages of interviewing with a partner. There are advantages to interviewing with a partner. Each of you may notice different things about the interviewee's answers and nonverbal elements. One can take notes while the other asks questions and notices nonverbal elements. The main downside of having a partner is the possible negative impact on interviewee rapport. Interviewees might feel "double-teamed," or it might be more difficult to build as a trusting a relationship as they might have with an individual interviewer.

Principle 7: Consider focus group interviewing. A focus group is a cross between a group discussion and an interview. A focus group usually consists of 5 to 10 members. The interviewer asks broad questions, and members are asked to discuss them. The interviewer plays the role of facilitator, constraining members who are too talkative, drawing out more reticent members, summarizing, and playing devil's advocate. A focus group is a rich source of data because participants are stimulated by one another's answers to think of things they would not have thought of in a one-to-one interview. Disadvantages include the greater complexity of scheduling, the potential for a few members to dominate the discussion, the reticence some have in talking about sensitive cultural issues before others, and the "bandwagon effect" in which members agree with a dominant member instead of thinking of ways their own perceptions might be different.

Special Considerations of Interviewing as an Insider or Outsider

In Chapter 2 we discussed the considerations in deciding whether to do an analysis of a culture of which you are a member, or a culture of which you are an outsider. In Chapter 5 we discussed various observer roles and how each role influences your strategy and the type of data you collect. Your relationship to an organization and its members will also impact your interviewing strategy.

Insider Considerations

If you are a member of the organization, you come to each interview with a relational context. The interviewee already knows you or at least knows you are a member of the organization. Hopefully you have a good relationship with the interviewee so will need to spend less time building rapport at the start. However, there are times that you may bring baggage. You may be part of management, and that could create social distance if you are interviewing a line employee, for instance. You may be a member of quality control, which has a perceived adversarial relationship with production. The biggest hurdle to overcome as an insider is the necessity to ask questions about things you think you already know. You must ask others about their perspectives, and you may find different parts of the organization have different conceptions of the culture than you do. It also is sometimes difficult for the interviewee to answer questions fully and directly for a fellow employee. If you ask them what employees are rewarded for, they will say, "Oh, you know that," and you will not harvest the rich stories and details that might be shared with an outsider. It is necessary for insiders, in the introduction to the interview, to ask interviewees to treat them as if they knew nothing about the organization, and for insiders to prompt and probe during the interview just as if they did not know anything about it.

Another advantage of interviewing as an insider is that you may know more specifics to ask about and be able to start at a deeper level of questioning than an outsider could. You might be able to ask an initial question that would take an outsider two or three probes to reach. You also have more context for interpreting answers. Another negative to being an insider, however, may be confidentiality. Interviewees may be afraid that you would share answers with others in the organization, or that their answers would affect your perception of each other and your continuing work relationship. Giving assurances of confidentiality are especially important for an insider.

Outsider Considerations

Outsiders will find it easier to adopt a genuinely naïve position in the interview on organizational culture. They will think of questions that the insider may not think to ask because the insider's cultural knowledge takes certain features of cultural practices for granted. The outsider will have to work harder in developing rapport and trust with the interviewee. Another disadvantage to overcome is substituting your own interpretation for the meaning within the culture. An interviewee might tell you that a stag is the representative symbol for an insurance company, and you might assume you know the reasons why, without finding what the symbol means to culture members. Therefore probes and paraphrasing are especially important when you are an outsider interviewer to be sure that you are checking your interpretations for cultural accuracy.

Connections: Linking Observation With Interviews

In addition to general interview guidelines, it is important to keep in mind the specific considerations for interviewing based both on the unique characteristics of the ethnographic interview and on the data you have already collected. Five specific guides are provided that should be considered as you prepare for interviews.

1. Review the cultural element summaries you drew from your observation in order to develop questions to gain further information about the cultural elements you have observed.

As a general rule, it is best to rely on interviews and surveys to gain information after you have collected other information. This guideline is based on the typical sequence of sense making: We notice something and then we ask about it to gain more detail or check our interpretations.

2. Construct a list of areas from your analysis of other data for possible inclusion. The list might include things like cultural data that

    (a) confuses you

    (b) lacks confirmation from multiple elements

    (c) merits further elaboration or clarification to see if your interpretation is shared by other organization members

    (d) indicates texts that have cultural significance that you might use for textual analysis (to be described in the next chapter)

    (e) can be explored only through direct questions and are not readily apparent through observation, things like metaphors, stories, history, and so on.

3. Determine members to interview who represent a variety of perspectives (position, tenure, etc.).

A common bias that enters our interpretation of culture is influence from our information sources. At times, random interviewing can have value in ethnographic interviewing. When you choose respondents for a specific reason, you can overlook important cultural sources. In cultural interviewing, every member of the culture has a perspective that may be valuable. The janitor may be in a position to overhear hallway conversations throughout the building. A part-time employee may have a boundary-spanning role that would be valuable to explore.

It is important to remember in interpretive research that every interviewee "counts." In quantitative survey research, you may treat a statistical deviant as simply an aberration to be dismissed. However, the interviewee who presents information that diverges from the mainstream might be telling you something important about the culture or subcultures within the organization.

One question our students often ask is, "How many interviews are enough?" The answer, of course, varies. It depends on the size and complexity of the organization. In small organizations (25 or fewer members), it makes sense to interview everyone. In larger organizations you must sample. If you were doing an academic study for publication of a very large organization, you might want to sample between 2% and 5% of the organization. In a class project, your sample will be smaller but should be as representative as possible. Ethnographic interviewing focuses more on depth than breadth. It is important to generate "thick" and rich descriptions from fewer people rather than having more, superficial data from a larger sample, as we might do in quantitative surveys. In a practical sense, we often know we've done enough interviews when we conduct three or four interviews without hearing anything new, anything that we haven't fully explored in previous interviews.

4. **Develop and focus on descriptive questions:**

Grand tour questions: Take me on a tour of the company by walking me through the doors at the start of a new day.

Mini tour: Take me on a tour of . . . (a specific department or a particular event, such as a meeting).

Example questions: What are the kinds of questions that are typically asked (by certain people, positions, times, settings).

Experience questions: Give me an example of experiences you have had (with, at, when).

Native language questions: *What does the title Associate mean here?* Asked to gain cultural definitions/uses of specialized language.

Hypothetical language: If I were to be late to a meeting, how would it be interpreted?

5. **Use contrast questions to understand how interviewees construct meaning:**

What's the difference between a _____ and a _____?
Example: *What is the difference between a new employee labeled as a "player" and one who is called a "gunner."*

These five guides should give you a sense of not only the ethnographic interview process but the content of certain types of questions you might elect to ask. Explore Rehearsal 6.1 to help you develop questions.

Rehearsal 6.1 Sample Interview
Questions for "Reading" a Culture

Use the following example to give you a start on your own cultural interview guide:

1. When you were a newcomer to the (name of organization), what was strange, or different, or unexpected about the way things were done here?

(Continued)

(Continued)

2. If you wanted to explain or illustrate to an outsider the essence of (name of organization), both the positive and the negative, what incident(s) would you describe? What do these incidents say about this organization?

3. What should visitors see and to whom should visitors speak if they want to understand this organization? What would they need to understand to "get along" and feel comfortable here?

4. When compared with similar organizations, what is special or distinctive about this organization?

5. What are the principal images or metaphors that people use to describe the organization?

6. What physical impression does the organization and its artifacts create? Does this vary from one place to another in the organization?

7. What kinds of beliefs and values dominate the organization? Officially? Unofficially?

8. What are the main norms operating here? What could people be fired for? What could limit a person's career success here?

9. What are the ceremonies/rituals and what purposes do they serve? What are members recognized for? How is this done? Do other organization members know when someone receives a reward or recognition?

10. What language dominates everyday conversation? What words do you hear in this organization that you wouldn't hear at other organizations? What do they signify about organizational values?

11. What are the dominant stories or legends that people tell? What messages are they trying to convey by telling these stories?

12. What reward systems are in place? What "messages" do they send in terms of what is valued here and what is not?

13. What are the favorite topics of informal conversation?

14. What do you know about the history of this organization? What has changed over the years?

15. Think of three influential people in the organization. In what ways do they symbolize the character and values of the organization?

16. Are there identifiable subcultures or cliques in the organization?

17. Is there a newsletter or similar written document in the organization? Do employees read it? What written source would really tell you something about what the organization is like?

18. How do people prefer to communicate here? If there were a new policy, how would you expect to hear about it? If your boss wanted to thank you for a good job, would you prefer him or her to tell you in a face-to-face meeting or in a note? Do most people communicate by e-mail? Is there anything you would not communicate via e-mail?

19. If you heard a rumor about layoffs or a major change, how would you check it out?

20. How does the surrounding environment (this neighborhood or this city or this country) influence the values and practices of this organization?

21. What is the climate for diversity here? Is there any specific group (African Americans, foreign citizens, Jewish people, women, gays, etc.) that would feel uncomfortable being a part of this organization?

22. Do members of this organization do things together outside of work hours? Who? What do they do?

23. What are special activities or events this organization sponsors for its members? What do they say about the nature of the organization?

Now add a few of your own:

_____

_____

_____

_____

_____

_____

_____

_____

Qualitative Surveys

The process of creating effective qualitative interview questions is identical to that of creating survey questions. For example, imagine not being able to catch a colleague in a "friendly conversation" or even a formal interview and instead sending an e-mail questionnaire. The important point is that just as in an interview, you have to be sure that you gain data that you then check against other information you have gathered about the culture. Although standardized surveys exist for measuring culture, our general conviction is that a grounded analysis is best because it encourages the consultant or leader to gain an in-depth understanding of the culture. Furthermore, a grounded analysis challenges you to devise your own interpretation of the culture rather then one constrained by factors already loaded into a standardized survey. Four reminders for survey development that parallels interviews include the following:

- Establish appropriate rapport for the question (i.e., you may need a brief introduction for your question to make sure interviewees understand your reason for asking)
- Explore question options (i.e., structural, contrast) so as to gain needed cultural information
- Word the question clearly
- Ask the questions of members who represent a variety of perspectives (position, tenure, etc.)

On a final note, remember that writing responses to open questions is time-consuming; thus it is best to narrow your survey to focus on a handful of most important questions. For instance, you might find that an electronic survey of from two to four questions will glean more cultural information from a wider array of members than seven or eight questions will from a handful of respondents.

Summary

You rely on question asking and responding almost every day. Method actors, like those interested in enhancing the quality of this informal interview process, must become more aware of their questions and how they interpret and respond to those they interview. The interview is an essential technique in gaining cultural knowledge because of its ability to allow you to learn from members about their interpretations and meanings. It is based on the assumption that members can comment reflectively about their own behaviors and interpretations. This chapter covered several key factors, principles, and guidelines relevant to the process.

1. Culture members may be at minimal, satisfactory, or optimal levels of consciousness about why members think and act as they do in the organization.

2. The quality of your interview data is dependent not just on rapport or technique and preparation, but on your ability to evaluate data in light of what you have learned from other players and observations.

3. Interviewers must be conscious of six interviewing principles:
   - Rapport is critical.
   - Question wording is important for eliciting the information you want.
   - Probes are critical for getting deeper cultural information.
   - Interviewers should avoid the common problems of leading questions, rushing into pauses, and discounting nonverbal communication.
   - The interviewer should carefully consider different methods of recording.
   - Interviewing with a partner has advantages.

4. Be aware of special considerations about interviewing as a culture member or as an outsider.

5. Be sure to review the specific guidelines offered about ethnographic interviewing that also apply to surveys (appropriate rapport for the question, explore question options, question clarity, select members who represent a variety of perspectives).

 Rehearsal 6.2 Alien Culture Interviews/Surveys

Purpose: To develop skills in qualitative data collection and analysis through interviewing a member of an unfamiliar culture.

Steps:

1. Review your notes from your visit to the alien culture from the previous Rehearsal.

2. Determine areas in which you have confusion or a lack of specific data on a given element (or no data on a certain element).

3. Prepare for your interview by creating a rapport section on an interview guide. Include ways you might build rapport through greetings, description of the purpose of the interview, explaining your role in the organization, assurances of confidentiality, general questions, analysis and note taking explanation, expressions of cultural interest and ignorance, and incorporating and restating informant's terms.

4. Create the following questions on your interview guide, but remember you will need to adapt to the interviewee by providing more detail in the question, repeating the question, and so on.

(Continued)

(Continued)

> 1 grand tour question; 1 native language question
> 1 structural question; 1 contrast question
>
> 5. Provide a closure/leave-taking section on your guide (appreciation, reminder of purpose and what is ahead, ask for any questions, etc.).
>
> 6. Like the observation assignment, develop a summary section that incorporates triangulated and new data and that
>   a. provides example data related to at least three of the elements of culture
>   b. interprets the data organized by elements by stating an overall theme
>   c. infers an overall definition of the culture based on themes and elements
>
> 7. Reflect on the strengths and limits of observation and interviewing. What did you understand differently/in more depth after the interview? What did you observe that would have been difficult to understand solely through an interview?

7

Method Acting

Textual Analysis

It is easy to create tension by trying a simple experiment. Try lifting something, such as an edge of a piano or a heavy table. At the same time, try to solve a simple mental problem, such as multiplying 75 by 6—an intellectual exercise that would normally involve little difficulty. You will discover it is nearly impossible to do so while lifting the heavy object.

—Strasberg, *A Dream of Passion*, 1987, p. 125

Step Three: Use a Variety of Methods to Collect Cultural Data

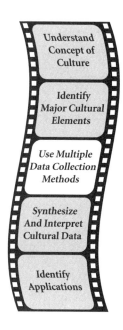

Understand Concept of Culture

Identify Major Cultural Elements

Use Multiple Data Collection Methods

Synthesize And Interpret Cultural Data

Identify Applications

Objectives:

- Learn to distinguish the major types of textual analysis
- Understand major guidelines for analyzing a text

Stage Terms:

- Textual analysis
- Content analysis
- Rhetorical analysis
- Critical linguistic analysis

"So, Jane, are you saying you read the company newsletter? Really?"

"Yes, Tom, and you would do well to pay attention to it. The HRD department takes a lead role in writing it and they often have the inside scoop on what is happening. They have a way of dropping hints in the newsletter they you may not get elsewhere."

Tom was shocked to learn that in his new organization the newsletter mattered at all. In his prior experience, the newsletter went in to the recycle bin without even a glance.

Textual Analysis

Textual analysis is a generic term used for the analysis of any written artifact. Just as an actor in a play must be adept at reading not only the script, but the reviews, biographies of the author, and so on, so also the effective organizational actor must be adept at analyzing texts that give insight into the culture. At an informal level, anytime you make observations about an organizational trend, pattern, strength, or problem based on reading a document (newsletter, report), you are engaged in textual analysis. The above example makes it clear that organizations differ in the weight given to various written media. However, determining what to read may not be as difficult as determining how to read. In other words, reading just for a quick update is different from reading for cultural information. For those conducting a cultural analysis, reading a newsletter for general updates while also trying to analyze it for cultural meaning may be like lifting the corner of piano while doing a math problem. Such a process creates tension until you learn to focus. This chapter is about getting you to set aside the math problem to focus on the heavy lifting of textual analysis. You will use textual analysis not only for newsletters and company Web pages, but also for analyzing your field notes and interview transcripts or summaries.

We briefly review three methods of textual analysis introduced in this chapter before providing more detailed guidance: content analysis, rhetorical analysis, and linguistic analysis. *Content analysis* is a method of developing categories from the text (such as interview transcripts and summaries) and developing a method of counting material related to each of the categories. For example, perhaps you have developed four categories of values you heard frequently during interviews: risk taking, public image, innovation, and profitability. You might then move systematically through your interview transcripts or summaries to see how many interviews mentioned each of the four categories, or how many times the terms came up in interviews. At the end of your categorizing, you might conclude that profitability had been mentioned twice as often as any other value.

Rhetorical analysis is more qualitative and less quantitative. In rhetorical analysis, the researcher examines the author, background, purpose, strategy, and effect of written or oral texts. Examples of this type of textual analysis are the study of apologies made by many sports and corporate figures in the era of public accountability—from Pete Rose to Kobe Bryant to Bill Clinton to Kenneth Lay (see Benoit, 1995; Harter, Stephens, & Japp, 2000; Patel & Reinsch, 2003; Prato, 2000; Scher & Darley, 1997; Sugimoto, 1997). The rhetorical scholar might investigate the public attitudes or climate in which the apology is offered, the nature of the person offering the apology, the characteristics of the message (Does it take personal responsibility? Does it contain excuses?), and the effect on the intended audience. Although this method of textual analysis is quite involved, it may be appropriate with certain important organizational texts that are cited as the moment of major cultural change or mission redefinition.

A final type of textual analysis is linguistic analysis. In this method, the researcher draws inferences from specific language and grammatical structures of messages. The linguistic researcher would pay attention to why a corporate leader chose one term rather than another; why one word was repeated over and over in a text; or the intent or effect of passive verb use, which tends to deny responsibility.

Perhaps the most powerful argument for using textual analysis is the unobtrusive nature of the method. You can, without influencing reactions from anyone, read and gain useful cultural data. Much can be learned from, for example, such organizational documents and artifacts as memos, written histories, and newsletters or even oral texts such as speeches or videos. Textual analysis also could be used to investigate a culture that no longer exists, or to analyze the past of a current organization through archival material. So, as you might imagine, wise leaders and consultants who want to be effective directors will do their homework at this stage. To make the most of a textual analysis, follow these guidelines:

1. Determine a valid/credible "text" for analysis.

For example, if you examine newsletters, get an organizationally relevant sample. Such a sample may need to include newsletters from both before and after a major change. Or relevance may mean samples from various stages or important periods in the history and annual event calendar of the organization. It is dangerous to draw conclusions from a single artifact or even from a small sample. The danger is much like that to be found in basing your understanding of an organization on one person's views. It is also important to consider official and unofficial samples of written artifacts. In one organization we had done an extensive analysis of a large sample of employee newsletters only to find that most employees considered the newsletter to be corporate propaganda and never read it. We then sought what culture members considered to be more authentic examples of corporate texts as viewed by culture members. You need to ask yourself who produced a particular text and for what reason in deciding whether it is a credible text for cultural analysis.

You should also consider the organizational communication style when deciding on texts for analysis. Organizational communication style was one of the cultural elements described in Chapter 4. If an organization has a written culture, you should have abundant texts to choose from—from policies and procedures manuals to memos to annual reports. If an organization style is more oral or interpersonal, you may have to focus on different types of texts. You may be able to find copies of speech texts or be able to find videos of corporate interactions. In an organization whose communication style is electronic, texts to analyze may include e-mail records or electronic system transactions.

Rehearsal 7.1 Selecting Texts for Analysis

Purpose: Identify relevant texts for analysis.

Steps:

1. Review the list of possible organizational texts to analyze.

2. Put a check mark by those that you have access to in the organization.

(Continued)

(Continued)

3. Put another check mark by those that observation and interviews suggest are particularly credible to organization members.

4. Jot down your sense of the type of cultural data available (values, heroes, etc.).

Example Texts	Available?	Credible?	Cultural Data?
Newsletter			
Annual report			
Web site			
Mission statement			
Bulletin boards			
Employee handbook			
E-mail transmissions			
Transcripts of speeches			
Memos			
Affirmative action/ diversity statement			
Employee orientation materials or videos			
Other			

2. Choose your method of analysis.

Content Analysis. The most common method for analyzing texts is content analysis. You will probably use this method for analyzing your field notes and interview transcripts or summaries. You may find it useful for analyzing other written texts as well. The basic technique of content analysis is to let categories emerge from the elements of culture or from your data, and then use those categories to count some feature of the text. You might have a sense after 15 or 20 interviews that you have heard three values most frequently: teamwork, excellence, and accountability. You will go back through the interview notes and summaries with these categories in mind, and perhaps a fourth category of "other." You will count the number of times each of the three values was mentioned, and place a tally mark beside that category for each time it was mentioned in the interviews. When you encounter other values in addition to the three you have chosen as categories, you will place a tally mark by the "other" category. If at the end of the process you find that "other" is larger than any of the three categories you started with, you might need to go back through the notes and decide whether there is another category you need to break out of the "other" category to represent the data accurately. Content analysis is often a trial-and-error process in which you may need to revise the category structure one or two times until you find the categories that fit your data best.

Some researchers use software to aid in content analysis. Thus, if your texts are in electronic format (newsletters, typed field notes, etc.), programs such as *Diction 5.0* (Hart, 2000) enable you to process 30,000 words in 1 minute. This type of software can examine texts for such features as "commonality"—language highlighting the agreed-upon values of a group, or "certainty"—language indicating resoluteness, inflexibility, and completeness.

As you perform content analysis on a text, either by hand or computer, you must decide your measurement unit. What are you counting? In the example above, your unit of analysis was "mentions" in an interview. In analyzing printed texts, different measurements might be more appropriate. You could count the number of pictures featuring management versus employees, or men versus women, or Caucasians versus African Americans. You could count the number of stories on certain subjects, or the number of column inches devoted to various topics. If you were analyzing a smaller document such as a speech, you might focus on counting actual words—how often the word *excellent* appeared in a 10-minute speech, for example. Within a lengthy newsletter, you may want to focus on one area, such as messages from the president or on member spotlights. You can analyze a written artifact at a micro or macro level. You might, for example, count the number of stories in an overall newsletter on various topics (macroanalysis) or analyze specific words used in a representative paragraph (microanalysis).

You may actually measure square centimeters or inches or do a word count; however, the percentage of an entire newsletter devoted to the issue in comparison to other topics is perhaps more telling. The key here is to use this analysis as *one gauge* of what is important to the organization, based on amount of space allotted in publications.

Rhetorical Analysis. Another technique of textual analysis is rhetorical analysis. Although there are many systems of rhetorical analysis, its simplest form involves an in-depth analysis of a specific speech or text given by an identifiable cultural figure. Since the process is so involved, you would use this only on a very significant organizational text. Suppose you are studying Hewlett-Packard's culture and come across an employee address that CEO Carly Fiorina gave on her assuming leadership of the company. Perhaps in employee interviews many individuals have cited this speech as the defining moment that turned the company around. In rhetorical analysis you would do research on that speech. You would find out more about Fiorina. What is her background? What did she do before this appointment? You would also find out more about the occasion. Who was in the physical audience? Was there another audience beyond the people physically present? What was the background context of the speech? What was Hewlett-Packard's financial situation and competitive place in the marketplace? What were challenges facing her in the position? Then with that appropriate background information you would analyze the message itself. What was the purpose of the speech? What arguments or persuasive appeals were made? How were they supported? What type of evidence was offered? What cultural elements were woven into the speech—History? Values? Metaphors? Symbols? Finally you would analyze the results of the speech. How did Hewlett-Packard change?

Critical Linguistic Analysis. The final method of textual analysis we discuss is critical linguistic analysis. In this method, based on the work of Fowler (1986), you take a small but culturally significant text such as a mission statement, an inaugural address, a press release, or a corporate apology and analyze the language and grammatical patterns to reveal underlying system logic. Although Fowler includes a number of linguistic features in his system, the following are particularly relevant to cultural analysis:

• Pronoun use: As corporate leaders talk and write, do they talk about "we" or "I"? Do they refer to employees as "them"? Do they use pronouns such as "you" that have the effect of finger pointing?

• Active or passive verb use: Do decision makers accept accountability for their actions by using names and active verbs or do they hide behind passive verbs that fail to identify agents of actions? (*The decision was made to eliminate 600 jobs.*)

• Overuse or underuse of certain words or type of words: For example, in a public statement Angi analyzed, leaders in one embattled organization used the terms *rational, orderly,* and *proper* more than 17 times. This was indicative of their resistance to cultural change led by the members of the culture.

• Verb tense: Do public statements talk more about the past with past tense or more about the future with future tense?

3. Link the results of your analysis back to cultural elements and cultural significance.

Like the interview and observation processes, this step is about summarizing your data into a form that is usable. For instance, you might have entries that state the following:

Heroes: Three of the four newsletters gave one eighth of their space to discussing the ex-CEO. This amount of space was about two times as much as for any other person or issue. Interview summaries and articles written by this ex-CEO all suggest that he remains a hero and perhaps a legend of sorts for this organization.

Values: One value was mentioned 43 times in interviews, four times as often as any other value discussed by employees.

Language: Certain terms are used repeatedly in discussing employee pay and benefit concerns. Such terms as *tenure, earned,* and *seen potential* are words used by management to explain a policy change that reduces benefits for employees who have less than 2 years of history with the organization.

4. Make a list of questions about confusing or contradictory issues.

Take time to reflect on information on the elements that do not fit or that stand out. For example, you might find an espoused value in the written documents that is different from the values expressed in employee interviews. The mission statement, for example, might stress the importance of employees, yet there is not one picture or story about an average employee in the company newsletter.

Summary

Systematic analyses of organizational texts are similar to the intense work an actor does with a script prior to crafting a performance. Textual analysis is an unobtrusive research method and can reveal a great deal about an organization. This chapter stressed the following points:

1. Three systematic ways to analyze organizational texts:
   - Content analysis
   - Rhetorical analysis
   - Critical linguistic analysis

2. It is vital that you choose a sufficient sample of organizationally credible texts to analyze to learn about culture. Organizational communication style may influence your choice.

Summary of Step Three, Using Multiple Methods to Collect Cultural Data

The major methods of observation, interviews and surveys, and textual analysis each provide a useful means of gathering cultural data. You should consider the following guidelines a way to provide a credible and valid interpretation. These methods and the call to integrate them into our cultural data collection process are provided as a way to combat a natural tendency we all have. Each of us tends to rely on initial impressions based on a limited number of observations or a cursory look at a newsletter. Optimal cultural performance is achieved when we sharpen our ability to collect and analyze data more systematically with each of these methods. If we have a clear grasp of the following guidelines, then we will be more effective in the culture interpretation process covered in the next chapter.

1. Use method "triangulation" to obtain credible and valid data.

2. Select a method of observation and write field notes with bracketed inferences and questions.

3. Try to adopt the curiosity of an outsider, especially when you observe your own culture.

4. Apply important principles in the conduct of interviews and surveys, such as selecting interviewees, developing rapport, wording questions in an open and clear fashion, using probes to dig deeper into answers, choosing recording methods, and negotiating the special roles of cultural insider or outsider.

5. Conduct textual analysis using one or more of the methods outlined: content analysis, rhetorical analysis, and/or textual analysis.

6. Draw inferences from each of the methods about cultural elements.

Rehearsal 7.2 Content Analysis

Purpose: To gain experience in noting the types of cultural elements that can be found in various organizational artifacts

Directions:

1. Identify an artifact for analysis (newsletter, etc.).

2. Analyze the artifact using content analysis.
   - Determine the unit of analysis or your focus within the text.
   - Pay attention to the amount of space devoted to certain issues from one document to the next.
   - Identify and give examples of specific cultural elements.
   - Make a list of questions about confusing or contradictory issues.

3. Write a brief summary of insights about at least three of the elements.

4. Write down specific challenges and questions you faced in the process. These issues can be shared with a colleague or instructor who is working with you in this process.

Rehearsal 7.3 Critical Linguistic Analysis

Purpose: To gain experience in using critical linguistic analysis in cultural studies

Directions: Compare the following language features in the two organizational texts provided, mission statements from Hewlett-Packard and Dell Computers.

- Pronoun use
- Passive or active voice
- Words that are overused or underused
- Verb tense—past, present, future

What differences do you note in these two mission statements? What tentative inferences might you draw about how the two corporate cultures differ?

Statement 1: Hewlett-Packard Computers

HP delivers vital technology for business and life. The company's solutions span IT infrastructure, personal computing and access devices, global services and imaging and printing for consumers, enterprises and small and medium business.

Our $4 billion annual R&D investment fuels the invention of products, solutions and new technologies, so that we can better serve customers and enter new markets. We invent, engineer and deliver technology solutions that drive business value, create social value and improve the lives of our customers.

The 2002 merger with Compaq Computer Corporation forged a dynamic, powerful team of 140,000 employees with capabilities in 178 countries doing business in more than 40 currencies and more than 10 languages. Revenues for the combined companies were $72 billion for the fiscal year that ended October 31, 2002. Chairman and CEO Carly Fiorina leads HP, which has corporate headquarters in Palo Alto, California.

SOURCE: Courtesy of Hewlett-Packard. Please see http://www.hp.com/hpinfo/abouthp/ for the most up-to-date information.

Statement 2: Dell Computers

Dell is committed to participating responsibly in the global marketplace. At Dell, we are committed to building value not only for our customers, but also for the communities that our company and our employees call home. We strive to participate responsibly in the global marketplace in which we operate.

At the core of this effort is the corporate philosophy that guides our conduct whenever we do business, which we call the Soul of Dell. Central to that philosophy is our efforts to hold ourselves to the highest possible standards when doing business. Our Code of Conduct details our efforts to hold ourselves to standards of ethical behavior that go well beyond legal minimums. Our Board of Directors has adopted Principles of Corporate Governance, which provide an effective corporate governance framework for Dell.

Dell relies on the diversity of its personnel, suppliers, and customer communities to maximize innovation, growth, competitiveness, and customer satisfaction. Our diversity programs help us to build a barrier-free workplace and we apply the same barrier-free philosophy to our supplier relationships through our supplier diversity programs.

Dell and our employees are committed to building technology that helps communities. Our global citizenship programs

(Continued)

(Continued)

and the Dell Foundation define our efforts to contribute positively to our communities.

Finally Dell is committed to a culture of environmental sustainability and responsibility. We continually reduce Dell's impact on the environment through product design, manufacturing, and operations, product ownership, experience and product end-of-life solutions.

8

Step Four: Synthesizing and Interpreting Cultural Data

Getting Inside the Character

Step Four:
Develop Your
Interpretation of
the Culture
Through Data
Synthesis and
Interpretation

I must have at least a dozen pages or more of just notes, and more notes. Of course, I also have draft after draft of cultural elements. The process has been interesting, but it is not realistic. No one can really spend this much time. The pay-off just cannot be worth it!

—Anonymous, Cultural Analysis Student

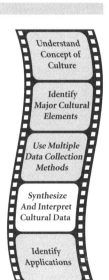

Objectives:

- Understand the interpretive nature of cultural analysis
- Learn how to combine elements to develop cultural themes
- Create an overall definition of the culture based on multiple themes

Stage Terms:

- Cultural themes
- Pervasiveness
- Salience
- Central paradox
- Master rule/value

A Time to
Interpret

The statement on the previous page about data overload reflects a common experience at this stage of the process. It is not uncommon for an initial effort at cultural analysis to become too much. Perhaps the sense of being overwhelmed can be compared to a dress rehearsal of a play when you have doubts about all the pieces coming together, about the ability of your characters to be accepted as "real." The process of "getting inside the character" means that you move to an actual interpretation. Until this time the method actor has been devoted to rehearsing the elements, but the time comes to put it together. In the cultural analysis process the challenge of finally interpreting the culture may seem daunting to some. However, the reality is that we all hold interpretations of our culture even before conducting formal analyses. The key at this point in the process is to check and change those interpretations by paying closer attention to a wider array of data. The following comments from a few alumni on the value of the process may help give perspective and maintain motivation:

- *Evaluating the organization's culture adds another dimension. Although the culture of the organization may not seem to have a direct impact on the immediate, short-term profit or bottom line, it does play a big part in the long-term effectiveness of the organization.*

- *The basic idea that an organization has a culture was an eye-opener. Since then I've seen the importance of person fit with the culture. "Problem employees" are often those who won't/can't adapt to the culture and have conflict with those who identify closely with the culture.*

- *I learned to ask questions in an interview to find out about the culture when I was considering making a job move. I also ask questions of people I'm considering hiring to see if they'll fit with our organizational culture.*

- *Just simply realizing that an organization has a definable culture has been helpful in dealing with the changes that have and are continuing to occur at the medical facility I work for.*

At this point in the process, if you have been collecting data on multiple elements, you likely have more information about your culture than may seem reasonable or "normal." Two factors should help you keep this data overload in perspective. *First,* this extensive process of analysis is usually appropriate at only certain points in time (e.g., selecting an organization, settling into a new position, during times of organizational crises or change). *Second,* as indicated in the alumni comments above, managing the overload of data can have meaningful payoffs. Leaders typically feel like they already operate on information overload, thus the process of collecting cultural data may mean times of feeling overwhelmed by the additional data. Yet recall that at the heart of the process is being a better observer—one who listens intently with ears, eyes, and heart. Becoming more adept at collecting cultural data involves bracketing biases and assumptions about what is the right or the best way to interpret and respond to events in the organization. Therefore, perhaps the most meaningful outcome, one worth wading through the data for, is the potential insight of more effective and ethical leader behaviors.

Not a Video Recording

Your final analysis may be viewed as a dramatic interpretation of the organization. Consider the drama metaphor as a way to remind you that when opening night finally occurs, when the curtain is being raised, the performance the audience sees will vary depending on the way a director has set the stage, cast the characters, and interpreted the tone and theme of the script. The notion of an interpretation is important in that a cultural analysis does not claim to be an objective and neutral video recording of organizational events. Indeed, the assumption with a cultural analysis is that such an objective and neutral rendering of culture is impossible and undesirable. Instead, the individual "researcher" (or team) works to provide a meaningful, valuable, and valid interpretation. Weick (1995) refers to an interpretive researcher's work as being driven by plausibility rather than accuracy. The researcher must make inferences beyond the directly observable facts and develop an interpretation that fits the facts, even if the fit is not perfect in all respects. At this point in the process you will return to reflecting on the major theoretic frames to guide your interpretation.

The following three-stage interpretive model, also shown in Figure 8.1, attempts to capture a process that is not easily systematized. The process of interpretation is difficult to delineate because interpretation involves insight and intuition. There may be points at which the process is much less linear and systematic than is portrayed in the following model. Nonetheless, it is important that you cover each of the steps in the model with the understanding that you may often move back and forth among the steps.

A. Creating the Actor's Script: The Elements

Each time you collect cultural information through any one of the qualitative methods, you should sort that data into summary sheets based on the cultural elements. These summary sheets can be seen as a first step in creating the script—a set of notes that influences the way the actor interprets the character. In order to create these summary sheets, you might take one pass through your interview notes, your observation notes, and your text analyses to consider references to place or to history. You might place each reference to history on a separate note card or in a separate reference citation on your computer. As you look across all those different references to history, you may find patterns, or even contradictions. You would then move to another element, such as heroes, and repeat the process. A few specific guides in this process include the following:

1. *Return to the same data set more than once to identify data on elements that may have been overlooked in the first analysis.* For example, if you focused on rules in your first analysis of the interview data, return to your data again to explore evidence of values or rituals, and so on. The same piece of data might be categorized under more than one element.

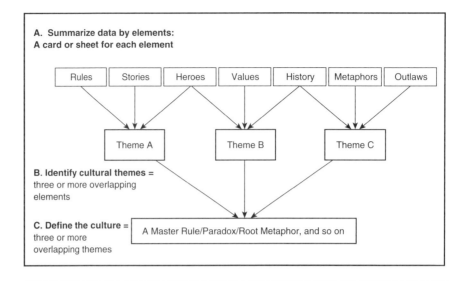

A. Summarize data by elements:
A card or sheet for each element

| Rules | Stories | Heroes | Values | History | Metaphors | Outlaws |

Theme A   Theme B   Theme C

B. Identify cultural themes =
three or more overlapping elements

C. Define the culture =
three or more overlapping themes

A Master Rule/Paradox/Root Metaphor, and so on

Figure 8.1   A Model for Interpreting and Defining the Culture

2. *Review data in each category to be sure you have collected sufficient information.* For example, your initial observations might surface information about all of the elements. A review of your data, however, might reveal limited or unclear information about certain rules, values, and communication styles. These gaps should be a focus of additional data collection efforts. If you do not have clear support or data on an element and you are not able to collect clarifying data, then leave the unclear data out of your final list of elements.

B. Sorting Subplots: Finding Themes

A list of elements does not constitute a final cultural analysis any more than a list of characters and subplots make a final play. The list of elements is a foundation for getting inside the character, for gaining a valid interpretation of the script, but without the next step all you will have is a list of elements. This second step is to infer cultural themes by surfacing ideas that are supported by three or more elements that also were derived from multiple methods.

Cultural themes can be viewed as similar to values in that they are under the surface, perhaps not ever spoken directly by a member. In other words, a cultural theme has to do with the "pervasiveness and salience" of some important aspect of the culture (Saffold, 1998). *Pervasiveness* has to do with the extent the theme is relevant to various units in the organization. Limited pervasiveness refers to those themes that are relevant to specific departments, while extensive pervasiveness refers to organization-wide themes. For example, in one organization, a theme like "work hard and play hard" may capture just one or two departments, for example, sales or marketing. It would have limited pervasiveness in the rest of the organization if the majority of the other units, such as Human Resources or Research and Development, were characterized by a "work hard, but not too hard" theme. In contrast, there may be themes with extensive pervasiveness that cut across units, like: "Getting it right the first time."

Salience, on the other hand, has to do with the importance of the theme or its "weightiness" in the culture. The assumption at this point in an analysis is that a theme, because of its repeated presence across elements and methods, is an important one in the organization. A theme might be identified as salient because of the large number of different people who mentioned it, or it might be salient because it was related to almost every element of culture as you analyzed them. It might be, for example, that a theme emerges from an understanding of heroes identified in textual analysis and interviews, rules from observations of meetings, and values from interviews. Across each of these elements you learn something about how the members have come to understand a proper response to conflict or disagreements. You might word the theme as, "silence is the best policy." However, you may find other themes that make the theme related to silence less important or significant. For example, you may learn of other rules and insights from meetings suggesting that conflicts and disagreements are handled in indirect ways, and thus you reword the theme: "Work out your differences without making a big scene." Again, the key here is to make an interpretation that is supported by your data—that stands out above other issues. Just as the actors must decide which aspects of a character to stress, so must the cultural analyst. Your discussion of the theme should give the reader a sense of pervasiveness as well as of salience.

Let's return to the earlier examples about "how hard to work." Let's imagine it is a different organization than the one discussed earlier that had mixed views on the subject. As you review data on values, rules, and rituals you might find consistent references to a common attitude about how hard one should work. You decide the attitude can best be captured in the following theme: "Work hard, but not too hard." To support this as a theme, you should be able to summarize data from the elements relevant to this theme (e.g., "Of the 10 people interviewed, all but one made some reference to the 'take it easy' *value*"). In addition, an implicit *rule* surfaced in these interviews that related to promotability. Employees agreed, "If you spend too much time on-task and don't spend time taking it easy and talking to other employees you will not get ahead." And finally, there was a daily *ritual* observed in the organization—a two-and-a-half-hour lunch and naptime was required (yes, this is a hypothetical example, but long lunch breaks are not uncommon in some countries).

Notice how, in the example above, *at least three elements were used that cut across more than one method*. Support from these multiple sources provides a credible reading of pervasive and salient themes in the culture. Support like this is also about finding data that will challenge or check your biases in an organization. Of course, as you develop support by reviewing field notes, realize that other examples and relevant observations may occur to you that you failed to record in your notes. If this happens, be sure to document these important observations. As you develop themes, remember that your analysis does not end there. These themes are used to help you provide a general definition of the culture or the "defining plot."

Rehearsal 8.1 Finding a Theme

Purpose: Take 5 minutes to practice developing themes

Steps:

1. Briefly state examples of three elements (heroes, rules, stories, etc.) from your observations, interviews, and/or textual analysis that appear relevant to one another.

Element A:

_____

_____

_____

_____

Element B:

_____

_____

_____

_____

Element C:

_____

_____

_____

_____

2. Identify connections across these elements by developing a theme that captures the core idea that links these elements.

_____

_____

_____

_____

3. Determine the relative pervasiveness of this theme. How widely spread is this theme in the organization? You may determine this by checking the sources you used for the various elements (e.g., organization-wide meetings vs. interviews in one department?).

_____

_____

_____

_____

4. Determine the relative salience of this theme. How important is this theme to organizational outcomes such as productivity or employee satisfaction? How often was it mentioned? How many elements supported it?

_____

_____

_____

_____

C. The Defining Plot: "What Is the Culture?"

You walk out of a play, an art gallery, a music performance hall and think about what you just experienced. The effort of translating the symbolic forms of music or art into words is difficult: something is always lost. For example, a book/opera like *Les Misérables* might leave you with a mix of feelings and ideas, such as "power in love," "the mystery of mercy," and "the self-destruction of evil." These word pictures attempt to capture themes in the play. Yet another step can be taken if you then distill these various themes and attempt to answer the question, "So what was that *Les Misérables* story about, anyway?" The process of distilling themes into a clear statement about culture is the third step in this interpretive model.

An overall definition of an organization may appear to fly in the face of the convention that organizations cannot or should not be reduced to specific labels or monoculture definitions (Martin, 1992). However, a general and overall definition does not mean that you must oversimplify the organization you have studied. Indeed, the answer to the question, "What is the culture?" may take a number of forms, each of which provides room for definitions that are complex and creative. We provide three major options to aid you in this process. Each of these methods for defining a culture should be seen a tool for thinking out of the box. We added a fourth method for defining the culture that encourages you to create your own interpretive approach.

1. Is there a central paradox underlying the themes?

A paradox is a contradictory statement that is nevertheless true. By a central paradox we mean a contradictory true statement that captures the core of the culture. Thinking about paradoxes in the organization can help you and members make sense of values and themes that may be the source of confusion or high levels of uncertainty. For example, "Chaotic Order" might capture a number of themes relevant to an organization characterized by standard polices and procedures that guide creative endeavors that are known for causing chaos in the organization. Often the crux of the culture lies in tensions and contradictions, for example, the contradiction between espoused values and organizational practices.

2. Is there a master rule/value underlying the themes?

The notion of a master rule or value implies that a number of themes merge to suggest an overarching guiding principle that permeates the organization. For instance, using the example above, if paradox is not the sense you get from your reading of the culture, you might note that the culture can best be captured by drawing attention to the way employees are expected to follow an implicit communication rule in all that they do: "Speak first of new ideas and ways of doing things before critiquing old ways." Or you might find that one value, such as, "The Customer Comes First," permeates descriptions of rituals, heroes, history, and stories.

3. Is there a root metaphor underlying the themes?

The idea of a root metaphor, like a master rule or value, suggests that one thing serves as the source or explanatory idea behind multiple themes. Root metaphors can capture multiple elements and provide a valuable way to examine an organization (Morgan, 1986). One church we studied was captured by the metaphor of "a healing community." This metaphor guided the theology of the church, the role of its leaders (often anointing sick members with oil and praying for their healing), the large percentage of disabled persons who regularly attended the church, the design and use of its building, and common rituals within the church.

4. Are there [*fill in the blank and be creative!*] underlying the themes?

The process of interpretation is a creative one. Interpreting a central paradox, a master rule, or a root metaphor may not be the most useful or meaningful approach with the set of elements and resultant themes you have identified. In fact, before you ever complete the process of identifying elements or themes you may have had a hunch or a word picture in your own mind that defined the organization. Recall that the intent of being more thorough or systematic in the process of answering the question, "What is the culture?" is to be able to provide credible support for your position. Yet we recognize that this process may be an intuitive one for some and that the formula or steps we encourage may work in the reverse. For example, you may have created your own definition before attempting a thorough data collection. If this is the case, the process of analysis is one of determining just how accurate or well supported your definition is once you dig deeper. Even if you did not begin this process with a sense of how you might define the culture, you may find it useful to go beyond the first three suggestions to create something of your own. Again, just be sure the overall definition is clearly supported by multiple themes and elements.

One last factor to consider in your interpretation is to ask yourself, "What is not here that I would expect to see?" Martin (1992) refers to this type of analysis as probing silences and empty spaces. Angi once served as a consultant to a children's home trying to survive a leadership transition. As she questioned the board members about the strengths and weaknesses of the organization, she was struck by the absence of any language about the care of children. Board members talked about the strength of leadership, the business plan, the endowment, and the new facilities, but no one talked about the children. The silence made it clear that the nonprofit organization had drifted from the clarity of its original mission and values.

When you write your analysis, you might experiment with creative forms of writing in presenting your results. Often the products of ethnomethodological research read more like short stories than formal research papers. They may include extensive quotes or narratives from interviews with culture members. They may include narratives of key episodes you observed.

Summary

At this stage of the analysis, your immersion in the data and your own creativity as an interpreter become all important. You should have a sense of seeing the organization you are studying in a new light or with a clearer understanding. Like an actor who has hung out behind the scenes to interact with other actors, who has studied the script and gotten inside the character, you should know more than the other actors about the set, the stage, the relationships among the players, and what makes this particular troupe and performance unique. The themes you have already discussed as well as other relevant data should support your general definition of the culture. Before moving to the application section, be sure you have a clear grasp of the following aspects of the interpretation process:

1. Cultural analysis is an interpretive process; definitions of the culture will likely vary from person to person.

2. Cultural themes grow from combining multiple elements and methods.

3. A general definition should be based on multiple themes and may take the form of paradoxes, master rules/values, root metaphors, and/or other ways to capture the organizational culture.

Rehearsal 8.2 A Practice Stage

Purpose: develop skills in observation and content analysis of data so you can make interpretations of an organizational culture

Major Steps:

1. Complete 2 weeks of observation notes.
    a. A minimum of 3–4 hours a week in observation
    b. A variety of observation settings (e.g., meetings, informal interactions, setting)
    c. Notes that include bracketed information (about inferences and questions)

(Continued)

(Continued)

2. Use interviews or qualitative surveys to explore cultural interpretations of organizational actors.
   a. Choose a representative sample of interviewees.
   b. Develop rapport.
   c. Use relatively open questions to elicit accounts, stories, and explanations.
   d. Follow up answers with probes.

3. Content analyze a representative text or texts.
   a. Choose representative and credible texts that match the communication style of the organization.
   b. Use content analysis, rhetorical analysis, or linguistic analysis.

4. Create a document summarizing data by elements of culture.
   a. Be sure to make clear reference to observation notes (date, etc.) and/or content analysis text (date of newsletter, section, etc.); the key here is to have summary data that can easily be traced back to notes.
   b. Be sure you have several examples of most, if not all, of the elements.

5. Analyze your summary of elements to determine major themes.
   a. A theme equals a description of the culture drawn from common ideas that surface in three or more of the elements.
   b. State the theme and the supporting elements. Be specific.

For example: In a day care organization a theme was: *"Supportive touch is a mandated and encouraged behavior." Rules and rituals indicate that teachers should initiate touch often during the day as well as encourage children to touch each other in appropriate ways. Furthermore, during a weekly staff meeting a story was told of a teacher's aide who was fired because he did not take time to hug and encourage children through positive and appropriate touch.*

   c. Aim for a minimum of three themes.

6. Create an overall definition of the culture based on themes and elements.
   a. An overall definition is a general statement that attempts to capture the core of the culture.

b. An overall definition does not mean that subcultures do not differ or that the culture is unified across all levels and divisions of the organization.

c. Themes and relevant elements provide support for the definition you have developed.

d. Review Chapter 8 for options in developing an overall definition of the culture.

7. Checklist for reviewing major steps of the Rehearsal:

_____ Interpretation section with themes and an overall definition

_____ Appendix with a paper trail (for validity and reliability/ consistency checks)

_____ A copy of your field notes

_____ A description or copy of the text you used for content analysis

_____ A copy of notes from any other method used (survey, interviews)

_____ A copy of your summary data for each element

_____ A completed reliability check by a trusted colleague, a mentor, a classmate, or a member of the organization to make sure your account is consistent with how organizational members interpret the culture

Note: Though the idea of a reliability check seems at first "too academic," it should be part of our interpretive processes—we check our perceptions with others. The following guide sheet can be used for a trusted colleague, mentor, or classmate to review your work.

Rehearsal 8.3 Reliability/Validity Check

1. Observation process:
   _____ Clear rationale for the observer role that was selected
   _____ Clear understanding of ethics involved in the choice

2. Check field notes: Check for improvement (from weeks 1–3) in the following:
   _____ Detailed descriptions
   _____ Use of brackets

(Continued)

(Continued)

3. Check text analysis:
   _____ Clear rationale for choosing this set of documents
   _____ Representative sample
   _____ Credible
   _____ Method of analysis documented and explained

4. Review summary of each element:
   _____ Are there gaps that indicate the need for more data?
   _____ Can you trace examples back to field notes, text, interviews?
   _____ Focus on descriptions? Free of judgment?
   _____ Examples clearly fit each element according to definition of element?
   _____ Missing details? (information sufficient, makes sense?)
   _____ Method triangulation on most elements: examples from both text analysis and observation and/or interviews/surveys?

5. Check themes for
   _____ Method triangulation: examples from both content analysis and observation and/or interviews/surveys?
   _____ Data triangulation: examples from three or more elements?

6. Check an overall definition for
   _____ Theme triangulation: support based on two or more themes (may include other well-developed elements)
   _____ Method triangulation: support from both text analysis and observation and/or interviews/surveys?

 Rehearsal 8.4 Cultural Analysis Write-Up Guides

Directions: This final checklist should guide rather than dictate your writing process. These suggestions are intended as guides to develop a highly credible report for other members of the organization. Of course, who your audience is (members of one department vs. executive leadership team) will dictate format. Remember, the goal is to "tell the story" of your analysis in a convincing manner. In this suggested outline, you are focused on elements, themes, and your definition of the culture. After we cover application topics, we will discuss ways to develop implications of your findings.

Introduction:
_____ Draw interest to your analysis
_____ Discuss the importance of your analysis
_____ Develop credibility—references
_____ Preview main sections

Body:

I. Overview of analysis
_____ Background of organization (mission, structure, brief history)
_____ Methods (discuss data collection, rationale, time spent)
_____ Refer to Appendix with notes on each element

II. Major Themes
_____ Minimum of three; each supported by data from three or more elements
_____ Clear, convincing support from Appendix/Text/Book
_____ Clear tables/data summaries
        (e.g., examples, frequency counts, quotes, paraphrases)
_____ Written to capture the richness of cultural data

III. Overall description of culture
_____ Supported by themes and elements
_____ Clear articulation of the rationale for the definition

Conclusion
_____ Restate major goals and major conclusions and benefits
_____ Review the process (strengths of analysis, lessons learned)

References (complete; consistent format)

Appendix
_____ Synopsis of inferences on all elements (e.g., list all the rules)
_____ Copy of interview/survey guide if used
_____ Copy of Executive Summary (when applicable)
_____ Field notes
_____ Texts used for analysis

PART IV

Cultural Analysis Application

An Introduction to Step Five

*Identifying Applications
for Cultural Analysis*

Good managers contemplating mergers today routinely consider cultural match as an important criterion in deciding whether to proceed or draw back. Major organizational changes succeed or fail depending on how well leadership grasps the symbolic details that are so easy to overlook and works to integrate them into the change strategy. All modern managers are expected to understand these concepts and practice them in their daily managerial life. Who would have thought it twenty years ago?

—Deal & Kennedy, "Introduction,"
Corporate Cultures, 2000, p. iv

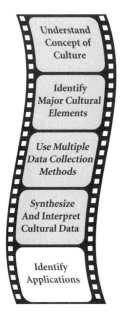

Objectives:

- Students will understand implications of culture for important organizational activities and processes.
- Students can use cultural data to assess their organization's commitment to diversity, approaches to change, leadership styles, and integration of ethical principles and overall organizational effectiveness.

Stage Terms:

- Diversity
- Organizational change
- Symbolic leadership
- Ethics
- Organizational effectiveness

An Approach to Answering "So What?"

Certainly actors undertaking the rigorous training of method acting must ask themselves at some points, "Will this really make me a better actor?" As they try to focus concentration on drinking a cup of orange juice, undertake animal studies, learn to channel emotions from previous experiences, and increase their concentration on stage, they have to wonder about their ability to transfer these activities into the creation of better stage and screen performances.

In the same way, students and organizational leaders often wonder if the rigorous study necessary to understand their organizational cultures has a payoff. What is the practical significance of understanding organizational culture? How does it lead to more effective individual and organizational performance? In Step Five of our five-part method, we address these questions.

Five Examples

In Chapters 9 through 13 we develop five examples of applications of cultural knowledge: diversity, organizational change, symbolic leadership, ethics, and organizational effectiveness. It is valid to ask, "Why these five?" If we understand culture as a root metaphor for the whole organization, as we explained in Chapter 3, isn't culture inherently tied to everything that goes on in an organization? We believe this is true. We chose these five as examples of cultural application because they are significant organizational processes or outcomes, and because they have a compelling and clear linkage to organizational culture. We hope that as you begin to see the connection between culture and these five topics, you will move beyond this textbook to consider other applications of the cultural information you now understand about your organization. For example, we hope you will begin to explore how culture relates to employee socialization, to technology innovation, to creativity, and to an unlimited number of other topics.

It is also fair to ask whether a cultural perspective brings anything new to the understanding of leadership, diversity, ethics, change, or other organizational processes. We believe that the cultural lens does have much to contribute to understanding organizational life. Take diversity as an example. Most organizations desire to become more diverse and to recognize the advantages of diverse perspectives among employees. Many organizations, however, approach diversity only through superficial training programs and organizational practices that never become rooted in the deeper levels of organizational culture, beliefs, and assumptions. Until diversity becomes deeply woven into the organizational culture, it fails to change the organization in fundamental ways.

Organizational ethics is a similar case. If an organization tries to become more ethical through training or adopting new accounting processes without changing the fundamental ideology coded into organizational stories and metaphors, the result will be superficial. We make arguments about the value of a cultural perspective on each of the topics covered in the next five chapters of the text. A cultural perspective is not the only perspective on diversity, change, effectiveness, ethics, and leadership, but it is a perspective that adds insight for the organizational leader.

In Chapter 9, "Casting Against Type: Diversity," we explore the linkage between organizational culture and embracing diversity. We approach this in two ways: how organizations can become more supportive of diversity through examining their organizational cultures, and how marginalized actors in an organizational culture can understand dominant cultures for the purposes of professional development and knowing how to gain a voice and initiate change. Too many organizations have launched diversity programs in a compartmentalized way—with an office that reports to the human resource director, several levels removed from the CEO. We point out that the culture as a whole must support a commitment to diversity if the value is to permeate an organization.

In Chapter 10, "Improvisation: Managing Change," we address the reasons why strong cultures often resist major change. We offer examples of organizational leaders who have initiated change without sufficient knowledge of the culture, leading to unsuccessful change efforts. We explain how change can be introduced more effectively by using key elements of the culture rather than changing in opposition to the culture.

In Chapter 11, "An Honest Portrayal: Ethics," we explain our perspective that ethical principles must be deeply ingrained in an organizational culture in order for them to exert an unconscious influence on employee decision making and behavior. We explain how recent ethical lapses such as WorldCom, Enron, and prisoner abuse scandals in the military can be understood as a reflection of organizational culture.

In Chapter 12, "The Director's Chair: Symbolic Leadership," we consider that culture creates a frame for viewing effective leadership performance. Effective leaders must understand how they are constrained by culture, as well as the role they play in creating, maintaining, and transforming culture. We argue that one of the most important characteristics of effective leaders is not only their technical expertise, but also their ability to use symbols to create identity and shared vision. We offer opportunities for you to evaluate your own symbolic leadership abilities and to assess leaders in your organization.

Chapter 13, "Reading Reviews: Organizational Effectiveness," summarizes the application of a cultural analysis to the organization by discussing effectiveness and how all the previous application topics contribute to organizational performance. We discuss different ways to evaluate the relationship of culture and organizational performance, and offer tools to assess the effectiveness of your organization in light of cultural data.

We hope that the chapters exploring Step Five will assist you in recognizing that cultural analysis is not only fascinating but also practical for organizations and their members.

9

Casting Against Type

Diversity

Step Five: Identify
Applications for
Organizational
Diversity,
Change,
Ethics,
Leadership, and
Effectiveness

Thus creativity has come to be the most highly prized commodity in our economy . . . Hiring for diversity, once a matter of legal compliance, has become a matter of economic survival because creativity comes in all colors, genders, and personal preferences.

—Florida, *The Rise of the Creative Class*, 2002, p. 5

Objectives:

- Explore the paradox of culture and diversity
- Promote skills for understanding organizational subcultures
- Understand the importance of diversity in today's creative economy
- Understand the essential nature of cultural understanding for minority subcultures within the organization.

Stage Terms:

- Diversity
- Marginalized groups
- Creative economy

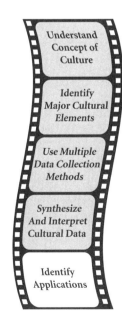

Understand Concept of Culture

Identify Major Cultural Elements

Use Multiple Data Collection Methods

Synthesize And Interpret Cultural Data

Identify Applications

Here's a trick: [Create a strong and vibrant culture in which values are shared, employees are socialized into a common way of creating meanings, and at the same time maintain a diverse workforce with enough tension to promote creativity and innovation.] This is the essential paradox of culture. Strong cultures tend to reproduce themselves. New employees are hired because they are a "good fit" with existing employees. Cultural values and norms are so strong that employees are socialized to accept the "company way" or they leave. Diversity is a clear example of Eisenberg and Goodall's (2001) concept of creativity and constraint. The very cohesiveness enabled by a strong culture can be a constraining force on difference and change.

The flip side also can be true. If a company strives for diversity in hiring and consciously chooses individuals quite different from the existing employee base, culture can become eroded over time. History is forgotten, rituals lose their meaning, and values fade. Subcultures compete for organizational dominance. Zak (1994) offered an ethnographic study of a blue-collar organizational culture newly diversified by race, gender, ethnicity, and class due to legal mandates. Veteran employees sought to maintain cultural identity and hierarchical position through linguistic strategies such as inside humor, exclusive language, and horseplay. Because of the frequent conflicts between newcomers and veterans, management stepped in to increase control and enforce punishments, leading to cultural fragmentation and resentment.

Defining Diversity

Cox (1993) defines cultural diversity as "the representation, in one social system, of people with distinctly different group affiliations of cultural significance" (p. 6). This definition is useful because it recognizes the role of perceptual identification and cultural significance in defining diversity. For example, an African American female who identifies more with her social class and gender than with her race might not add to the diversity of an organization in which her race is underrepresented. A European American male who identifies more as a disabled person than as a majority male might add to diversity. Cox's definition also stresses cultural significance of the group affiliation. For example, in a traditional church structure that is composed predominantly of intact nuclear families, introducing a church leader who identifies himself as a single or divorced male would have great cultural significance and add to diversity, while a divorced individual in another organization would have little cultural significance. In a male-dominated profession such as systems engineering, a female employee who identifies with her gender might contribute to cultural diversity, while a female employee in a less male-dominated field such as elementary education might have less cultural significance.

We take two different approaches to diversity in this chapter. The first approach helps you to assess the commitment to diversity within your organization and helps you to understand the importance of culture in shaping a truly diverse organization. The focus of this first approach is on organizational change. The second approach is an individual strategy that recognizes that not all organizations embrace a culture of diversity. If you are part of an organization that does not embrace diversity, how can you enhance your own organizational performance if you are a member of a marginalized organizational group?

Creating Organizational Cultures That Embrace Diversity

Creating cultures that can embrace diversity is an imperative for organizations in the next 20–50 years. As Table 9.1 indicates, the Caucasian population of the United States is projected to become a "majority minority" by 2040. According to the 2000 U.S. Census, those who identified themselves

Table 9.1   Projections of U.S. Population by Race/Ethnicity

Race/Ethnicity	Current Population/%	2040 Population/%
African American	35 million/12.4%	55 million/14.0%
Hispanic	35 million/12.4%	87 million/22.2%
White	195 million/69.1%	210 million/53.7%
Asian American	10 million/3.5%	28 million/7.2%
Others (American Indian/Native; Multiracial)	7 million/2.5%	18 million/4.6%
Total	282 million/100%	391 million/100%*

SOURCE: 2000 U.S. Census.

* Author's note: These numbers do not add up to 391 million; however, these are the figures provided in the Census data.

only as "white" presently constitute 69.1% of the population, but will be only 53.7% by 2040. The Hispanic population is projected to increase most dramatically, from 12.4% of the current population to 22.2% in 2040. The African American population will increase more slowly from its current 12.4% to 14.0%. The Asian American population will also increase, from 3.5% to 7.2%. Population gains will come from higher birthrates among some minority populations as well as immigration patterns. Foreign-born citizens and legal immigrants will also constitute a growing portion of the U.S. workforce. It is also interesting that by 2040 4.6% will identify themselves as multiracial or American Indian as traditional categories of race/ethnicity lose their descriptive power.

The trends and projections captured in Table 9.1 are commonly mentioned in the news and in classes on management and organizational development. The common assumption is that these U.S. demographic shifts will result in organizations that enjoy the benefits of increased diversity—multiple perspectives from differing cultural value sets and/or synergy from increased contact and collaboration between different cultural and ethnic groups (Harris & Moran, 2000; Moran & Harris, 1982). While these outcomes are hoped for, two cautions should be noted when studying multinational or culturally diverse organizations. First, racial and ethnic diversity in an organization does not necessarily result in diverse values and/or perspectives. Cultural generalizations about value differences may or may not hold true from person to person. Thus, while an organization may appear diverse in terms of color or nationality, the value sets of those individuals may or may not be dissimilar. A Thai immigrant who has spent his whole life in Bangkok working for Citibank, for example, may have more organizational values in common with a native from New York City than with his own countryman who has spent his life in rural area of Thailand. This point echoes Cox's (1993) definition, earlier in this chapter, of cultural identification in defining diversity.

Dodd (1998) suggests that caution in generalizing about differences must be balanced by another equally important second caution—acting as if differences do not exist or do not matter. In his research, Gerald has heard comments from more than one manager revealing the assumption that "we are really the same," or "yes, I see some differences, but it is really just a personality thing, not a cultural issue." At one level it is important that supervisors recognize a difference even if they attribute it to a personality difference. At another level, however, being blind to the pervasive influence of cultural differences can handicap an organization.

In one multinational company Gerald found that the minority Asian Indian population, as well as the majority U.S. population, tended to overlook differences with two results—mismanaged conflict and missed opportunities for creatively tapping into value differences. In one situation, differences in supervisory style were creating tensions with employees. Asian Indians in management roles assumed that close, immediate supervision was effective. U.S. employees tended to prefer less "over the shoulder" approaches. Neither side had an understanding or acceptance of this national cultural difference. Furthermore, neither side realized that if managed well, not only could these tensions be lessened, but both supervisors and employees would have the opportunity to tap into their value differences to solve problems more effectively. Rather than remain in a stalemate over the difference, dialogue might have resulted in more creative approaches to supervision and teamwork (Driskill, 1995; Driskill & Downs, 1995).

This organizational culture lacked a vision for managing differences in a way that could result in creative responses to difference. Thus, casting a diverse set of players on the organizational stage with the hopes of creative outcomes involves more than just having diverse cultures or personalities present. Creative outcomes also involve more than being aware of differences or effective cross-cultural conflict management. Leadership must develop core and defining values about valuing and using diversity. Such a view is in opposition to assumptions and values on which most organizations have been built. Cleveland, Stockdale, and Murphy (2000) express the feminist viewpoint that despite their differences, most organizational cultures have been built upon male stereotypes and assumptions. They write,

> American organizations tend to expect and reward high levels of dedication and commitment, long hours, and placing the demands of work ahead of the demands of nonwork responsibilities. . . . Most U.S. organizations were built by and for men (usually White men), and it should come as no surprise that men fit better than women in many instances. Perhaps the biggest challenge is in building organizations that fit women as well as men is to examine critically the values and assumptions that define work and work organizations. (pp. 381–382)

They advocate pluralistic rather than monolithic organizational culture. Rather than expecting each culture member to adapt to a single set of values and expectations, a pluralistic culture will create systemic organizational change to adapt to the dynamism of a diverse workforce.

Solving the dilemma of culture and diversity takes on additional urgency in the present "creative economy." Richard Florida (2002) has written an intriguing book, *The Rise of the Creative Class (and How It's Transforming Work, Leisure, Community, and Everyday Life)*. In it he argues that the U.S. economy (and to a large extent the world economy) has become based not only on information but also on creativity, an economy in which hardware and software innovation, biomedical research, e-commerce innovation, and entertainment are driving our total economic growth.

Florida points out that an essential ethos of the new creative class involves diversity. Members of the creative class feel that innovation can flourish only in an environment of stimulation and creative tension. As companies compete for the top creative talent, diversity is a key edge. Florida has conducted extensive statistical research showing that the fastest growing economic areas show excellent statistical fit with areas rich in diversity. Florida (2002) writes,

> One indicator of this preference for diversity is reflected in the fact that Creative Class people tell me that at job interviews they like to ask if the company offers same sex partner benefits, even when they are not themselves gay. What they're seeking is an environment open to differences. . . . When they are sizing up a new company and community, acceptance of diversity and of gays in particular is a sign that reads, "nonstandard people welcome here." (p. 79)

> When they are sizing up a new company and community, acceptance of diversity and gays in particular is a sign that reads, "Nonstandard people welcome here."

Methods for Integrating Diversity as a Cultural Value

So how can an organization create a strong culture that fosters diversity and creativity? One way is to make sure that diversity and tolerance are among the core values, reinforced by heroes, stories, rituals, and artifacts. It is this imperative, rather than political correctness, driving companies toward more inclusive multicultural holiday parties, same sex partner benefits, paid time off for a variety of religious holidays of choice, and other tangible signals that demonstrate they value talented employees of various national, ethnic, and religious backgrounds. Such signals must be consistent and must be supported and articulated from the top of the organization to permeate the organizational culture.

Florida (2002) writes that this evolution of culture in some of America's largest corporations has indeed occurred to attract and retain creative employees. The cultural transformation is marked by casual dress codes, flexible work schedules, open loft-style office spaces, communal hangout spaces, abundant art, and new perks such as concierge services.

A second way to reconcile strong organizational cultures with the need for diversity is to support and encourage organizational subcultures within the overall culture. Steve Jobs did this at Apple Computer when he developed the subversive, renegade team that created the Macintosh computer. This group was supported and encouraged in flouting organizational norms to foster creativity and a sense of being "outlaws." Most creative teams in advertising agencies are granted similar latitude in breaking organizational norms of dress, scheduling, and work habits to foster an environment that nourishes creativity.

The danger with the second approach is evident. If more and more distinct subcultures flourish, employees may come to identify more closely with the subculture than the overall parent culture, and the subculture's values and norms may eclipse and/or change the dominant culture over time. Different subcultures can also compete with one another, as the Mac division did with the Lisa division at Apple Computer. While competition is not always negative and some cultural change and evolution may be positive, if competition is not effectively managed it can fragment and weaken cultures.

Enhancing the Ability of Marginalized Groups to Read Dominant Cultures

In addition to making sure that organizational culture supports diversity, it is also crucial for members of marginalized groups to understand the dominant organizational culture. Marginalized groups are those whose interests and styles are not privileged within the organization. Rosabeth Moss Kanter (1977) in her classic book *Men and Women of the Corporation* offered a numerical minority hypothesis, that tokens (one of only a few representatives of their category in a larger dominant group) face similar pressures whether it is a woman in a male-dominated profession, an African American executive in a European American–dominated team, or an American manager in a Japanese subsidiary of a multinational corporation. One obstacle facing each of these tokens is the lack of access to informal channels of information that would yield tacit understanding of organizational norms. Allen (1995), based on her review of the literature, concluded, "persons of color tend to have limited access to social networks, blocked mobility and often do not have mentors or sponsors" (p. 150).

Rehearsal 9.1 Are You a Privileged Member of Your Organizational Culture?

Consider asking the following questions if your organizational culture creates hurdles for diversity.

1. Have you ever left an employment interview wondering if your race or sexual orientation was a factor in not getting a job?

2. How likely is it that your direct supervisor will be of your race and gender?

3. Do you have to use two languages or idioms, one for social and the other for professional?

4. How many times in a year do you walk into a meeting in which you are the only member of your representative group?

5. How likely is it that someone of your group would be available as a mentor within your organization?

6. Are holidays associated with your religion standard organizational holidays, or do you have to ask special permission to observe them or take personal vacation days?

7. What would be the reaction of your colleagues if you took the person you live with to an office party?

8. How many times have you been asked to speak for all members of your race or gender in a business conversation?

9. Would questions be raised if you chose to select or promote a member of your race or gender?

10. Are you ever invited to a club or restaurant for an organizational function at which you feel uncomfortable as a member of your group?

11. Do you have to rely on laws to ensure equal treatment of your group?

12. Do you ever have to seek assistance or alternatives to be able to enter an office or to use a restroom because the facilities were not designed for you?

13. Do you often feel you are chosen for committees or assignments not because of your qualifications or interests but to represent your minority group?

O'Brien (1980) noted that women in male-dominated workplaces faced the double jeopardy of being less likely to understand informal norms in the workplace and being judged more harshly than their male counterparts when they violated informal norms. In Angi's dissertation research (Laird, 1982) she found that female supervisors working in an oil-well cable manufacturing plant could articulate organizational norms and values as well as their male counterparts in oral interviews, yet when asked to enact the rule in an applied episode they did not show the same situational intelligence as almost all their male counterparts. In a consulting study a few years ago, she asked all the tellers in a large bank chain what it took to become an officer of the bank. All the white males knew it took hard work, good results, face time, and service in certain "approved" community organizations. Every woman and racial/ethnic minority she interviewed declared with confidence that they would become an officer with hard work and diligence. Not one mentioned the expectation of face time or community service. How did all the males know? It likely is because this "tacit" information is learned through informal communication networks—on the golf course, at the Friday happy hour, at the company hunting lodge—all venues that too often the tokens are excluded from. It is this very "social networking" that Richard Florida's Creative Class rebels against as they seek a meritocracy built on talent and performance rather than social connections.

We recognize an ethical dilemma as we propose strategies for marginalized groups to understand the dominant organizational culture. Numerous critical theorists (see Clair, 1993, 1998; Mumby, 1997) have pointed out that when marginalized groups adapt to the dominant culture, they reinforce the legitimacy of unjust cultures that privilege the interests of some groups over others. They call this process hegemony, the participation of marginalized groups in their own domination. Our response is that marginalized groups must understand the dominant culture in order to change it. Often the means of domination through unconscious cultural patterns can be the means of liberation when marginalized groups understand and use cultural patterns to support their own interests.

Either organizations or individuals can take primary responsibility for ensuring that members of culturally significant minorities have resources to learn about cultural expectations. Organizations have sought to level the playing field for women and minorities in a variety of ways. One is by formal mentoring programs, in which a senior member of the organization is paired with a new employee to "show him [or her] the ropes." These formal mentoring relationships rarely produce the same results as naturally occurring mentoring relationships based on perceived mutual benefit and professional attraction. The assigned mentor spends less time with the mentee and doesn't interact in the informal ways that would produce a cultural understanding of the informal relationship.

Chao, Waltz, and Gardner (1992) and Cotton (1995) compared results and levels of satisfaction between individuals who had been involved in informal and formal mentoring programs. While they found that both groups expressed greater socialization and career progress than employees who had not been mentored at all, satisfaction was much higher in informal mentorships, and those relationships also resulted in higher salaries for mentees.

Kreps (1983) writes of another interesting way that organizations have sought to help all new employees with enculturation. RCA developed extensive video orientation programs, not only telling the new employee of policies and corporate data but also cultural information about history, rituals, heroes, and norms.

Another strategy has been developed by minorities themselves in organizations such as minority fraternities and sororities, all-female professional networking groups, and communities of immigrant populations. These alternative information networking groups may give the edge that formal programs lack.

African American fraternities and sororities are an especially interesting social networking phenomenon. More than 1.5 million members, predominantly African Americans, are members of nine fraternities and sororities associated with the National Pan-Hellenic Council, according to its Web site (www.nphchq.org). The fraternities include Omega Psi Phi, Kappa Alpha Psi, Alpha Phi Alpha, Phi Beta Sigma, and Iota Phi Theta. The sororities include Alpha Kappa Alpha, Delta Sigma Theta, Zeta Phi Beta, and Sigma Gamma Rho. Unlike many Caucasian college sororities and

Table 9.2   Creating Diverse Cultures

Method	Advantages	Disadvantages
Creating diversity as a central organizational value	Ends duality of culture and diversity	Difficult to change culture
	Sends clear message through multiple channels	Top leadership must support and lead by example
Encouraging diverse subcultures	Creates pluralistic cultural values and norms	Can erode community and identification
		Can set up battles for organization identity
Formal mentoring programs	Give equal access to informal cultural information	Not same effect as natural mentoring relationships
Organizational orientation including cultural information	Recognizes the importance of culture	Much cultural information is tacit
	Gives all access to cultural information	
Minority networks for personal and professional development	Empowering	May not have cultural insight to share

fraternities, the organizations of the National Pan-Hellenic Council are formed as lifetime networking groups to give members an alternative to exclusive corporate and social networks. Its Web site states,

Each of the nine NPHC organizations evolved during a period when African Americans were being denied essential rights and privileges afforded others. Racial isolation on predominantly white campuses and social barriers of class on all campuses created need for African Americans to align themselves with other individuals sharing common goals and ideals. With the realization of such a need the African American Greek-lettered organization movement took on the personae of a haven and outlet which could foster brotherhood and sisterhood in the pursuit to bring about social change through the development of social programs that would create positive change for Blacks and the country. Today the need remains the same. . . . A lifetime commitment to the goals and ideals of each respective organization is stressed. The individual member is also expected to align himself with a graduate/alumni chapter following graduation from college, with the expectation that he/she will attend regular chapter meetings, regional conferences and national conventions, and take part in matters concerning and affecting the community in which he or she lives.

Members of the National Pan-Hellenic Council have become an economic, political, and social force. The organizations also create a strong and effective alternative networking structure. Recently we interviewed an African American applicant for a tenure-track teaching position at the university. Angi was fascinated when her associate dean greeted the young man and proceeded to tell him every member of his fraternity on campus and leading members of the community who were also "brothers." Listservs for the fraternity offer opportunities to seek career guidance, reestablish connections after moves, or offer social support.

Such constructive efforts provide alternative networking structures to counteract the exclusion of many women, racial/ethnic minorities, international employees, and other marginalized groups from informal communication networks in many organizations. They may offer the best long-term opportunity for learning cultural information in alternate ways. In this chapter we have summarized a variety of approaches for integrating the value of diversity into organizational culture. Those various approaches, along with their advantages and disadvantages, are summarized in Table 9.2 on the previous page.

Summary

1. Strong cultures can prevent organizations from embracing diversity because of hiring biases and expectations for new employees to embrace cultural norms and expectations.

2. Women, racial/ethnic minorities, international employees, and other marginalized groups are often disadvantaged because they are not part of informal communication networks that transmit cultural norms and values.

3. Working toward pluralistic cultures in which diversity is a central organizational value seems the best long-term solution. In the meantime, mentoring or conscious culture socialization processes can help to level the playing field.

4. Naturally occurring mentorships have advantages over formal mentoring programs. Networks specifically formed to advance the interests of women and minorities also show promise in creating cultural change.

Rehearsal 9.2 Diversity Survey

(Created by Angela Brenton for a hospital client)

Please respond to each of the following questions on a 5-point scale in which 5 indicates Strongly Agree; 4, Agree; 3, Neither Agree nor Disagree; 2, Disagree; and 1, Strongly Disagree.

1. My job is important to this organization.		1 2 3 4 5
2. I enjoy my job.		1 2 3 4 5
3. I have received adequate training to do my job.		1 2 3 4 5

4. My opportunity for advancement   1   2   3   4   5
    in this organization is good.

5. Hiring and promotion decisions   1   2   3   4   5
    are made fairly here.

6. Top management supports respect   1   2   3   4   5
    for diversity.

7. This organization has a clear   1   2   3   4   5
    policy on sexual harassment.

8. I know how to file a harassment   1   2   3   4   5
    complaint.

9. I know how to file a discrimination   1   2   3   4   5
    complaint.

10. Individuals guilty of harassment in   1   2   3   4   5
    this organization are disciplined
    appropriately.

11. Individuals guilty of discrimination   1   2   3   4   5
    in this organization are disciplined
    appropriately.

12. Employees of different racial and   1   2   3   4   5
    ethnic groups are treated equally
    in organizational policies and
    practices.

13. This organization treats men and   1   2   3   4   5
    women equally in organizational
    policies and practices.

14. Discrimination on the basis of   1   2   3   4   5
    race, gender, religion, age,
    disability, or sexual orientation
    is not tolerated here.

15. I have experienced discrimination   1   2   3   4   5
    in this organization.

16. Someone I know has experienced   1   2   3   4   5
    discrimination in this organization.

17. I have heard offensive comments   1   2   3   4   5
    of a sexual nature here.

18. I have heard offensive racial or   1   2   3   4   5
    ethnic language used by
    employees in this organization.

(Continued)

(Continued)

19.	Employees of different racial/ethnic groups and genders communicate well with one another.	1	2	3	4	5
20.	My supervisor shows appreciation for individual differences (i.e., ethnic, gender, age, disabilities, sexual orientation, etc.).	1	2	3	4	5
21.	My supervisor accommodates the needs of employees who are responsible for the care of children or older adults.	1	2	3	4	5
22.	I have the opportunity for flextime on my schedule.	1	2	3	4	5
23.	I have the option of job sharing.	1	2	3	4	5
24.	I find it difficult to balance work and family responsibilities.	1	2	3	4	5
25.	This organization would benefit if more women were promoted to managerial or leadership positions.	1	2	3	4	5
26.	This organization would benefit if more racial/ethnic minorities were promoted to managerial and leadership positions.	1	2	3	4	5
27.	I would feel comfortable working with someone who is openly gay/lesbian.	1	2	3	4	5
28.	My supervisor shows respect for me.	1	2	3	4	5
29.	This organization makes accommodation for employees with disabilities.	1	2	3	4	5
30.	My supervisor shows favoritism to some employees.	1	2	3	4	5
31.	I have input into decisions that affect my job.	1	2	3	4	5
32.	This organization is a good place to work.	1	2	3	4	5
33.	This organization cares about the health and welfare of employees.	1	2	3	4	5

34. What is your employment status?
    A. Part-time
    B. Full-time

35. What is your gender?
    A. Male
    B. Female

36. What is your racial/ethnic classification?
    A. Caucasian
    B. African American
    C. Hispanic/Latino
    D. Asian/Pacific Islander
    E. Middle Eastern
    F. Native American
    G. Other

37. How long have you worked at this organization?
    A. Less than 1 year
    B. 1–5 years
    C. 6–10 years
    D. 11–20 years
    E. More than 20 years

We computed cross-tabs of each question by employment status, gender, race/ethnicity, and tenure to determine if there were differences in job satisfaction, relationship with supervisor, training opportunities, or reactions to diversity by demographic characteristics.

10

Improvisation

Managing Change

Step Five: Identify Applications for Organizational Diversity, *Change*, Ethics, Leadership, and Effectiveness

Objectives:

- Understand the major forces that drive change
- Understand the four perspectives on the way organizations view change
- Understand the insights on how to manage change

Stage Terms:

- Substitution
- Evolution
- Loss
- Integration
- Differentiation
- Fragmentation

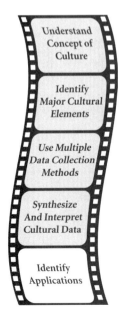

Understand Concept of Culture

Identify Major Cultural Elements

Use Multiple Data Collection Methods

Synthesize And Interpret Cultural Data

Identify Applications

A standard part of the training for method actors involves improvisation—creating scenes and characters without the security or structure of a script. In improvisation, characters must draw on their creativity and inner experiences to create a reality with one another when neither knows what is coming next. Although improvisation is seen as creative and fun for many method actors, it is often stressful for organizational actors. It is our position in this chapter that understanding organizational culture is essential to achieving substantial and lasting changes in organizations. The cultural perspective is a unique viewpoint on organizational change for several reasons: (a) It focuses on how organizational practices are interwoven with deeper (but unseen) layers of organizational beliefs and assumptions, (b) it helps organizational leaders understand resistance to change and helps them develop strategies for coping with resistance, and (c) it suggests symbolic strategies necessary for successful organizational change. This section reviews some of the forces that prompt change before providing a model for understanding responses to change. We also provide suggestions for change management in light of your cultural themes and overall definition.

Forces Driving Change

A list of factors that cause or result in organizations making changes in policies, practices, and perhaps attempting changes in core values is not difficult to generate. If you generated your own list of change-inducing forces, what would you include?

Rehearsal 10.1 Forces Driving Change

1. _____

2. _____

3. _____

4. _____

Your list probably includes such things as competition, changes in the environment and technologies, government regulations, generational changes, globalization, mergers, and/or rapid growth. You may also have included factors that cause an individual in an organization to undergo adjustments and changes that are beyond typical organization-wide changes, for example: promotion, firing, transfer, or retirement.

Reactions to Change

Regardless of the force behind it, change is a pervasive aspect of organizational life. As indicated in the opening statements, varied responses and reactions to change are part of all our experiences. Marris (1974) argues that disruptions in "meaning structures" are what people most resist in change processes, not the change itself. Put differently, individuals hold different levels of "psychological safety" in response to change depending on how they view or interpret the form of the change. Forms of change, according to Marris, can be categorized as follows:

- **Substitution:** a change in which one item of meaning is exchanged for another (e.g., a new boss)
- **Evolution:** gradual shifts in values, meanings (e.g., a gradual move from a family business to a larger business employing non-family members)
- **Loss:** significant change in the avenue a person had used to achieve attachment, success, and competence (e.g., job loss due to a plant closing or a transfer resulting in new duties and new colleagues)

In substitution, the organization member gives up one cultural meaning for another. Smith and Eisenberg (1987) give the example of Disneyland, which shifted from a theater metaphor to a family metaphor with some harmful consequences for the organization. A family metaphor became inconsistent with hard business decisions management had to make. You don't lay off family members. The authors suggest that Disneyland could recover its original culture by substituting the original theater language and rituals for the family elements that had replaced them. At times, when change is perceived as substitution rather than loss, it may be easier for organization members to accept because they are not left with a void. When there is strong ego attachment to the culture, however, even substitution may be difficult to accept.

In evolution, change seems gradual rather than abrupt. In the taken-for-granted reality, employees may not even be aware of gradual changes. Those most likely to react negatively are employees with longer tenure who are most likely to remember "the way things used to be." At times there is a moment of cultural comparison that may make organization members more aware of the change.

In loss, change is sudden and shocking, producing resistance and grief. Recognizing these different forms of change can be useful in recognizing normal and expected reactions. Depression, grief, denial, anger, sadness, and holding on to the past are all responses to loss. Thus, in managing changes viewed in terms of loss, communication skills of reflection and paraphrasing may be more appropriate than arguing with someone to "get over" a normal process.

Deetz, Tracy, and Simpson (2000) offer an insight on the different reactions of management and employees to major change:

Business leaders rarely anticipate the extent of the resistance to planned changes. One reason for this is that the leaders have had more time to think about the change and more fully understand the reasons for it. But equally important, leaders often have less to lose from it. Employees, on the other hand, are surprised, do not understand the reasoning, did not participate in the choice, and see themselves as having much to lose. (p. 39)

Bridges (1991) likens the change process to a marathon with thousands of runners. Runners start in tiers. The competitive runners start first. The

"Sunday runners" are so far in the back of the pack they can't even hear the starting gun. By the time the Sunday runners have eased into a trot, the competitive runners have neared the finish line. Too many managers are typical of the frontrunners; they are impatient with employees who can't seem to catch a vision of the finish line.

Bridges (1991), in an excellent and practical book on change, offers several suggestions to help employees let go of the past:

- Identify who's losing what.
- Accept the reality and importance of the subjective losses.
- Don't be surprised by "overreaction."
- Acknowledge the losses openly and sympathetically.
- Expect and accept the signs of grieving.
- Compensate for the losses.
- Give people information, and do it again and again.
- Define what's over and what isn't.
- Mark the endings.
- Treat the past with respect.
- Let people take a piece of the old way with them.
- Show how endings ensure continuity of what really matters.

In all, the value of paying attention to change management as a meaning-management process places a greater emphasis on understanding the organization's culture(s), since symbolic ("sense-making") processes are at the core of understanding change. After reviewing a framework for understanding change processes in organizations, we provide several activities to aid you in examining your cultural data and drawing implications for change management.

Three Perspectives on Culture (Plus One)

Martin (1992) provides three perspectives or ways that researchers and organizational members interpret culture in light of three variables: "the relationship among cultural elements or manifestations" such as values and rules, the degree of consensus among organization members about the culture, and the "orientation to ambiguity" or uncertainty (p. 190). Based on these three variables, Martin characterizes organizational cultures as integrated, differentiated, or fragmented; we introduced these perspectives in Chapter 4. These perspectives can also help in understanding why one organization experiences change so much differently than another organization. After reviewing each perspective, we will present implications for this framework in the change management process.

First, the *integration* perspective focuses on consistency in cultural elements, organization-wide consensus on issues or policies, and has a negative orientation toward ambiguity. A researcher taking an integration perspective toward the study of culture would look for broadly shared values and themes and would assume that meanings were shared across organization members and groups. Ambiguity would be seen as a sign that values and meanings were imperfectly shared. These shared values come from inspirational leaders who unite organization members, often in response to the external environment. The strength of the culture is often seen in its stability and in the continuity of organizational values and practices. It is clear from this perspective how change is seen as destabilizing and threatening to group identity.

The *differentiation* perspective focuses on the differences in values and assumptions among members of the organization, and the tensions among subcultures competing to define organizational values and practices. For example, you may have noticed differences in your analysis between a marketing department and a research department about the values or norms of the organization. One of your themes might have been paradoxes or tensions among organizational values. Change, from this perspective, is viewed differently by various subcultures in the organization. Some subgroups may applaud a change consistent with their values while others may feel loss and disconfirmation.

Finally, a third perspective, *fragmentation,* assumes an inherent complexity in cultural elements, accepts a multiplicity of views on organizational issues rather than organization-wide or even subcultural consensus, and accepts ambiguity and change as normal. A researcher operating from a fragmentation perspective assumes that values and meanings are only partially shared among organization members and that cultural consensus is more surface than real. For example, while all organization members say they value diversity, the term may have completely different meanings and implications among employees. Members of a divergent culture welcome diverse views and do not see problems with varying values or interpretations of events. For example, a computer research laboratory may thrive because it accepts the norm of uncertainty and embraces such uncertainty as a resource and motivation for creativity. Change, from this perspective, would not even be noticed since change is par for the course.

The underlying assumption behind this analytic model or metatheory on organizational cultures is that to understand how an organization experiences change, you must understand more about the underlying culture. Change may be seen as expected and normal in one organization but traumatic or difficult in another. By way of analogy, consider taking someone's pulse and discovering that the person's heart was beating at about 40 beats per minute. If an inexperienced person took this rate without knowledge of the person's history (exercise and eating habits, age, etc.), he or she might conclude the person had a weak heart and needed a pacemaker or medication. Such a conclusion might be appropriate for an older, still active individual, but for a younger athlete, a low resting heartbeat of 40 might be normal. In a similar vein, Martin's model provides a way to *contextualize change* by directing attention to the meaning organizations attach to uncertainty or ambiguity in the environment.

Table 10.1 highlights examples of each of these perspectives by providing a metaphor, the degree of consensus within the organization about how change is viewed, how ambiguity is viewed, assumptions about the source of change, and finally implications for each perspective.

The jungle metaphor for each of the three perspectives captures the importance of understanding how an organization views change. Each metaphor holds implications for how the organization views effectiveness and what, if anything, needs to be done to manage change. The difference, for example, between an organization seeking and accustomed to organization-wide consensus on issues (integration) versus an organization accustomed

Table 10.1   Three Perspectives on Organizational Culture and Change

	Integration	Perspective Differentiation	Fragmentation
Metaphor	Clearing in a jungle	Islands of clarity in a sea of ambiguity	Jungle
Consensus	Organization-wide	Within subcultures	Issue specific
Ambiguity	Denial	Channeling	Acceptance
Change	Revolutionary	Incremental	Continual
Source of change	Leader-centered	External/internal catalysts	Individual catalysts
Implications	If superficial, controllable; if deeper, difficult to control	Predictable and unpredictable sources and consequences of change	Uncontrollable due to continual change

SOURCE: Adapted from Meyerson and Martin (1987).

to continual change (fragmentation) is clear. For one, change typically must be monitored and initiated by top leaders; for another, change is something everyone is involved in adapting to each day. Thus, a new leader not tuned in to a fragmentation culture with the norm of accepting change may run aground. Her failure may be inevitable if she attempts to manage change based on an integration perspective with the focus on top management taking charge and managing the process.

 Rehearsal 10.2 Cultural Approach to Change

Take a minute to reflect on your organization in light of Table 10.1.

Which of the three perspectives best captures how the organization you analyzed views ambiguity?

_____ Culture is seen as a stable force with high consistency among manifestations of culture? Thus, change equals a loss of psychological safety if clarity is not maintained.

_____ Culture is stable within units, but diverse and unpredictable across units? Thus, change is accepted unless viewed as an effort to disturb subculture clarity or autonomy.

_____ Cultural manifestations are accepted as unclear and inconsistent? Change is not noticed as a problem unless an underlying value system disturbs perspective of acceptance.

> *We should not confuse our analytic frameworks with reality.*

Martin's three perspectives provide a valuable categorization system that reflects the way each of us interprets the culture of an organization based on our own biases and comfort levels with ambiguity. Those who seek out consistent, unambiguous interpretations fall at one end of the continuum. However, if you as a researcher have imposed your own order on an organizational culture better characterized as differentiated or fragmented, you may not have fully captured the richness of the organizational culture. In Rehearsal 10.2, your effort to make a connection with one of these perspectives might have caused you to feel boxed in by the three choices. You may have seen differences across the organization. Martin (1992) realizes the limitation of her model and argues for the merits of examining an organization from all three perspectives. How would you examine a culture from each of the three perspectives? Consider again each perspective in light of our discussion of subcultures. There may be individual employees and/or subcultures that view the organization from an integration view—you may hear from members of this subculture about consistently held values and leader-led initiatives. Others may hold a differentiation view, suggested by their stories of heroes that indicate a lack of organization-wide consensus on values or themes. And finally, individuals throughout the organization might suggest greater comfort with innovation and constant change, thus implying a fragmentation perspective. In other words, if you felt boxed in by the three choices or found yourself checking more then one box, you were on track with a key insight. As you seek to interpret the culture, it is imperative that you not fall into just one vision of how change is viewed by members of the organization. Applying these different perspectives, listening for divergent viewpoints, will give you a richer reading of the culture and thus provide important insight for change management.

Plus One

Martin (1992) provides a critique of these three perspectives and in doing so reminds us that reality is not contained in just one of the three boxes. Her expansion reflects the challenges of creating a model or framework for interpretation. With her, we realize that any framework may cause you to fail to ask other important questions of your cultural data. While Martin does not provide a clear "fourth box," she does suggest questions that you might ask that get beyond her boxes. For example, she suggests examining cultures in light of the focus or intent of changes that are introduced by management: Does management introduce change solely for its own interests? Do they seek change that would be less oppressive to lower ranked organization members? (Stablien & Nord, 1985). These questions combined with the notion of applying multiple frameworks underscore a key component of effective change management: We should not confuse our analytic frameworks with reality; they, like culture, are constructs intended to help us manage meaning.

> *"The choice that individuals and societies ultimately have before them is thus really a choice about the kind of contradiction that is to shape the pattern of daily life"* (Morgan, 1986, p. 267).

Connections: The Metaphor Game

Chapter 3 highlighted the role of metaphor in the way we define organizations. We stressed that organizational culture can be seen as a metaphor for understanding an organization. Viewing culture as a metaphor encourages the identification of elements of culture, as we explored earlier. The notion of metaphor for understanding organizations also finds value in change management. Researchers and theorists accept the powerful influence implicit and explicit metaphors have on the way we think about and communicate in organizations (Bolman & Deal, 1998; Fairhurst & Sarr, 1996; Morgan, 1986). A metaphor provides a lens or frame for the way we think about and respond to symbols in our organizations. For example, a manager might operate under a frame or lens that implies an organization should operate like a machine. Such a focus then would necessarily focus on managing change in a way that improves efficiency or makes sure each part is functioning correctly. This same machine metaphor in the context of managing change might prompt the same manager to overlook or deemphasize individual or personal motivation factors that influence performance or the way power inequities shape the way changes are accepted or managed.

The limitations of any one lens or metaphor for managing change suggests the importance of multiframe thinking—applying multiple perspectives. Effective leaders, optimally competent communicators, should learn to move between frames as well as blend and develop additional approaches to managing change. The value of multiframe thinking is supported by research on communication competence. Studies have found that competent communicators are able to generate a greater variety of communication interpretations and options for dealing with complex and challenging situations (Clampitt, Lemke, & Hazen, 1992; Driskill & Honey, 1994; Spitzberg & Hecht, 1984).

Beyond Martin's (1992) three-perspective framework, metaphors provide another means for enhancing our ability to generate a wider array of interpretive options. Bolman and Deal (1998) take a metaphor approach to organizations. They focus on four frames—structural, human resource, political, and symbolic—each of which is embedded in an implicit metaphor. The competent or ideal change agent will use multiframe thinking and see organizations through more than one of these frames simultaneously. However, the reality is that we tend to assume one of the frames is the better approach to understanding an organization. For example, a structural manager may tend to approach change through reorganization of functions, reporting relationships, or geographic locations. A human resource manager will think of the human element and explore training, clear job descriptions, and the calming of insecurities. This manager will realize that change produces feeling of incompetence and will work on clarifying expectations and equipping employees with requisite skills. A political leader will understand that change affects power currencies. Some organization members gain power by the change and others lose. This leader will carefully analyze the effect of change on various players and will build coalitions of those who will be favorably impacted by change. Finally, the symbolic leader understands that change is about meaning and works to shape the way employees interpret the change through various symbolic means—stories, rituals, heroes, and other elements of culture. The bottom-line implication is to use insights from all of the frames. Just as you should gain an awareness of the way the organization views change, you should also be aware of multiple perspectives or frames for managing change.

Practical Suggestions for Considering Culture in Organizational Change

We offer a few practical suggestions for managing change from a cultural perspective. *First, recognize that culture can facilitate change as well as inhibit it.* Once the leader understands the importance of culture and has a good understanding of her current organizational culture, she can use cultural elements to support change efforts. For example, current values can be used as a bridge to new rituals or practices. Angi was a management consultant for a bank for several years. It was known for its exceptional customer service. As banking was deregulated to offer more financial services, the bank rolled out a plan to encourage employees to "sell" more products and services to bank customers. They offered significant financial incentives and were surprised when few employees achieved their selling goals. After interviewing several employees, she concluded that the resistance to selling was based on employees' perceptions that selling compromised their service to employees. She encouraged the bank to drop the financial incentives and to focus instead on explaining to bank employees how the new products could serve existing customers, to tell stories about the elderly lady getting 1.7% on a large balance in a regular savings account who could earn 6% with the same money in a mutual fund. Sales soared once employees "reframed" the new sales practices within the strong cultural value of service.

Cultural elements such as rituals can also assist in grieving losses or symbolically welcoming new practices. You can ground the change within elements of history, or position cultural heroes as leaders of change.

Second, recognize the value of the "neutral zone." Bridges (1991) identifies the neutral zone as an inherent part of any major change effort. It is the time in which employees have left behind the familiar but have not fully entered the new. He writes,

> Given the ambiguities of the neutral zone, it is natural for people to become polarized between those who want to rush forward and those who want to go back to old ways. And given that polarization, it is natural for consensus to break down and the level of discord to rise. Teamwork may be severely undermined, as may loyalty to the organization itself. Managed properly, this is only a temporary situation. Left unmanaged, it can lead to terminal chaos. (p. 79)

Bridges notes that the neutral zone is important because old ideas and practices have to have time to die before employees are ready to embrace the new. It can also be a time of innovation and creativity when old norms and restraints are loosened and new rules have yet to develop. Communication strategies such as reframing metaphors, sharing information, reducing uncertainty, and building connections assist employees in realizing the positive potential of the neutral zone.

Third, be aware that process is everything during periods of cultural change. It is not so much where you end up as how you get there that will impact employee's reactions to change. Even a good change that is badly handled will be damaging. Two keys to good process are communication and participation. Change processes are destabilizing and increase uncertainty. Providing as much information as possible, as often as possible, helps reduce this uncertainty. Employees tend to support what they help create. Involving employees in every stage of the change effort will reduce their feelings of being passive victims and will encourage their ownership of the change effort. One medical organization contacted Gerald for assistance in the midst of a merger process. The lack of focus on the process had resulted in one physician becoming the scapegoat for much of the grieving and sense of loss in the organization. To complicate matters, this physician was from another country. Thus, HRD managers and senior managers found themselves trying to determine if part of the problem was to be found in employees' having to adjust to a national culture difference. A closer examination of the two organizations that had merged showed that the issue was not as simple as the collision of two national cultures. The core issue was that the controversial physician represented an organizational culture that valued research productivity while the other organization valued patient care. In short, the merger got on track only when HRD focused on process and gave more time to training rituals that allowed discussion of value differences.

Fourth, effective change requires a vision and a plan. Most employees are reluctant to set out for foreign territory unless the leader can share some inspiring vision of what lies ahead. Deetz and colleagues (2000) stress the importance of communicating a vision that is linked to shared values within the organizational culture:

> A vision without the voice of a prophet can neither inspire nor guide. Under-communication usually occurs when the vision remains a property of upper managers. They may be clear about where they are going, but the various instructions and directives they send out do not carry the vision. These often make little sense and fail to inspire. (p. 45)

Bridges (1991) notes that even an inspiring vision can be frustrating without a specific transition plan. Such a plan should serve as a roadmap for realizing the vision. The vision and the plan must work together. Either without the other is incomplete.

Kotter (1995) outlines eight steps for major organizational transformations:

1. Establish a sense of urgency.
2. Form a powerful guiding coalition.
3. Create a guiding vision.
4. Communicate the vision.

5. Empower others to act.
6. Create small wins along the way.
7. Consolidate improvements and create more change.
8. Institutionalize the new culture.

His steps, of course, would need to be filtered through the information you gather about how the organization views change. If change is par for the course, the organization likely already has a strong framework and norm of empowering others to act to manage change.

If you were to review your cultural analysis, including elements, themes, and an overall definition(s), you would likely find embedded in it insights on change management. A major effort at change in an organization (merger, acquisition, and so on) should give some thought to these insights for leadership or management strategy. For example, one medical specialty organization experienced major difficulties when they expanded to work with a state-run agency. In initial interviews, comments were made about who was to benefit from this new association. It was clear that most of their energy was being used to negotiate the new political territory. Even as they continued to spend energy there, leadership had become aware of a higher turnover rate and much lower employee satisfaction. They noticed that employees called on to spend more time in the state agency did not feel valued and that they were experiencing a loss of meaning in that some of them had worked with the smaller, "family" culture of the home organization for more than 10 years. Efforts to manage this expansion were soon augmented with greater employee support through more regular ritualized meetings that allowed them to grieve for their loss. These same meetings became an opportunity to reaffirm the employees' value to the organization. We provide a Rehearsal at the end of this chapter to encourage thought about ways to manage change across multiple perspectives or metaphors. Your goal should be to devise a multimetaphor approach that does not limit your interpretation or change management strategy to a single approach.

Summary

Change management will no doubt remain one of the most critical leadership skills. Regardless of the source of the change (merger, resizing, and so on) or the form it takes (substitution, evolution, or loss), the following guiding principles are useful tools for change managers:

1. Understand the perspective the organization holds concerning change (integration, differentiation, or fragmentation). Failing to realize that organizations hold assumptions about how change is viewed can result in a cookie-cutter and typically flawed approach to managing change.

2. Adjust change strategies based on the organization's experience or perception of the change. For example, loss of meaning rather than role confusion may be the primary perception. Paying attention to the variety of change management strategies implicated by varying perceptions of change will result in a tailored and effective response.

3. Understand how cultural elements can be used to implement change.

4. Use the neutral zone as a positive time to allow employees to let go and to stimulate creative thinking.

5. Realize that process is critical to successful cultural change, particularly communication and participation.

6. Combine a clearly communicated vision with a practical transition plan to inspire and offer guidance.

7. Adopt multiframe thinking to view change and change strategies through multiple perspectives.

Rehearsal 10.3 Adapting
Change Messages to the Culture

Purpose: Develop communication strategies based on the way an organization views change.

Steps:

1. Review your analysis data to determine organizational perceptions of change. Examine each of the three options: integration, differentiation, fragmentation.

2. Develop a communication strategy appropriate for the organization, remembering the concept of multiperspective thinking. In other words, go beyond the boxes to synthesize an approach sensitive to the way change is viewed in the organization. For example, the organization may place a high value on consistency and clarity, which suggests certain top management efforts to establish direction. However, there may be subcultures or minority cultures that have a greater acceptance of uncertainty. Thus, change management strategies should go beyond a simple approach that addresses a unitary or integrated view of the culture.

Metaphor A: It Is a Jungle Out There

Culture: A stable force with high consistency among manifestations of culture

Change: Results in a loss of psychological safety if clarity is not maintained

Subculture Variation: _____

(Continued)

(Continued)

Strategy: Leadership creates messages to indicate control over change process, reduces ambiguity by clarifying roles and norms and processes in place to maintain stability and meaning.

Metaphor B: The Jungle Is Not All Out There

Culture: Stable within units, but diverse and unpredictable across units

Change: Accepted unless viewed as an effort to disturb subculture clarity or autonomy

Subculture Variation: _____

Strategy: Leadership stresses and defines sources of change that can be controlled by the organization and those factors that are beyond their control. Organizational responses are developed as a longer-range incremental approach that will be viewed and adjusted as new information is gained. Messages focus on maintaining clarity and meaning in areas most significant to the organization.

Metaphor C: We Are Part of the Jungle

Culture: Cultural manifestations are accepted as unclear and inconsistent

Change: Not noticed as a problem unless underlying value system disturbs perspective of acceptance

Subculture Variation: _____

Strategy: Leaders encourage continued acceptance of the reality of change process. Policies are reviewed that encourage empowerment of subcultures and individuals to respond to change and to serve as catalysts for future change.

Metaphor D: Conflict in the Jungle

Culture: Cultural manifestations perceived by workers as manipulated for management interests or gain

Change: Viewed as a tension between management and employee interests

Subculture Variation: _____

Strategy: Leadership encourages dialogue and negotiation on issues of importance to the employees and management. Symbols and rituals are used to unify and find common ground to encourage sense of value in the process of making sure the change brings benefit to the entire organization.

Rehearsal 10.4 A Change Plan

Choose a project that would be a significant cultural change within either your own organization, your cultural analysis organization, or another organization with which you are very familiar. Outline a plan for how you would approach leading the change, using principles from your reading. Make sure that your project narrative addresses the following issues:

1. What change is envisioned? Why is this change a cultural change?

2. Discuss how you would prepare individuals in the organization for change.

3. Describe the change process. How long would it take? Who would be involved? What would be the steps toward change?

4. Describe how your plan would accomplish the following:
   a. Encouraging employees to confront and deal with losses
   b. Using a neutral zone creatively
   c. Making a new beginning involving purpose, picture, plan, and part in the plan for each member of the organization
   d. Ensuring continuity of cultural values
   e. Using cultural rituals to support and enable change
   f. Ensuring as much security as possible during transition
   g. Keeping the lines of communication open

Rehearsal 10.5 A Change Case

Dean John Smith was hired by a research-intensive university to become Dean of the College of Science and Mathematics. He had served as a program director for a major national science foundation for 10 years before assuming this role. He had previous held a tenured faculty position at a university, but had no

(Continued)

(Continued)

university administrative experience. He inherited a college in which 40% of the faculty were older than 55, the college was dead last in the university in grant activity, the numbers of majors were declining, and the quality of facilities for instruction and research were substandard. The college had been led for 4 years by a series of interim deans during unsuccessful searches for a permanent dean.

During his first year as dean he led the faculty (in the face of some resistance) in a major and ambitious strategic planning process. The plan produced by the process set ambitious goals that would require about $3 million in new investment. He also instituted the following actions:

- He required all faculty members to integrate Internet instructional tools into their classes, with the goal of developing online instruction that would attract new students.
- He overruled a faculty decision to award promotion to a popular faculty member he considered did not have sufficient research productivity.
- He made public comments disparaging the quality of the current faculty, and put pressure on senior faculty members to consider early retirement.
- He requested that the university offer his faculty no summer teaching contracts to force more faculty members to seek outside grant support to provide summer income.
- He developed assertive (some perceived them as aggressive and competitive) appeals in the Dean's Council for why his college should receive additional funding for salaries, graduate assistantships, and facilities.

Results of his efforts were mixed. The number of majors and student semester credit hours increased in the college. The number of grant submissions increased, although his faculty did not have a high percentage of awards to submissions. A number of senior faculty members chose early retirement, and the dean hired bright new faculty members to take their places. His evaluations by faculty members in his college were the lowest for any dean in the university. Many of his colleagues on the Dean's Council viewed him as brash and noncollegial.

Questions:

1. How would you evaluate these change efforts?

2. Which of Bolman and Dean's four "frames" or metaphors (structural, political, human resource, symbolic) did the leader use? Fail to use?

3. Were such reactions by members necessary and to be expected?

4. What type of cultural orientation to change existed prior to the change efforts (integrated, differentiated, fragmented)? How did this affect reactions to change?

5. What might have been done differently to gain more acceptance of change? Reflect on Kotter's guidelines from the chapter.

11

An Honest Portrayal

Ethics

Step Five: Identify
Applications for
Organizational
Diversity,
Change, *Ethics*,
Leadership, and
Effectiveness

Business practitioners . . . confront many daunting problems. Some [face] . . . lagging productivity, burdensome social and regulatory costs, discontented and disloyal work forces, a rising tide of global competition, geopolitical turmoil, unreliable currency systems. . . . A deep knowledge of how values impel business practitioners, their workers, their firms [attempt] to survive present difficulties but also to ride the powerful social and technological currents. The task and challenge are considerably more formidable than . . . a simple, "discover your organizational culture's values," as salable formulas suggest.

—Frederick, *Values, Nature, and Culture in
the American Corporation*, 1995, p. 5

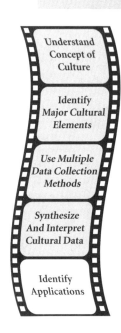

Objectives:

- Learn the major value tensions that influence communication and ethics
- Understand critical questions to ask concerning culture and ethical value tensions

Stage Terms:

- Value tensions
- Economizing values
- Power aggrandizement values
- Ecologizing values

Too Much
Bad News

When the curtain is raised or when the screen lights up, as audience members we hope for nothing more and nothing less than an honest portrayal. Method actors are trained to develop a devotion to the "power of truth in acting" (Vineberg, 1991, p. 7). In short, effective acting is not about pretense but honest portrayals that bring truth to the heart and mind.

When the curtain is raised on cultural performances, we hope for the same. In fact, what we deem not only as right and wrong, but what should or ought to happen, is at the heart of many complaints about life in organizations. Labor unions continue to battle management for power and resources. Disenchanted citizens hear again and again of CEOs with incomes that rival the budgets of third world countries. Daily news reports bring bad news about another CEO indicted or sentenced. The names of the organizations and their respective CEOs are now too numerous to track as news of Enron sentencing blurs into ongoing cases with ImClone and Tenet Health Care. In this chapter we make the argument that ethical principles must be deeply woven throughout the organizational culture in order for ethics to be part of the taken-for-granted reality of corporate actors. We also suggest for your consideration that ethical lapses in the news are not, for the most part, moral failings of individuals, but reflections of cultural values and practices deeply ingrained in organizational cultures.

It is not a surprise that organizations continue to call for assistance in dealing with the problems associated with unethical behavior and value conflicts since more than two thirds of Fortune 500 firms have been convicted of serious crimes, ranging from fraud to illegal dumping of hazardous wastes (Eisenberg & Goodall, 1997). In the search for guidance in the ethical arena, attention is sometimes drawn to an occasional moral or ethical hero, such as the case of Malden Mills' president Aaron Feuerstein. After a fire destroyed his textile plant, he kept employees on the payroll despite the cries of shareholders to do the opposite (Ulmer, 2001). The "1996 Botwinick Prizes in Business Ethics and in Ethical Practice in the Professions" was presented to Feurstein for his ethical leadership (retrieved from the World Wide Web, January 19, 2004, http://www.columbia.edu/cu/1996/0918/c.html). More recently, despite speculation that bankruptcy could have been avoided had he not been so generous with his employees, he maintained his position of no regrets. The guiding ethical principle for Feurstein, growing from his religious faith, was that of acting for the larger goal, not for the moment, for doing the right thing (Shafron, 2004).

It is our view that ethical values and assumptions must be deeply grounded in organizational culture to have a guiding influence on employee decisions and behavior. If ethics become compartmentalized, or if they reside only in organizational practices at the surface level of culture, they will fail to become a guiding force for the organization.

Identifying guiding principles from ethical heroes such as Feurstein provides one approach to ethics. In the context of deciphering cultural data, such principles may provide a benchmark or a place to reflect on themes or cultural values that merit revision. The approach we take in teaching and consultation is to examine cultural data in light of value tensions in the organization. We focus on a value tension model that informs ethical decision making. We close this section with Rehearsals that encourage reflection on cultural data with these value tensions in mind.

Value Tensions and Ethics

We have stressed throughout this workbook that organizational cultures do not exist in a vacuum. Effective organizations must find ways to exist and thrive in the national and international cultures that they seek to serve. The challenges organizations face in adapting and responding to the external culture are especially salient in the case of ethical issues. As an organization develops its own value system for evaluating ethical behavior, it must at the same time be responsive to the larger societal value system (Nicotera & Cushman, 1992). Examining the norms of a given culture via customers and business partners, however, is not sufficient. The lament of sales, marketing, and development specialists in multinationals is often that bribes and corruption appear to be the norm in certain societies. The U.S. government has passed laws and interpretive guides (e.g., http://www.usdoj.gov/criminal/fraud/fcpa.html,http://www.mac.doc.gov/tcc/anti_b/oecd2001/BriberyReport2001.pdf, http://www.bisnis.doc.gov/bisnis/fcp1.htm), and other intercultural specialists provide additional insight on how to respond to bribery and corruption (Knoten, 1999). Nonetheless, the challenge of knowing when to "do as the Romans do" and when to take a stand for a certain principle is not easily resolved. For example, if you learn that it is the norm to pay an extra fee to build an additional storage building for your company, do you take on a local bureaucrat about the ethicality of the fee knowing it may mean months of delay, or do you pay it realizing that you may be hit with other hidden fees later? Furthermore, what do you do if you learn that your own organization has developed a culture that allows for practices such as paying bribes that you know the society "back home" would not consider ethical? A cultural relativist position would encourage you to view the fee as a tip, while a cultural universalistic position would challenge that view by noting the differences in power relationships and motives between a tip and a bribe.

Given the challenges faced in a diverse and multicultural society, organizational cultural leaders need to be equipped to meet ethical challenges. One approach to communication and ethics is to gain an awareness of values tensions that are an inescapable part of organizational life. Frederick (1995) discusses three general value clusters in light of human culture and evolutionary processes. He argues that these value clusters are tied to each other and inform our efforts to encourage good decision making about ethics and value conflicts.

According to Frederick (1995), businesses have typically been aware of and operated within the confines of two of these value clusters: economizing—concerns over sufficient profit versus human values of sustainable cooperation; and power aggrandizement—concerns over the extent power is dispersed versus held by a few. Often overlooked is the value set related to ecologizing values—concerns over the macroenvironment versus the microenvironment. Reflection on the interdependency of each of the three values sets can provide a foundation for understanding ethical dilemmas and values conflicts. Adapting William Frederick's work, we discuss these value clusters as tensions or dialectics as a way to promote reflection on ethics and organizational culture. The three tensions include (a) economizing—short-term profit versus human values, (b) power-aggrandizing versus equality, and (c) ecologizing—macroenvironment versus microenvironment. As we present each value tension, we include a section of application questions designed to promote reflection and connections to your analysis. We end this chapter by challenging you to give thought to other value tensions.

Economizing

Economizing is short-term profit values versus human values of sustainable cooperation. This value tension, like the others, is an essential societal dialectic. The values in this cluster support activities that cause individuals and groups to act efficiently in using resources required for survival and material prosperity. The accepted measure of economizing is monetary profit and loss. However, as we argue in the discussion of organizational effectiveness in Chapter 13, the bottom line of profits is insufficient as a measure of effectiveness. Other measures revolve around the interests of employees, customers, and other stakeholders. Indeed, as Frederick (1995) notes, "Though desired, profits appear not to be essential to a particular firm, although some minimum (varying) number of companies need to be profitable if their host economy is to grow" (p. 54).

One international company, Acxiom, places honesty and open relationships with stockholders, clients, business partners, and associates at the core of their values. Their company Web site provides access to charters and governance documents that guide their company. Charles Morgan, the "Company Leader," states that "integrity results in the establishment of trust, which in turn results in good business" (Morgan, 2004). An independent, external marketing report is provided that cites Acxiom as an industry leader, substantiating the validity of their focus on integrity as a good business strategy. Informal interviews with employees of Acxiom suggest that this core value is not just one espoused by leadership, but one found throughout the company.

Economizing, therefore, demands a degree of cooperative interactions to promote goals that do not work against other, important societal values (Gardner, 1990). Without such cooperative interactions, decisions will often fall far below an ethical "high-water" mark. For example, Enron, before the ethical scandals went public, was a strong culture, in a negative sense. A strong value set kept those at the top embedded in a value that focused on short-term profit to the detriment of employees and other stakeholders. The lack of integrity as a core value meant that the company lost its balance in its efforts to realize the economizing value (Seeger & Ulmer, 2003).

In short, economizing suggests that profit is one value, but is not the end itself. Economizing suggests an essential role for values that promote cooperative interactions such fairness, equality, and caring for both individual and group needs.

Rehearsal 11.1 Applying the
Economizing Value Tension

Based on your cultural analysis, explore the following questions
to gain insight on this value tension.

What rationales for decision making are dominant in the
organization?

_____

_____

_____

What is said (or not said) when a team member suggests a
strategy that may reduce profits in the short run?

_____

_____

_____

What examples can you find of heroes who are known for
achieving productive goals while maintaining other values,
such as fairness and equality?

_____

_____

_____

Power Aggrandizement

Power aggrandizement is hierarchy values versus equality values.
Organizations impose a hierarchy or rank order and coercive power on the
economizing process. This value set refers to the acquisition, accumulation, and
retention of coercive power (rank order, managerial decision power, power
system equilibrium), for both instrumental and domineering purposes. This
value set assumes that humans tend to seek coercive power and in the process
of doing so can actually hamper the economizing value (Bellah, Madsen,
Sullivan, Swidler, & Tipton, 1992). The power-focused values "are not inherently necessary for business' economizing mission to be carried out successfully.
Giving allegiance to such values almost invariably diverts a company from making effective use of resources" (Frederick, 1995, p. 57). Consider, for example,
organization leaders who become too concerned with maintaining position and
power and in the process cease to adapt strategically to the interests of customers
or employees (Kotter & Heskett, 1995). The tragic tales of Enron and ImClone
provide examples of power imbalances that harmed the economizing value.

The need to organize and align human resources for growth is clear, yet the way such alignment happens varies by national culture. Thus, a distinction must be made between a power "aggrandizing" organizational culture and one that values hierarchy. Hofstede (2003) describes national cultures with a "high power distance" versus a "low power distance." In a high power distance culture there is a tendency to accept inequality between members of that culture. A high power distance culture holds norms that value hierarchy or vertical patterns of organizing and communication (e.g., Mexico, India, Singapore). In contrast, a low power distance indicates a national culture that values equality, thus it tends to be horizontal or less focused on hierarchy in relationships (e.g., New Zealand, Ireland, Australia).

Organizations within a culture with a low or high power distance value set are likely to share the norm with the national culture. However, the exceptions to this norm are obviously organizations whose mission and history combine to create a contradiction to the norm. For example, while the United States tends to have a lower power distance value, organizational cultures like the military and some religious groups tend to value hierarchy. Again, it may be helpful to use a Rehearsal activity to reflect on a few core questions to apply this value to understanding a culture.

Rehearsal 11.2 Applying the Power Aggrandizement Value Tension

1. What is the power distance value in the national culture to which the organization belongs?

   • For instance, do employees tend to value close supervision?
   • Is "effective management" viewed as close supervision?
   • Is the chain of command clear and does it tend to include multiple levels?

   _____

   _____

   _____

   _____

   _____

2. What role does a newcomer or someone in a "lower position" have in decision making?

   _____

   _____

(Continued)

_____

_____

_____

3. To what extent do managers and executives empower subordinates to make their own career building decisions?

_____

_____

_____

_____

_____

Ecologizing

Ecologizing is macroenvironment values versus microenvironment values. As the term suggests, this value set is concerned with the impact and
relationship of the organization to the external environment. Ecologizing
includes values, on one hand, that focus on a larger macro value for the
environment, a learned survival trait of human communities. Ecological
relationships interweave the life activities of groups in ways conducive to
the perpetuation of an entire community, including the flora, fauna, and
physical features that constitute the groups' ecosystem. On the other hand,
in tension with the macro value is a concern over the microenvironment,
which includes accepted allegiance to stockholders seeking profits.

Seeing how this value tension interweaves with other value clusters is
important to understanding intersections and conflicts, and ways to manage
them. The number of creative organizations suggests a trend toward greater
attention to the external environment. In a shift from just a few decades ago, it
is now popular for a company to boast of its attention to the environment, both
social and physical, beyond the walls of the organization. The macroecologiz-
ing value suggests a longer-term orientation to time and effectiveness. A series
of rehearsal questions relevant to the culture of the organization should aid you
in deciphering the relevance of this value in light of the other two.

Rehearsal 11.3 Applying the
Ecologizing Value Tension

1. To what extent do company documents explicitly discuss
   environmental policies?

_____

_____

_____

_____

_____

2. How are ecological concerns weighed when making decisions about stock profit margins?

   _____

   _____

   _____

   _____

3. To what extent is it permissible to criticize a policy or
   decision based on larger environmental concerns?

   _____

   _____

   _____

   _____

Connections: Other Tensions?

Paying close attention to these value conflicts is not an easy leadership task. Yet time spent reflecting on these value tensions provides new insights into finding effective ways to manage the ethical landscape. In an effort to connect these value sets with your own cultural analysis, consider instances when your data indicate an implicit or explicit tension existing across the three values: economizing, power aggrandizing, and ecologizing. For example, are there stories that indicate concerns over management treatment of the environment or use of power? Or do any of your themes suggest a tension between profits and ecological values?

However, as we opened this chapter, we indicated that these three value tensions are not intended to be exhaustive. For example, based on Chapter 9, another value tension could be diversity versus uniformity. Or in this same context, a tension could exist between resistance versus withdrawal in response to mistreatment. In one study, minority members who perceived maltreatment faced a dilemma: Resistance might result in more mistreatment whereas reacting by disengaging might result in strengthening the power structure that kept them from being heard in the first place (Meares, Oetzel, Torres, Derkacs, & Ginossar, 2004). Rehearsal 11.4 provides a place for you to brainstorm additional tensions that you see as critical in the process of making ethical decisions.

REHEARSAL   **Rehearsal 11.4** Other Value Tensions

1. Value tension:

_____

Questions to ask: _____

_____

_____

Ethical implications: _____

_____

_____

_____

2. Value tension:

_____

Questions to ask: _____

_____

_____

Ethical implications: _____

_____

_____

_____

Summary

Leadership in shaping organizational culture performance that enacts enduring ethical values remains a pressing need in our society. The statistics are alarming, as is the significance of ethical abuse in terms of fairness and safety. However, enacting an honest portrayal involves more than being aware of these abuses. The study of ethics takes us back to an application of the first step in the cultural analysis process: We all act out our ethics based on implicit frames, metaphors, or theories. Reviewing the ways we can maximize a positive influence and minimize the negative influences embedded in each of the metaphors or implicit theories is critical.

This chapter provides several analytic tools to aid in the process of identifying possible areas of value conflicts. Managing these tensions is a basic part of our job descriptions. We cannot avoid them. As you reflect on these value tensions, consider completing the Rehearsal at the end of the chapter that is intended to prompt reflection on ethics and culture.

1. Economizing: Short-term profit versus human values

2. Power aggrandizement: Hierarchy versus equality values

3. Ecologizing: Macroenvironment versus microenvironment value tensions make ethical dilemmas a reality.

4. Other value tensions: We encouraged you to explore value tensions within our discussion of diversity as well as others you might identify.

Rehearsal 11.5 Ethics and Communication Leadership

Purpose: Identify leadership practices that contribute to an ethical or unethical organizational communication pattern.

Steps:

1. Review your cultural analysis, including elements, themes, and overall definition(s).

2. Write down instances when your data indicate implicit or explicit examples of positive and ethical leadership behaviors. For instance, are there examples of when a cultural hero stood for a constructive, ethical principle despite the potential loss of money?

3. Write down instances when your data indicate implicit or explicit examples of negative and unethical leadership behaviors. For instance, are there norms and rules in place that make disclosure of ineffective or unethical practices difficult?

4. Brainstorm another short list of implications drawn from the observations you made. For example, if you noted ethical leadership strengths, how might these be useful in introducing changes you see the need to implement? Conversely, if you noted certain unethical leadership behaviors, how might these be addressed?

12

The Director's Chair

Symbolic Leadership

Step Five: Identify
Applications for
Organizational
Diversity,
Change, Ethics,
Leadership, and
Effectiveness

Caring for the culture cannot be delegated. It can be shared but not left for someone else to do. . . . The leader is the fountainhead. This is true whether that individual is the entrepreneurfounder who first lays out the guiding beliefs, or the current CEO who has been given the right to reinterpret the guiding beliefs and state new ones. If the leader is a great person then inspiring ideas will permeate the corporation's culture.

—Stanley M. Davis (1984),
Managing Corporate Culture, pp. 7–8

Objectives:

- Understand the role of leader as "manager of meaning"
- Explore symbolic forms through which the leader shapes meanings within the culture
- Recognize ideology and identification as forms of unobtrusive control
- Develop optimal competence as a leader through multiframe thinking
- Evaluate yourself as a cultural leader or potential cultural leader

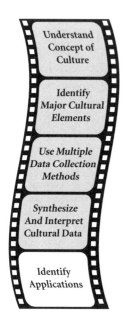

Understand
Concept of
Culture

Identify
Major Cultural
Elements

Use Multiple
Data Collection
Methods

Synthesize
And Interpret
Cultural Data

Identify
Applications

Stage Terms:

- Framing/reframing
- Vision
- Symbolic leadership
- Contrast
- Spin
- Unobtrusive control

In theater or film the director plays a critical role in shaping the performance of actors to create a unified artistic vision. To be effective, the director must have a clear interpretation of the work he wishes to produce and the skill to communicate that vision to the actors who will help him realize that vision. His skill includes the ability to communicate and to motivate the actors to call on their best efforts in realizing the vision. In the end the production is a cooperative venture between the talents of the director and actors. In earlier management literature, the role of a manager was seen as planning, control, and coordination of organizational resources and systems. However, much of current leadership theory places more emphasis on the intangible leadership functions of creating the organizational mind-set and influencing how employees interpret organizational events, very similar to the way the director shapes and encourages the performance of actors.

Bolman and Deal (1998) offer a relational view of leadership: "Leadership is thus a subtle process of mutual influence fusing thought, feeling, and action to produce cooperative effort in the service of purposes and values of *both* the leader and the led" (p. 296). They note that an important function of leadership is interpreting and reinterpreting experience within the organization, much as President Franklin D. Roosevelt performed on a national level when he assured citizens, "The only thing we have to fear is fear itself." Bennis (1986) concurs that

> the single most important determinant of corporate culture is the behavior of the chief executive officer. He or she is the one clearly responsible for shaping the beliefs, motives, commitments and predispositions of all executives—from senior management to the operators of the organization. (p. 64)

Schein (1992) went so far as to state that the only thing of real importance that managers do is to create and manage culture.

Reframing

The term *framing* or *reframing* refers to adopting a different perspective or interpretation of an event or person. When we refer to reframing as a central function of leadership, we mean that leaders often have the ability to help organizational actors change their perspective on organizational events. Some leaders, when facing a financial crisis in their organizations, might frame the emergency as a time to seek out and eliminate weak programs, a perspective that would lead to turf protection and competition. Another leader facing the same challenge could frame the crisis as "a time for the family to pull together and make joint sacrifices for the common good." This framing might lead to stronger ties and a common commitment to making it through the financial crisis. Each of these ways of framing has constraints. The leader who uses the crisis to set organizational priorities may have relational fallout, but will also avoid the democratic pitfall of weakening all programs rather than making hard decisions. The second approach will build common ties and commitments but may result in overall weakening. Each might be the appropriate response in a given organizational situation.

What kind of meanings or interpretations can leaders influence? Leaders set organizational perceptions on a number of important areas that affect every other decision within the organization. *Leaders can manipulate perceptions of external threat.* History is rife with leaders who have used perceptions of external threat to divert attention from internal problems or to create internal unity to deal with a common enemy. Sometimes employees have become complacent and need to be more aware of potential threats than they currently are. A perception of external threat gives urgency and focus to their work. *Leaders can also influence perceptions of competitors and benchmark institutions.* One university president we observed had a massive impact on his school when he influenced faculty to accept they were no longer competing against small in-state colleges, but should consider larger regional universities as their "benchmark" comparisons. This changed views of faculty salaries, research expectations, student admission standards, and many other decisions within the university. *Leaders often create the internal perceptions of accountability and stakeholders.* A central question for any organization is to whom are we accountable? Who has an interest in what we do? A state agency, for example, that sees the legislature as their primary stakeholder will perform much differently from one that views the citizens of the state as its primary stakeholders. *A leader through overt and subtle messages also shapes the sense of the organization as to what is most valued here.* Is it profit and efficiency? Is it service? Is it people? Too often the leader may send inadvertent messages about what is most valued by where he spends time, what he talks about, and what he rewards. Shockley-Zalabak and Morley (1994), in a longitudinal organizational study of the influence of the founder on organizational values and rules, concluded that organizational founders were influential in shaping both management and worker values and rules over time.

Finally and most important, a leader creates meaning by casting a vision for the future. Bolman and Deal (1998) write,

> One of the most powerful ways in which leaders can interpret experience is by distilling and disseminating a vision—a persuasive and hopeful image of the future. A vision needs to address both the challenges of the present and the hopes and values of followers. Vision is particularly important in times of crisis and uncertainty. When people are in pain, when they are confused and uncertain, or when they feel despair and hopelessness, they desperately seek meaning and hope. (p. 315)

Bolman and Deal (1998) make the point that leaders do not create a vision in isolation and then persuade organization members to adopt it, but rather gather the vision by listening to hints throughout the organization of needs, deficiencies, dreams, and goals and synthesizing all that varied input into a compelling image of the future.

Deetz, Tracy, and Simpson (2000) contrast mission, strategic planning, and vision. They define mission as the direction the organization wants to go and the strategic plan as a roadmap for getting there, but say that the vision is the compelling image of what it will be like once you arrive at that destination. They conclude,

In short, a good vision is realistic enough to create a recognizable picture of the future, powerful enough to generate commitment to performance, coherent enough to provide coordination, and open enough that others can make it their own. If this is done the vision can inspire and motivate, provide direction and enable benchmarking progress toward the future. (p. 52)

Consider an individual identified as a cultural hero in your cultural analysis. How did he or she influence meanings for other culture members?

_____

_____

_____

_____

_____

_____

Symbolic Dimensions of Leadership

Not only do leaders greatly influence the organizational culture through shaping meaning and interpretations, but they also achieve this influence by symbolic means. They shape the culture by the very cultural elements you have been studying throughout this text. Schein (1992) discusses five ways leaders embed and transmit organizational culture: (1) by what they pay attention to, measure, and control; (2) by their reactions to critical incidents and crises; (3) by deliberate role modeling, coaching, and teaching; (4) by their choice of criteria for allocation of reward and status; and (5) by their choice of criteria for recruitment, selection, promotion, retirement, and "excommunication." Schein also discussed five "secondary mechanisms" for creating, displaying, and maintaining culture: (1) the organization's design and structure; (2) organizational systems and procedures; (3) the design of physical space, façades, and buildings; (4) stories, myths, legends, and parables about important events and people; and (5) formal statements of organizational philosophy, creeds, and charters.

We offer seven implications/suggestions describing how effective symbolic leaders shape and define organizational culture. *First, symbolic leaders recognize that all their actions and statements will convey cultural significance.* If the CEO's office is much more opulent and luxurious than offices of other employees, it sends a message. If a nonprofit manager throws a fund-raiser at an expensive hotel while claiming the nonprofit is in dire need of funds, it sends a message both without and within that organization. One large organization hosts a company picnic at which all the corporate officers serve the meal to janitors, secretaries, and other employees. They are serious about servant leadership. What the leader spends time doing, what she talks about in public addresses, who she interacts with, what information she asks for, what she spends money on, and a variety of other seemingly insignificant choices send clear value messages. If you want to show you value employee input, eat in the company cafeteria. If you want to emphasize customer service, serve as a role model yourself, talk about it in every message you give, and appoint the most important members of the organization to a task force you chair yourself.

What values and lessons would employees learn by observing the example of the leader of the culture you studied?

_____

_____

_____

_____

_____

_____

_____

Second, symbolic leaders tell stories. They understand the power of the narrative structure. Bormann (1969), in his theory of symbolic convergence, states that when we participate together in telling or hearing a powerful story we share a common experience that binds and unifies us. Stories are powerful because they are memorable, multifaceted, and dramatic. We can draw multiple messages from a story. Stories can tap into a rich historical legacy to interpret the present, or can paint an inspiring picture of the future in imagery to which listeners can relate. Bolman and Deal (1998) write about the power of stories of the past or future:

> The past is usually a golden one, a time of noble purposes, of great deeds, of heroes or heroines. The present is a time of trouble, challenge, or crisis: a critical moment when we have to make fateful choices. The future is a dream, a vision of hope and greatness, often linked directly to the past. That is just the kind of story that helped Ronald Reagan, a master storyteller, become president of the United States. Reagan's golden past was the frontier, a place of rugged, sturdy, self-reliant men and women who built a great nation and took care of themselves and their neighbors without the intervention of a monstrous national government. (p. 316)

Angi heard a university provost of a small university tell an especially poignant story about one of his predecessors. The former president had retired, and on his last workday, unknown to him, every member of the administration and staff gathered in a long line outside the building to wish him well and show their love and respect for him. The provost ended the story by saying, "That's who we are at this university. That's what makes us different."

Often stories told about the leader are as important as the stories the leader tells. In one cultural analysis we performed, we heard the same story about the CEO from several interviewees. The company had a regional meeting at a hotel in the Southwest. The CEO noticed when one of the regional managers didn't arrive at dinner and called his room. When he didn't answer the door, the CEO got the manager to open the door and found the regional manager barely alive after a heart attack. The CEO cancelled an international conference to stay at the hospital with the family for 4 days until the manager was out of danger. Then he paid for all medical expenses and travel expenses for the family. He became a legend, and the story did much to create and display the organizational value of caring and responsibility for others.

Many stories may not be completely true, and at some point it doesn't matter if they are or not, as long as organization members believe them. Stories must be credible, however. Many politicians, trying to seize on the communication success of Reagan and Clinton, have integrated storytelling into important addresses, parading the subject of the stories past national audiences. Some of the stories seem so contrived and manipulative that they not only lose their impact, but may even have a negative one in that listeners may discount the speaker all together. To be credible, a story must be relevant and believable to the intended audience.

Did the leader of the organization you studied tell stories? What did they convey relative to the culture? Did you hear stories about the leader of the organization you studied?

_____

_____

_____

_____

_____

_____

Third, symbolic leaders capitalize on the significance of rituals. We described rituals in Chapter 4 as the "acting out of cultural values." Rituals can be everyday routines such as a daily religious observance at a parochial school or a weekly staff meeting at a camp. They can also involve organization-wide events such as family picnics, awards banquets, celebrations of achievements, or retirement rituals. Rituals are windows on a culture, and demonstrate values in action. Whether an organization has traditions and the nature of those traditions tells us a great deal about its values. A company with a tradition of rowdy Friday afternoon happy hours is different from a company with an annual family picnic. It is very important that an organization's rituals, especially recognition rituals, line up with the values the leader wants to imbue in the culture. For example, one of Angi's clients was in the midst of a cultural transition shifting to a team-based culture and was frustrated that employees were still emphasizing individual action over team cooperation. After a review of the culture, she noted that all their corporate awards were for individual achievement rather than team accomplishments. In another organization, a leader wanted to emphasize a performance-based culture. Yet the only corporate-wide event that employees attended was an annual retirement dinner at which employees were honored for length of service rather than excellence of performance. Symbolic managers know what you reward says more to employees than the formal mission statement. They reward employees in public ways that emphasize values the culture wants to encourage.

What rituals did the leader of the culture participate in? What rewards did he present to employees? What did these rites and rituals indicate about the culture?

_____

_____

_____

_____

_____

_____

Fourth, symbolic leaders understand the value of historical continuity. Our first clue to a weak or fragmented culture is when employees in interviews know nothing of an organization's history. Cultural values and vision are rooted in history. Even if an organization had a dismal history and has reacted by changing core values and practices, it is essential to remember that history in order to ground and understand the current values. One large university hospital, for example, had lost its focus on caring for the most fragile and underserved populations through an emphasis on managed care, Medicare reimbursement formulas, funded research, and the bottom line. Few employees knew that the hospital had once been a private charity hospital formed as a health care safety net for the poor. Leaders became intentional in including that history in employee orientations, in posting pictures of the first hospital throughout the current facility, and in telling stories about the early heroes.

Did the cultural leader you studied make reference to organizational history? To what purpose?

_____

_____

_____

_____

_____

_____

_____

Fifth, symbolic leaders use language as a tacit way of shaping meanings and values. Fairhurst and Sarr (1996), in their book *The Art of Framing: Managing the Language of Leadership*, discuss language tools for leaders. They include metaphors, jargon or catch-phrases, contrast, spin, and stories. Metaphors a leader uses consciously or unconsciously will shape employee perceptions and meanings. One university president assumed leadership of a university that was second in the state to the "flagship" research campus. In his inaugural address he said, "I don't care that we're not the flagship. Flagships are an anachronism in today's military. They're large, unwieldy, and difficult to turn. Let's be a starship." That imagery and metaphor started to overcome a "second-best" mentality among the faculty, staff, and students and probably served as a basis for a number of initiatives during his presidency to create a modern, flexible, and technologically sophisticated university. Some metaphors are unconscious and emerge through language patterns. A leader, for example, who talks continually in athletic terms may create an athletic metaphor for the organization that has positive and negative implications. It may foster team commitments but may also encourage competitiveness and exclude employees with less experience with team sports.

Fairhurst and Sarr (1996) define jargon as "language that is peculiar to a particular profession, an organizational culture, or a well-developed vision or program" (p. 108). Our university defines itself as a "metropolitan" university. That had the internal connotation to organization members when it was first used to refer to the responsiveness of the university to the community, consisting of a diverse group of nontraditional students, and an emphasis on applied scholarship. Over the years, however, the concept of a metropolitan university has been difficult to translate to the community and has taken on less positive connotations internally. To some, "metropolitan" has come to mean second-class education, open admission of unqualified students, and a lack of support for academic research. In a strategic planning process we are struggling with new terminology to capture the intent of the old term without also carrying its baggage.

Contrast is the opposite of metaphor. Rather than explaining the common elements of two unlike things through comparison, the leader highlights an essential trait by placing one object, person, or idea in opposition or contrast to another. Just as we talked about the power of a leader to define competitors for an organization, or to suggest similar benchmark institutions, contrast can define an organization by what it is not. In one church organization that Gerald has researched, leadership used contrast to call the church to a new vision. The church was no longer to be a country club but a bridge. The contrast was intended to help the members move away from a focus on taking care of themselves to being a bridge to segments of the community not being served.

Spin is a term that has come from politics, as political handlers compete to place their own interpretations on speeches, debates, or political contests. Is finishing third a good or bad thing? Spin is also an important tool of symbolic leaders. Is a 10% drop in revenues a crushing blow, or an opportunity to evaluate which functions are most efficient and essential to the organizational mission? Are layoffs a betrayal of employee trusts or the chance to create a leaner, more competitive organizational structure? Spin has its limits. Most organization members are sophisticated enough to see through an obviously self-serving interpretation. Yet many events can be seen in both positive and negative ways, and the leader can help organization members see events in different perspectives by "spin."

What types of language behavior did you notice in the leader you studied? Can you give examples of metaphor, contrast, stories, spin, or jargon?

_____

_____

_____

_____

_____

_____

_____

Sixth, symbolic leaders recognize identification with organizational values as a form of unobtrusive control of employee behavior. Tompkins and Cheney (1985) write of unobtrusive control as a "third generation" of organizational control systems. In earlier eras, employees were controlled directly by a supervisor watching every action and correcting errors. In the second generation, bureaucratic rules replaced direct supervision. If we could make rules for every possible situation, then employees would be controlled by rules rather than direct supervision, making possible larger spans of supervision. We suspect we are now in an era of technological control in which software can count and trace every action in a way that monitors performance. Tompkins and Cheney's argument still applies. Leaders can influence employee behavior more powerfully through identification with values than with any control mechanism. If you control by supervision, then I will comply only when I am in your line of sight. If you control by rules, you are successful only to the extent I believe you will enforce the rules and know if I have broken them. If you control by technology, I may find ways to modify the technology or to manipulate counting systems. However, if I understand and believe in an organizational value like service, and that value is strong and unequivocal, then I will know what to do in any situation. Many credit Johnson & Johnson's ability to survive an incident of product tampering with strong and consistent organizational values that placed patient safety first. Thus there was no question that all products would be pulled from the shelves and new product packaging developed.

One of Angi's hospital clients has an employee policy that employees must call in the day before to be eligible for a sick day. Otherwise if they are absent, they must count the day as a vacation day. The rationale for such a policy is valid since it is critical to public health that hospitals maintain sufficient staffing levels on any given day. However, the effect of the policy is that employees come to work sick and view the sick days as an entitlement that they take when they want to have a day off. How much more effective would it be if leaders would truly inculcate a value of how important each and every employee is to the hospital's mission, and employees really believed that? They would come to work because they felt their work was important and would take responsibility for making arrangements if they could not come to work.

Did the culture you studied use rules or values to influence employee behavior? What was the effect?

_____

_____

_____

_____

_____

_____

Seventh, symbolic leaders demonstrate optimal competence by demonstrating the ability to take multiple points of view on the organizational culture. We discussed levels of competence in Chapter 7. An individual with minimal competence may demonstrate culturally competent behavior without being able to articulate the underlying logic or rule. An individual with satisfactory competence can explain the rationale but will not be able to see the situation from multiple points of view. A leader with optimal competence can see the culture from multiple points of view and thus be in a position to help others understand the culture in multiple ways. A leader can be competent in being aware of, and being able to take the point of view of, various subcultures within the organization. Because she understand the power of the metaphor or story, she also knows its limits, and how such symbolic forms could be "read" or understood in multiple ways.

One approach to helping leaders adopt multiframe thinking is in the excellent book by Lee Bolman and Terry Deal, *Reframing Organizations* (1998). They explain how organizations can be seen through structural, human resource, political, and symbolic frames. They apply the frames to leadership styles and show how leaders managing from each of the frames might bring strengths to the organization. They point out, however, that a leader who is able to see the organization through multiple frames at the same time can incorporate the strengths of all the perspectives. *Structural leaders* are architects and analysts who are skilled in restructuring the organization to perform more efficiently. They do their homework, are skilled at analysis, and see the connections among structure, function, and environment. They pay attention to the details of implementation and are not hesitant to reorganize if their data and analysis indicate another structure might be more efficient. A downside of this style is that they may lose sight of the human consequences of continual structural changes, they can be micromanagers, and they may not be as adept at seeing the synergy between human and system elements in performance.

A leader who operates primarily from the *human resource frame* is a "facilitator and catalyst who motivates and empowers organization members" (Bolman & Deal, 1998, p. 308). Leaders who excel in this way of seeing the organization often adopt a servant leader model and see their role as supporting organization members to achieve goals. Strengths of human resource leaders are communication abilities, accessibility, serving as visible role models, and anticipating impacts of change and motivation on people. Weaknesses can include oversensitivity to how they are viewed by others, insufficient decisiveness, and failure to see that many problems have both human and system components.

Political leaders are pragmatic and realistic. They are adept at analyzing power and in determining whose interests are being served by any particular initiative. They are good at developing coalitions to support change, and in gaining the support of opinion leaders within the organization and key stakeholders without. Bolman and Deal (1998) point out that political leaders "persuade first, negotiate second, and use coercion only if necessary" (p. 312). Political leaders are effective in getting things done, but they can fall prey to pragmatism over idealism, and can be seen as divisive and manipulative.

Symbolic leaders as defined by Bolman and Deal (1998) are master image weavers. They write,

> This frame sees organizations as both theaters and temples. In the theater, every actor plays certain roles and tries to create the right impression to the right audience. As temple, organizations are communities of faith, bonded by shared beliefs, traditions, myth, rituals and ceremonies. (p. 313)

Symbolic leaders exemplify many of the skills we have described throughout this text of framing meaning, considering the importance of symbols, and recognizing the durable fabric of organizational culture. The downside is that without substance, the focus on forms can feel empty and meaningless.

When leaders are able to see the organization through multiple points of view, they are better equipped to understand the implications of various cultural choices and to interpret the culture to others, recognizing their different perceptions. In short, an optimally competent leader is not only able to reframe situations but is adept at interpreting events and casting vision in ways that transcend the diverse national and subcultures within an organization.

What frame seemed to be the strength of the leader you studied? What were his or her deficiencies?

_____

_____

_____

_____

_____

_____

_____

Summary

Too many organizations leave culture to chance and haphazard development. The leader who understands the importance of culture is better equipped to use symbolic forms to create organizational vision and strategies to achieve their vision, to embody organizational values, and to use a variety of symbolic tools for transmitting those values to others. To be effective, the leader must be sure that cultural elements are consistent in conveying values. Of course, as we have stated throughout this text, there are limits to manipulating culture. While the leader has an important role to play in establishing, modifying, and protecting culture, organizational meaning is an interactive process between leaders and organizational members. Members must identify with values and vision for the culture to penetrate and guide the organization to desired outcomes.

In this chapter you should have learned the following:

1. The most important job of a cultural leader is shaping meaning.

2. The leader can shape many types of meanings
   - Perceptions of external threats
   - Perceptions of competitors and benchmark organizations
   - Accountability to stakeholders
   - What is valued in the organization

3. The leader is influential in synthesizing a vision and communicating it to organization members.

4. Leaders use several types of symbolic means to reflect and shape the organizational culture:
   - Personal modeling
   - Telling stories
   - Using rites and rituals
   - Understanding the impact of history

5. Leaders can use language to influence meaning
   - metaphors
   - jargon
   - contrast
   - spin

6. Identification with organizational values can exert unobtrusive control over employee behavior.

Rehearsal 12.1 Assessing Yourself as a Leader

Assess yourself as a cultural leader or potential cultural leader. Consider each of the leadership qualities below, and rate yourself on a 1–10 scale with 10 highest if your leadership style reflects this quality. On items on which you rate yourself 6 or lower, consider an action plan for how you can cultivate this cultural leadership behavior in yourself.

1. Use personal example to convey values or norms.

Culture members can watch what I do and get a sense of what the organization values.

Rating on 1–10 scale:_____

Action plan if score is less than 7:

_____

_____

_____

_____

_____

_____

_____

2. Tell stories to convey culture.

I make points dramatic and memorable by telling stories in speeches and remarks that reinforce organizational values and expectations.

Rating on 1–10 scale:_____

Action plan if score is less than 7:

_____

_____

_____

_____

_____

_____

_____

3. Use rituals to reinforce values.

I participate in rituals and give employees rewards that are consistent with organizational values and priorities.

Rating on 1–10 scale:_____

Action plan if score is less than 7:

_____

_____

_____

_____

_____

_____

_____

4. Use language elements of metaphor, jargon, or spin to shape organizational meanings.

Rating on 1–10 scale:_____

Action plan if score is less than 7:

_____

_____

_____

_____

_____

_____

_____

5. Use shared values rather than rules to guide employee behavior.

Rating on 1–10 scale:_____

Action plan if score is less than 7:

_____

_____

_____

_____

_____

_____

_____

(Continued)

(Continued)

6. I have a clear vision for the organization, developed with input from employees, and I have clearly communicated that vision to the members of my organization.

Rating on 1–10 scale:_____

Action plan if score is less than 7:

_____

_____

_____

_____

_____

_____

_____

7. I use at least three of the four leadership frames described by Bolman and Deal (structural, human resources, political, symbolic).

Rating on a 1–10 scale:_____

Action plan if score is less than 7:

_____

_____

_____

_____

_____

_____

_____

Rehearsal 12.2 Case Study of
Cultural Leadership

David Tate is dean of a College of Arts and Sciences at a Midwestern university. He guides his college according to two clear values: excellence and community. He stresses the value of excellence in a number of ways. He maintains his own professional scholarship at a high level even with his heavy administrative demands. He participates personally in the hiring of every faculty member in the college of almost 200 faculty members. In the interview process he stresses the expectations of the university. He has been known to veto hiring candidates if he feels the department is settling, and he has been known to extend searches if the right candidate cannot be found. In his 10 years in the position, he has fired three department chairs because they did not meet the standards he set for college leaders. In each case this was done after extensive counseling, and in each case he met with each member of the affected department to explain his actions and solicit their views on a new departmental leader. He encourages faculty members and chairs to compete for university-wide awards, and faculty and students in the college are represented disproportionately each year in university-wide awards.

He also reinforces the value of community in a number of ways. He knows each faculty member in the college and is aware of their activities and accomplishments. He often drops by faculty members' offices to hear about their classes and professional activities. He personally hosts a first-year orientation program for all new faculty members in the college to get to know them, and to socialize them to expectations and practices within the college. These orientation sessions include a couple of Friday afternoon happy hours in his home. He hosts a dinner and tent theater performance each summer for all faculty and staff members and their families. He states that he makes the college calendar his own and is almost always present at concerts, performances, readings, and other college events. His collegiality and sense of community extends to other deans in the university. Although he is assertive about the needs of his college, he is seen as a cooperative and knowledgeable colleague who is a trusted team player. He recently developed a strategic plan for the college with extensive input from every member of the college. He also allocates all discretionary funding in the college through a democratic process in which all of the department chairs in the college explain their needs to one another, and then as a group the chairs vote on spending priorities. The norm is very clear in the group that competitive behavior is not expected or valued.

Questions:

1. In what ways does David Tate demonstrate symbolic leadership?

2. How do his actions create cultural values and expectations?

3. Which of Bolman and Deal's four frames seem especially strong in his leadership style?

4. Are there any drawbacks to the culture in David Tate's leadership style?

13

Reading Reviews

Organizational Effectiveness

Step Five: Identify Applications for Organizational Diversity, Change, Ethics, Leadership, and *Effectiveness*

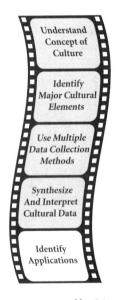

We forget that the primary function of language, if we have something to say and are not merely babbling, is to uncover something within the world, to bring it into the open . . .

—Barrett, *The Illusion of Technique*, 1979, p. 158

Objectives:

- Understand three major perspectives on the relationship between culture and effectiveness
- Gain insight into the dimensions of an effective organizational culture

Stage Terms:

- Strong versus weak cultures
- Strategically appropriate cultures
- Adaptive cultures

Full Circle

We began our work by examining expected payoffs or benefits of conducting a cultural analysis. We noted that the simple process of describing a culture aids an organization in such areas as hiring and socialization practices, managing change, and planning. We also noted how such a process is an essential aspect of being an effective and ethical leader. We have provided tools for you to link your cultural analysis findings to relevant aspects of organizational cultural performances: diversity, change, ethics, and leadership. Each of these areas contributes to overall organizational effectiveness, and thus our final application of organizational culture to effectiveness will draw together leadership, ethics, diversity, and change.

With a final application chapter on effectiveness we have come full circle. Performance reviews in the workplace, like reviews of dramatic performances, are not always productive and useful. Sometime managers get off on tangents; sometimes a reviewer has a personal bias against an actor. Yet a review of overall organizational effectiveness in light of cultural data should not be discarded or discounted because the process is sometimes flawed. In fact, we would argue that effective organizational performances always involve review. Like a thorough review of a play, a review of organizational effectiveness should provide a perspective on the organization that is both convincing and enlightening. The hope is that this review process will inspire new insights into ways to improve communication within the organization. We believe that you should leave this process with a clearer sense of how you can improve your own effectiveness from being an observer of your own thinking (Singe, 1990). Such improvements should provide a greater sense of direction, meaning, and value for your organizational experiences. As one CEO, writing about the process of leadership and organizational success suggests,

> *Listen*
> *In every office*
> *you hear the threads*
> *of love and joy and fear and guilt,*
> *the cries of celebration and reassurance,*
> *and somehow you know that connecting those threads*
> *is what you are supposed to do and business will take care of itself.*
> (Autry, 1991, p. 26)

You may have noted important aspects of your own communication that contribute to or distract from certain organizational cultural values. For example, you may realize that you tend to discourage innovation by focusing on failed projects. You may also have noticed cultural themes that are consistent or inconsistent with ethical values that are espoused. Or you may have observed how an organization marginalizes minority populations in decision making. Such insights, whether personal or organization-wide, are major payoffs in the analysis process.

Regardless of your organizational role, you may be in a position to provide specific recommendations; that is, trainers, "internal performance consultants," or external consultants. Furthermore, even if your analysis is never to be formally presented to the organization, this chapter will encourage applications of value for your own development as a leader.

Organizational Effectiveness

Terms like *the bottom line, productivity/profit,* and *return on investment* are perhaps the most commonly used rationales for making changes or justifying the existence of an organization. You may have said or heard the phrase, "If we don't make a profit, what are we here for?" ROI, or return on investment, continues to be a hot topic in the training industry as human resource professionals seek to justify the expense of training and other organizational development (OD) efforts. Definitions of productivity vary, but the approaches of short- versus long-term productivity (Crandall & Wooten, 1978), the attainment of organizational goals (Steers, 1977), or the highest level of performance with the least expenditure of resources (Mali, 1978) share a common emphasis. Not surprisingly, the concern over maximizing profits and increasing efficiency is either implicit or explicit in most discussions about productivity and performance. Leaders in organizations, like directors bringing a play to the stage, seek a payoff—they want their work to have some sort of success beyond opening night.

We accept the importance of the bottom line as a given; however, there are three problems with making the bottom line the primary rationale to drive changes in culture. First, *organization members typically react to and resist efforts at change that they view as manipulative for management gain.* Employees may actually counter such efforts and resist changes. In fact, it is critical to realize that the cultural analysis process may reveal information that the organization or individuals in the organization are not ready to hear (Deetz, Tracy, & Simpson, 2000). Thus, even if your analysis is a convincing one, grounded in careful consideration of multiple elements gathered over time, how you make sense of the analysis and present it to others is a challenging process that merits planning and preparation. Your preparation should take into consideration one particular fact: Culture change grounded in a profit motive alone is likely to backfire.

A second consideration in linking organizational culture to effectiveness is the fact that *effectiveness may be seen in different ways in the organization* (Brenton & Driskill, 1991). Was Enron an effective organization? It certainly was profitable over the short run. Yet because of unethical practices and lack of concern for employees and stockholders, its house of cards eventually collapsed. Many organizations are coming to realize that environmental impact, community citizenship, financial stewardship, global development, and corporate responsibility are as important to evaluate as profitability in determining an organization's effectiveness. Recall the two mission statements from Hewlett-Packard and Dell Computers that you analyzed in the linguistic exercise in Chapter 7. Did you observe that the latest generation of corporate mission statements has as much to say about ethics and values as about profitability? It is particularly important to consider definitions of successful organizational outcomes in terms other than profitability because of the growing nonprofit sector of our economy, which now accounts for approximately 6% of the national GNP. Obviously nonprofits do not exist to make a profit, but they can be examined by a number of other outcome measures.

Rehearsal 13.1 How Do
You Measure Effectiveness?

Steps:

1. Select an organization you have worked in or participated in (from business, to nonprofit, to faith based).

2. Write down the statements you can recall from members, memos, and so on, that best capture how effectiveness is/was measured.

> 3. Do you agree with those measures? If so, why? If not, what would you measure?
>
> _____
>
> _____
>
> _____
>
> _____

A third issue with trying to manipulate culture to improve performance is that research paints a rather complex picture concerning the relationship between culture and performance. A review of this research provides a backdrop for the model of organizational effectiveness we find useful in the application of cultural data. Research in this area can be captured in terms of three major perspectives on the link between culture and performance.

Perspective 1: Strong Cultures Are Good

Early discussions of the link between culture and performance argued for the notion of "strong cultures" being associated with excellent performances. Deal and Kennedy (1982) popularized this argument by defining strong cultures as possessing the following themes: (a) shared vision and values, (b) supportive business environment, (c) recognized corporate heroes, (d) effective rites and rituals, and (e) effective formal and informal communication networks. These authors highlighted organizations like IBM and Tandem Computers for their strong cultures. Peters and Waterman (1982) also popularized certain characteristics of strong cultures based on their study of 62 successful companies. For instance, they noted things like a "bias for action," "close relations to the customer," "simple form, lean staff," and "hands-on value driven or strong core values."

Though dated, the work of Deal and Kennedy (1982) and Peters and Waterman (1982) still resonates. Who can argue against strong core values or effective networks? Still, further exploration of the strong culture concept has shown that some of the organizations identified in these studies have not been strong performers over the long haul. Strong cultures, paradoxically, may honor certain values or communication patterns that are actually detrimental to the organization (Kunda, 1993). In the worst case, unethical practices may become embedded in the culture. As Kotter and Heskett (1992) point out, "the strong culture theory" fails to account for the success of weak cultures. Such organizations as McGraw-Hill and Pitney Bowes, for example, received "weak corporate culture" scores but had impressive performance records.

Perspective 2: Strategically Appropriate Cultures Are Good

A second perspective argues for the notion of "strategically appropriate cultures"—the contents of the culture "fit" the context (conditions of the industry, degree of competitiveness, amount of change, degree of government regulation, degree of uncertainty). This "contingency" notion, like the strong culture, has appeal in the logic presented. It makes sense that an effective organization would somehow adapt its strategies to fit specific economic conditions. However, research has shown that while short- and medium-term performance can be predicted by the notion of "fit," prediction of long-term effectiveness remains as elusive to predict with this theory as the "strong-cultures" perspective (Kotter & Heskett, p. 43). In fact, Collins (2001) based his theory of great organizations on trying to predict what distinguishes companies that perform well in the short run versus those that have moved from "good to great" over a longer period of time. His analysis indicates that strategic fit is not the key to being a great organization.

Rehearsal 13.2 Finding the Drawbacks of the Best Fit

Steps:

1. Reflect on the discussion of strategically appropriate cultures.

2. Identify an instance in your experience or that you have read or heard about when an organization worked to adapt to its environment yet did not prove to be an effective organization over time.

   _____

   _____

   _____

   _____

3. Review the facets of the culture that may have contributed to this lower-than-expected performance.

   _____

   _____

   _____

   _____

Perspective 3: Adaptive Cultures Are Good

A third and final perspective, "adaptive cultures," presents arguments for cultures that can "help organizations anticipate and adapt to environmental change . . ." (Kotter & Heskett, p. 44). In these organizations (e.g.,

Hewlett-Packard, Golden West, American Airlines), leadership is the key to maintaining and passing on a value set focused on making the changes needed to satisfy the legitimate interests of stockholders, customers, and employees. In contrast, less adaptive cultures tended to have leadership that was absorbed in self-advancement or protection of position and status.

Collins (2001) documented 11 organizations that made the move from "good to great." He argues that leadership is at the core of this "leap." These organizations, according to Collins's careful market analysis, stood out from competitors in their markets over a 15-year time period. His research team, despite instruction to downplay the role of top executives, found each of these organizations had a type of leadership that blended "personal humility and professional will" (p. 20). In short, their ambition was for the institution, not for themselves. They tended to leave behind an organization that could be great without them. For instance, 75% of the comparison companies, those that did not make the leap from good to great, had executives who set their successors up for failure or chose weak successors (or both).

In summary, an organization is likely to be effective because of its ability to adapt. While certain traits of strong cultures, such as effective communication practices, make sense, they do not provide sufficient direction. Furthermore, the ability to "fit" current market conditions, while a critical component, fails to account for long-term effectiveness. So a core question remains. What about adaptive cultures do we need to pay attention to in relation to the data found in a cultural analysis? Leadership has been mentioned, but what other characteristics might be used to guide the analysis of organizational culture data? What are the themes likely to surface that encourage an organization to be adaptive?

Adaptive cultures do tend to share certain characteristics. Table 13.1 highlights a model of organizational effectiveness that captures themes and qualities that should be considered in determining implications of your organizational analysis. These themes grow from the review presented above but focus on communication "habits" of organizations that have proven track records in the marketplace for great long-term performance. Remember, however, that any insight or potential recommendation for change needs to be sifted through the lenses of diversity, ethics, and change management. For instance, it would be a mistake to assume that national cultures do not have an influence on taken-for-granted values such as a relationship versus a results focus. In the United States, a value is placed on the management of objectives (e.g., working toward clearly established goals). Thus, success is determined and measured by time-efficient goal achievement. In contrast, in other cultures, such as Mexico, business is not conducted until partners have a chance to get to know one another (Varner & Beamer, 1995). Effective organizations find ways to adapt to and manage these cultural differences when engaged in global environment.

As you review this model, think about the extent to which your cultural analysis contains themes and values that encourage or discourage moves toward being effective through being adaptive.

The themes you interpreted in your analysis as well as the overall definition of culture often give hints as to the extent to which an organization is enacting the cultural themes and communication practices indicated in Table 13.1. Embedded in the themes you identified, for example, may be value statements about how stakeholders are to be treated, or about communication rules regarding customer communication. For instance, if you

Table 13.1 Linking Effectiveness With Culture

The organization adopts strategies and tactics for:

Employees

- High value on developing vision based on facts/truth
- Leading with questions—using informal networks to develop vision
- Consensus building rather then coercion
- Open forum for discussing differences, disagreements
- Learn from failed efforts without assigning blame
- Understanding and sharing a vision of what the organization does best
- Selecting and keeping the best
- Merit-based (rather than political) rewards and advancement
- Tapping into strengths of cultural diversity

Customers

- Communicating a clear vision to customers of what the organization does best
- Channels for receiving customer input and feedback
- Always listening and changing based on feedback

Stakeholders

- Balancing demands of stockholders for profits with concerns for the physical environment
- Balancing demands of stockholders for profits with concerns for employees and customers

Leadership

- Empowering and shared leadership functions
- Based on principle and values rather than personal charisma
- Focus on leadership identification and development
- Plans for leadership succession

Organizational Structure

- Flexible and dynamic structure
- Permeability to allow environmental input and scanning

identified a theme related to conflict ("Customers are heard only when they file formal complaints"), you might generate a list of possible applications since this theme has such clear ties to important organizational performance issues. You might note as a strength that this theme makes it clear that customer complaints are important. Yet, in contrast, other important information from customers may be downplayed. Any number of insights and potential interventions might be suggested by such an analysis. Aspects of the organization's history that contribute to this theme would be worthy of examination. Furthermore, leadership would have to determine the overall impact of the practices implied in this theme. Leaders may determine the need to review employee orientation and training practices related to customer service. This process of cultural analysis should be about a willingness to hear themes that contribute to effectiveness as well as those that are detrimental.

Summary

Research on organizational culture and effectiveness has prompted a revision of earlier, overly simplistic ideas. We covered two major approaches to defining an effective culture before introducing the one that is best supported by research. We also encouraged your own review process. The following summary points capture the main ideas presented.

1. Problems may arise if profits become the driving rationale in making changes to culture. Employees may resist such efforts if they are seen as solely for management's gain.

2. In the wake of corporate scandals, top corporations now realize that corporate responsibility and values must be evaluated as well as profitability in determining long-term organizational effectiveness.

3. The first approach to defining an effective culture is the notion that "strong is good." Reviews of long-term strong performers show they do not always fit this model and, in some cases, unethical practices can be embedded in a strong culture.

4. A second approach suggests that a "contingency" or strategically appropriate culture is a good one. Again, the long-term high-performance companies that were reviewed do not fit this approach.

5. The final approach, and the one argued for in this workbook, is that efficiently adaptive cultures are the most effective. This perspective finds support for long-term, high-performing organizational cultures maintaining and passing on a value set focused on changing as needed.

6. We encourage you to review your themes and overall definition of culture to gain clues about the extent to which the culture you studied is efficiently adaptive.

Rehearsal 13.3 Gauging Effectiveness

Purpose: Identify cultural themes that contribute to effective organizational communication patterns.

Steps:

1. Review your cultural interpretation, including elements, themes, and an overall definition(s).

2. Write down instances when your data indicate implicit or explicit examples of *in*effective communication practices based on Table 13.1.

3. Write down instances when your data indicate implicit or explicit examples of effective communication practices based on Table 13.1.

4. Brainstorm a list of two or more implications of the observations you made in your data. For example, if you noted effective communication patterns, how might the values inherent in these patterns be further strengthened? Conversely, if you noted ineffective behaviors, how might these be addressed?

14

Opening Night

Conclusion

> *The kind of concentration necessary for acting demands the ability to recreate something which is not there. It leads not only to the workings of the imagination, but also the presence of that kind of belief or faith which has often been characterized as the essential element in acting.*
>
> —Strasberg, *A Dream of Passion*, 1987, p. 131

Objectives:

- Apply your cultural analysis to professional communication goals
- Apply your cultural analysis for organizational development

---

- I cannot believe all that I am seeing here. I really have a better sense of how to make it in this organization. I realize now why things seem to be going faster than the speed of light. I am not as stressed as I once was and I am far less critical of management. I began my analysis as I began my second week here and now I feel like an insider after just a few months. In fact, I was able to make some suggestions on how to manage our recent transitions to a new facility.
- I think it was a mistake doing this study. Well, I knew before I started that I held some strong biases, but now I have to face them. The truth is that I would rather not address these issues at this time. It is hard to admit, but it really is easier not changing my communication habits even when I see from my study that they need changing.
- This analysis has pretty much convinced me that I do not belong in this organization.

Back to Change

Change often begins with one single, solitary insight. The challenge of enhancing your own performance or that of an organization is to act on that insight. Opening night is that moment when an insight, an interpretation of a role, is put into action. After much thought, planning, and rehearsal, a role is enacted, a script is brought to life. As the statements on the previous page suggest, the outcomes of paying close attention to culture vary greatly—from aiding in a transition to a new organization to finally assessing a lack of self-motivation in the change process. If these insights are to have value, it is essential to remember that regardless of the insight, significant organizational and professional communication developments come only from developing and enacting a plan. As the following quote indicates, the challenge of taking responsibility for such action is both significant and meaningful.

> [A] lasting organizational community requires more than commitment and communication. It requires discipline and mastery. This mastery is achieved as each person makes his or her contributions and assumes responsibility for them. Instead of a solitary leader responsible for performance, each member becomes a leader depending on the skills, knowledge, and experience needed in each situation. (Eisenberg, Andrews, Murphy, & Laine-Timmerman, 1999, pp. 145–146)

You have gained knowledge of how to conduct a cultural analysis as well as how to identify applications for your cultural insight. As a change agent even, if you are not formally presenting results to your own organization or to the organization you analyzed, you have gained insights that merit further reflection and application (DeWine, 1994).

Goal setting and the process of developing an action plan can give the illusion that we can know exactly where our plans will take us. The tendency is to think that an action plan is like a map to be followed; for instance, take I-30 west from Little Rock, Arkansas, to Dallas, Texas. Using this map analogy, we might think to ourselves: *I know where I am going, and I am not lost.* In contrast, we view action plans as more in keeping with the statement: *I don't where I am going, but I am not lost.* Action plans are more like a compass than a map. A compass gives you the confidence that you are not lost; you know the general direction you are going, but you may not know exactly where that direction will lead you.

In the business of culture change, and more particularly making changes in professional or organizational communication, usually the best that can be done is gaining an awareness of where you are through an analysis and then using an action plan to point you in the direction of desired change. The process of implementing such changes involves continual readjustment. For example, you may identify a goal for professional development that involves setting up a conflict management ritual in the workplace. Once initiated, this change may make you aware that you have not adequately addressed the issue of motivating coworkers or employees to engage in productive conflict. Thus, new goals relevant to creating support for effective conflict management may need to be developed. Nonetheless, the process you engage in, a process of awareness, action, and adjustment, is at the heart of enhancing your organizational culture performances.

The compass illustration suggests that we have a sense of a desired direction (i.e., a goal to implement an organizational change), and we have an awareness of where we are now (i.e., as a result of the cultural analysis), but even the best action plans cannot predict the future (e.g., what will the actual result of the change be?). Students and practitioners have shared with us the variety of outcomes that have come through their cultural analysis process: promotions and transfers; business as usual; others speak of personal insights or being more effective in adapting to the culture; still others have left their organizations for various reasons.

In short, action plans do not guarantee certain outcomes, but they should be developed to make certain desired changes possible. We provide Rehearsals 14.1 and 14.2 as means for reviewing your cultural analysis experience with the intent of helping you visualize results. The process of writing an action plan is familiar turf for many of you. The final product will be of your own making; still, the checklists include reminders on writing an effective action plan. The first rehearsal focuses on professional communication development goals and the second rehearsal on organizational development. Each section includes space for writing a rough draft of your goals.

Summary

You made it! The stage is now set for you to make use of your analysis in ways that make the most sense to you. Remember, as you engage in discussing your analysis and informal and/or formal recommendations, you are involved in a process of shaping communication patterns that are part of your organization's culture. In this process, you have an ethical responsibility to act on your awareness of your culture, and to act in ways that improve and enhance organizational life. Our hope is that both the process and the outcome of cultural analysis will surprise you. We began this workbook by reflecting on the span of experiences we have in organizations, from the cradle to the grave, with tragic and comic stories. Both the training tools of method actors and the process of cultural analysis encourage you to keep awareness of communication in the foreground. We have found the outcome of this process to be no less than greater participation in the meaning-creation process.

> Life is many days, day after day. But it is not, we hope, a mere succession of days. We long that these days will somehow add up to a meaning or a drama that we can call a life. (Barrett, 1979, p. 154)

A compass gives you the confidence that you are not lost, you know the general direction you are going, but you may not know exactly where that direction will lead you.

Rehearsal 14.1 Action Plan for
Professional Communication Development

Purpose: Develop an action plan for at least two communication goals important to your leadership development.

Step 1: Identify two communication goals that have the following characteristics.

Specific communication behavior, rather than general attitudes or values. For example, a theme may have made you aware of the types of tensions and value dilemmas existing in the organization. If your first draft of the goal is something like, "Gain a better perspective on the problems faced by the organization," revise this goal to focus on a communication behavior. For example, you might revise it to be, "Tell my immediate supervisor of my awareness of certain organizational challenges/dilemmas. Ask what role I can have in managing these challenges."

Contextualized communication behavior (appropriate setting, purpose, etc.), rather than general statements of what you plan to do. The above example does not provide a sense of reflection on the most competent way to approach this topic with a supervisor. For instance, consider the different interpretations and impact of a statement about your awareness of a specific organizational challenge made to a supervisor informally spoken over a morning cup of coffee versus a formal discussion during a performance review. Thus, a revised version should contextual your plan and might read like this: "I will connect the cultural theme of conflict over values with my own performance goals to improve communication with my co-workers. I will plan on having this discussion during my next review."

Your communication behavior, rather than something that requires a change in someone else. The goal, "To get my supervisor to provide clearer feedback," would be better worded as, "To provide paraphrases of my supervisor's feedback to ensure understanding."

Inspiring or motivating—Remember these are your goals. Go for what is most important to you—something you know will be good for you to do, something you believe the data indicate would be right for you to do, something you will be glad you did or at least glad you attempted.

Step 2: Identify a time frame with action steps.

For example, one *goal* might be: "During my upcoming review this June, discuss my professional development goals in light of specific cultural themes."

Dates	Steps
May 15	a. Summarize data on theme one as it relates to my ability to negotiate differences between work groups.

(Continued)

(Continued)

June 1   b. Review my ideas and goals with a colleague and mentor.

June 15   c. Make revisions in goals and gather resources (books, training, etc., that may be needed).

July 7   d. Present my goals at my performance review.

Step 3: Set a time frame to review results of your action plan and evaluate appropriate next steps.

An evaluation step is a way to encourage you to picture desired results and then determine ways to revise and develop a plan. Drafts of this step may actually prompt revisions of the earlier steps. The following example illustrates elements that might be included in this step.

Follow up by October 1.

    a. Discuss with key parties the effectiveness of recent meetings that depended on my negotiation skills.

    b. Keep a journal of meetings—review impact of integrating alternative negotiation tactics based on each of the four frames.

    c. Revise goals as needed.

Write a brief follow-up plan that relates to the steps you wrote earlier. Again, remember that a compass allows you to adjust your plan as you gain more information. The adjustments should be considered part of your ongoing commitment to acting on your awareness of ways to enhance your communication in the context of the overall performance of the organization.

Step 1: Communication goals that identify specific and contextualized communication behavior and focus on your own rather than others' behavior.

Goal A: _____

_____

_____

_____

_____

Goal B: _____

_____

_____

_____

_____

Step 2: Identify a time frame with action steps.

Goal A: _____

Date	**Steps**
_____	_____
_____	_____
_____	_____
_____	_____
_____	_____

Goal B: _____

Date	**Steps**
_____	_____
_____	_____
_____	_____
_____	_____
_____	_____

Step 3: Time frame for reviewing action plan results; evaluate appropriate next steps.

Date	**Evaluation Comments**
_____	_____
_____	_____
_____	_____
_____	_____
_____	_____

Rehearsal 14.2 Organizational
Development Action Plan

Purpose: Identify two organizational development goals important for the effectiveness of your organization.

Imagine the sense of loss if you have information that is pertinent and important for organizational effectiveness but you are not able to find the appropriate channel for introducing that information. Further imagine the sense of wrong or misdirection if you are aware that a failure to translate your insights into action may not only cost the organization money, but may also mean unethical practices continue unchecked. However, introducing ideas based on your own detective work, your own artistry in action, is not an easy chore. This section will guide you through a set of steps intended to make the process comprehensible and more likely to succeed. Remember, however, that this process should not be treated separately from the first section. Recall that formal and informal recommendations are more likely to be received if you have already demonstrated meaningful changes in your own communication behaviors. If, for example, you see the need for improved meeting management skills among all supervisors, and if you have already begun to improve your own skills in this area, recommendations are much more likely to be heard. Because of the breadth of questions reviewed in the next section, space is not provided for all of your responses. We encourage you to draft your ideas, review them, and check them against your cultural analysis before deciding on a final plan of action.

Steps for Developing Recommendations

1. Reflect on insights gained from the application chapters (Chapters 9–13). Write down specific themes that relate to issues in each of these chapters.

Chapter 9: Diversity _____

_____

_____

_____

_____

_____

Chapter 10: Change _____

_____

_____

_____

_____

Chapter 11: Ethics _____

_____

_____

_____

_____

Chapter 12: Leadership _____

_____

_____

_____

_____

Chapter 13: Effectiveness _____

_____

_____

_____

_____

2. Select no more than two issues that you see as most important and most likely to be accepted if presented as organizational development (OD) goals. Such focus will increase the likelihood of application. Develop these issues into OD goals. The intent here is for you to brainstorm and envision an OD initiative that would enhance or develop a cultural theme that supports effective communication in your organization. For example, you might have concluded from several elements of culture that the organization culture is inconsistent in supporting diversity initiatives. However, you did learn that one cultural hero encouraged diversity initiatives and that a diversity strategy was in place. Thus, you might brainstorm a next step that would include additional rituals and training in the area of diversity.

(Continued)

(Continued)

Possible Areas of Focus:

_____

_____

_____

_____

_____

_____

_____

_____

3. Decide if these OD goals would be best presented in a formal manner or introduced informally. (Note: You might have aspects that you present formally and others that are best introduced informally.) A few criteria to check to determine if you are in position to make formal recommendations:

- Your organization knows of your study and expects you to present your findings.
- Your position allows you such freedom.
- Your relationship with management makes it possible.

If you are not able to answer yes to at least one of the above, then develop your action plan for this section according the guides provided in the informal recommendation section. *If you were able to answer yes,* then create your action plan based on the suggestions in the formal recommendations section.

Informal Recommendations

Informal recommendations take on numerous forms. These recommendations, the process you engage in, challenge you to be more than an observer. Wearing the "hat" of a change agent, a leader willing to find ways to bring meaningful changes is invigorating and challenging. The following set of questions, if thoroughly considered, will guide you in dealing with this challenge. You should answer these questions in conjunction with each of the two applications you selected for organizational communication development.

Questions for Analysis: Informal Recommendations

What are you presenting?

- What has been the content of past attempts (your own as well as those of colleagues) of making informal recommendations?
- In what ways, if any, does the content of your current recommendation relate to past recommendations?
- Is your recommendation positively worded? Restate one of your recommendations in positive language.

Who are you presenting your ideas to?

- Is there more than one person who would be receptive?
- What aspects of diversity or national culture should be considered?
- Who can you rely on to champion your ideas?
- Who in your organization is known for implementing change? Who is listened to/respected?
- Who will be reluctant to accept or is against this idea?
- What can you learn about their reluctance to accept it?
- How can you deal effectively with the reasons for resistance?

Why should they listen?

- Why are these changes of value to the organization?
- Are the changes connected with employee, stockholder, and/or customer satisfaction data/issues? Explain.

When will you present?

- What time of day will you be best received?
- Is there a time in the week or year that you are most likely to be heard fully?
- Is there a time in the day when the person you present ideas to is most receptive?

How will you present?

- What are the expectations of those to whom you will present your ideas?
- Do they expect detailed, written support of the ideas?
- Do they prefer to be involved in shaping the idea?

(Continued)

(Continued)

Action Plan:

1. Review your responses to each of the above questions.

2. Write/rewrite at least two of your *informal* organization-wide applications, in single-sentence, positively worded statements.

3. Write down the date(s), place(s), and person(s) important to implementing these goals.

Formal Recommendations

Writing and presenting a formal recommendation requires an analysis of your audience, setting, purposes, and so on, in a way much like that of preparing for informal recommendations. The following set of questions mirrors the informal recommendation development exercise with only minor differences. If thoroughly considered, it will guide you in preparing effective recommendations. Each question encourages you not only to examine your own recommendation, but the history of past recommendations. The reason for doing this additional history step is so you will be able to determine what was effective or ineffective. You should answer these questions in conjunction with each of the two applications you selected for organizational communication development.

What are you presenting?

- What has been the content of past OD recommendations (your own as well as those of colleagues)?
- In what ways, if any, does the content of your current recommendation relate to past recommendations?
- Is your recommendation positively worded? Restate your recommendations in positive language.

Who are you presenting your ideas to?

- Is there more than one person who would be receptive?
- What aspects of diversity or national culture should be considered?
- Who can you rely on to champion your ideas?
- Who in your organization is known for implementing change?
- Who is listened to/respected?
- Who will be reluctant to accept this idea?

- What can you learn about their reluctance to accept it?
- How can you deal effectively with the reasons for resistance?

Why should they listen?

- Why are these changes of value to the organization?
- Are the changes connected with employee, stockholder, and/or customer satisfaction data/issues? Explain.

Where will you present?

- Where will you be presenting your recommendations?
- Will media equipment be expected in this setting?

When are you most likely to be best received?

- Is there a time in the week or year that you are most likely to be heard fully?
- Is there a time in the day when the person(s) you present your ideas to is most receptive?

How does this organization define an effective presentation?

- How have successful recommendations been presented?
- Formats used? Audiences? Time length?
- Other audience expectations?

Action Plan:

1. Review your responses to each of the above questions.

2. Write/rewrite at least two of your formal organization-wide applications, in single-sentence, positively worded statements.

_____

_____

_____

_____

_____

_____

(Continued)

(Continued)

3. Write down the date(s), place(s), and person(s) important to implementing these goals.

Date: Place: Contact Names:

____   _____   _____

____   _____   _____

____   _____   _____

____   _____   _____

____   _____   _____

____   _____   _____

____   _____   _____

____   _____   _____

Appendix

Example Student Cultural Analysis*

Z Bank, Right Town, USA

Introduction

We have found a third "sure thing" in life besides death and taxes: *change*. In exploring the organizational culture of Z Bank in Right Town, USA, we have been fascinated by the number of times we have come across examples of changing times. In fact, the importance of this study can be seen primarily in its applicability to other organizations in small towns where changing times are influencing the way they do business. From humble beginnings and a legacy of sacrifice, Z Bank has grown to employ 100 people and have deposits of more than $250 million. With such growth come "growing pains" that change the way people relate to one another and the way business is conducted. This study is offered as a tool for understanding and relieving these growing pains.

This cultural audit consists of an overview of the organization's background and a discussion of methods of analysis. Next, it explores the major themes discovered through observation and interviews. A definition of the culture follows the discussion of themes. Last, it addresses both the strengths and limitations of the study.

Overview

Historical Perspective

Z Bank began in 1904 as Bank of Right Town. In 1906 it burned and was immediately rebuilt. James William was the founder; his son Daniel assumed ownership in 1920. The effects of the Great Depression reached Right Town in 1931. At the time, there were four banks in Right Town; the only one to survive was the Bank of Right Town. In fact, it was the only Bank in River County that never closed its doors during the Great

* Reprinted with permission from Lara Schock-Keck and Amy H. Amy.

Depression. Its survival depended upon the personal sacrifice of James William, who mortgaged his own home to keep the Bank in operation.

In 1943, W. D. Gregg purchased the Bank and renamed it The Right Town Bank. In the late 1960s, it sought national bank status and became Z Bank. From the late 1960s to the early 1970s, Z moved its headquarters to its current location and began building branches throughout Right Town. Since the 1980s, Z Bank has opened branches throughout River County. Z Bank currently has six locations in Right Town plus three outlying branches. From deposits of $3 million, Z has grown to a financial institution with deposits totaling more than $250 million. For 92 years, the bank has maintained a constant presence in the community under the guidance of only five presidents.

Organizational Mission

Technically, Z Bank has no formal, publicized mission statement. In our interviews, we discovered that one had been devised in a *marketing* class taken through the State Banking Association. Although an exact copy could not be located, several officers suggested the following: "To provide friendly, efficient customer service; to meet the financial needs of the community; to provide a return for the stockholders; to foster a strong work environment for employees." In addition, all those interviewed were asked to offer their version of Z Bank's mission statement, if it were to be used as a marketing tool. An overall consensus centered on providing friendly customer service.

Institutional Structure

Z Bank employs nearly 100 people. There is a tier of upper management that reports to a board of directors. The controlling ownership of the bank, however, lies in the hands of the Gregg family. The day-to-day operations of the Bank are overseen by a president/CEO who is assisted by two executive vice presidents, one in charge of lending services, the other in charge of personnel and operations. Other officers include four vice presidents, three assistant vice presidents, and 11 assistant cashiers (most are department supervisors).

Six of the nine branches have designated managers who also serve as loan officers in their particular locations. Bank demographics reflect a population that is predominantly male in upper management and primarily female in middle management and non-management. Out of 10 loan officers, three are female. Conversely, 13 of the 18 middle management positions are held by women. The Bank as a whole is approximately 85% female. Reflecting the population of Right Town, Z Bank employs very few racial minorities.

Methods

From the beginning, we brainstormed how best to utilize a team approach. We wanted to make the most of the insider/outsider dynamic. As an organizational insider, Amy decided to observe and interview in several of the branches. As an outsider, Lara spent most of her time in the main bank (located in downtown Right Town) and at one out-of-town branch, in Raytown. The rationale employed was that Amy would be less familiar with the individual subcultures of the branches but could draw from her knowledge of the larger culture. Lara, on the other hand, could spend time in the main bank where Amy was already too immersed in the culture to maintain objectivity. The arrangement served our purposes perfectly.

In an attempt to ensure a representative sample, we observed in the main Bank and in four of the outlying branches. Lara divided her time in the main Bank between various departments located on all three floors. Since Z's lobby is a three-story atrium, she had the opportunity to absorb the essence of the culture by observing the activity of several facets of bank life. She could see and hear simultaneously the goings-on of the teller line, note department, loan officers, and customer service representatives. She also spent time observing in bookkeeping and the proof department. Lara continued her observation by spending an afternoon in the Raytown branch.

In keeping with our efforts to be representative in our observations, Amy spent time at N. Central (by far the busiest branch), S. Main, and the Downtown branch. We believe that other Right Town locations were represented by observing at N. Central and S. Main. The Downtown branch, however, had to be experienced by one of us because banking inside the Downtown Supercenter is far different from that in any other Z Bank environment. We also believe Raytown gave us a feel for how the outlying branches differ from the Right Town locations. We explored these beliefs further in interviews. Observation took place in five of the nine locations.

In our interviewing process, we faced the challenge of representing the opinions of nearly 100 employees. Because Lara was traveling from another city, we scheduled all of her interviews in just two locations, the main Bank and the Raytown branch. Amy supplied a list of people from various locations who, with the support of upper management, were scheduled to be interviewed in the conference room in her department. She talked with management and staff from the locations where she had observed. In addition, she interviewed members of upper management along with an employee from each of the other two out-of-town locations. She also had the opportunity to speak with Tom Gregg, one of the brothers who has a controlling interest in Z Bank.

Between the two of us, we spoke with all three levels in the organizational structure: upper management, middle management, and staff. (See Appendix Figure 15.1.) Interviews represented employees from seven of the nine locations. We actually spoke with 25 employees, which is also 25% of the entire Z Bank staff. (See Appendix Figure 15.2.)

Lara made a special effort to conduct artifact analysis during her observations. She picked up various brochures with the intention of also conducting content analysis. She later realized that most of the brochures are from various banking organizations. Only a handful of them were actually generated by the Z Bank. She also discovered that the latest brochure was written and designed by Amy, making it difficult to comment on what it reveals since Amy had completed the brochure when she was first hired and knew little about the actual Z Bank culture.

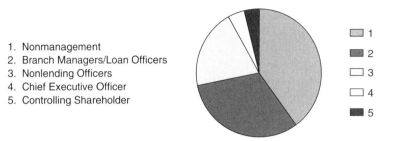

1. Nonmanagement
2. Branch Managers/Loan Officers
3. Nonlending Officers
4. Chief Executive Officer
5. Controlling Shareholder

Appendix Figure 15.1   Interview Sample

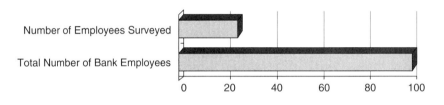

Appendix Figure 15.2   Sample Size vs. Total Population

"Framing" the Analysis

Throughout a semester of studying organizational culture, we have heard repeatedly about the four frames that can be used as "windows" through which to view a culture. In describing our own frame of reference, we believe the human resources frame is most appropriate. We did not find role instability (a structural issue) or power-related conflicts (a characteristic of the political frame) in Z Bank's culture. Instead, we saw inadequate training, support, and involvement as the most pressing issues in the culture. While we have examined the culture from all four perspectives, we realize the human resources frame is the one through which we have brought the picture into view.

Major Themes

Theme 1: Community-Centered Focus

Reaching out to the community through interest, involvement, and contribution is one of Z Bank's highest values.

As one branch manager put it, Z Bank's focus is "to help the *people* of the community to prosper and grow and to meet their financial needs." In other words, one of Z's top priorities is reaching out to the community of River County, assuming that helping them to prosper will also help the bank grow financially. Several cultural elements support this focus. First, during observation, we noted that the *physical setting* revealed this as a priority. Various community artifacts were displayed at several locations. For example, at the Raytown branch they had a community bulletin board publicizing local events. They also had a copy of the local school newspaper in their lobby area. Conversations overheard during observation often revealed a personal interest in the goings-on of the local schools, churches, and civic organizations. This focus on community was heard numerous *times* and in numerous ways during interviews. Three elements in particular revealed this theme, most explicitly from interviewees who reported an organizational *rule* that states, "If you wish to do well in this organization, you need to be active in the community." This is, according to Schall (1983), a regulative rule that guides goal-directed behavior. Out of the 19 people who responded to the question regarding rules, 5 mentioned community involvement specifically. One branch manager said he handles himself "as representing the bank at all times." When asking employees to name their organizational *hero,* we had an excellent opportunity to learn indirectly about organizational *values.* Like Meyer (1995), we found this indirect method especially revealing because value statements so often cannot be expressed explicitly. A more accurate revelation is found by identifying them indirectly in stories, such as those about heroes. In explaining their rationale for choosing a mentor, many commented not only on the individual's character traits, but also on his or her ability to understand and address the needs of the community. For instance, the current president of Z said E. P. Gregg (former owner/president) was his hero because Gregg was "a person who understood the community." Two other employees mentioned the current president as having a community-directed attitude, indicating that a heritage of community involvement began in top management and has worked its way down through the organization. One middle manager mentioned the expectation for community involvement, indicating that he often makes decisions based on, "How does it look for the Bank?" Another manager indicated an unstated expectation that all branch managers live and actively participate in the towns where they work.

About half of those interviewed mentioned the Christmas Open House as a *ritual* that reaches out to the community. Each branch advertises free apple cider and homemade goodies. They also offer complimentary calendars for the following year. Another common custom evidenced at Raytown is the annual honoring of graduates throughout the area. On a larger scale, in support of the state's collegiate sports programs, all locations wore Razorback red during the NCAA playoffs.

Through physical setting, rules, heroes, and rituals, it is obvious that community involvement is both expected and delivered. Branch managers in particular feel the pressure of joining civic organizations and taking leadership roles. This focus makes sense, of course, since customers come from the local community.

Theme 2: Customer-Orientation

Responding to customer needs and making customers happy at virtually any cost characterizes Z Bank's intense customer focus.

It is this spirit that pervades Z Bank and that has influenced organizational members to adopt an attitude of intense customer focus. As an organizational theme, this has led many to evaluate the effectiveness of their days by counting how many people they have helped. The most explicit *value* statements made during our interviews came in response to the question, "What is the best/worst thing that happens at work?" Sixteen of the 25 respondents indicated that the best kind of day is one where customers are happy. Related to that, several elaborated by saying a day they feel good about is one where they are able to meet the customers' needs or help solve their problems. One employee said he enjoyed "helping people accomplish what they couldn't do without the bank's help." Along the same lines, 11 out of 25 said their worst days were those where irate customers could not be appeased. Several loan officers indicated that having to turn someone down or send someone away constitutes the worst kind of day. Interestingly enough, the 8 who did not list helping the customer as the best kind of day indicated that task accomplishment was the criterion for a good day.

On occasion, the desire to promote a positive banking experience for customers comes in direct conflict with the need to accomplish daily tasks. One department supervisor responded, "There's such a hectic pace, we have time to slay only the biggest dragons." One secretary responded that the best day is a busy day, "because I feel a sense of accomplishment." However, for her the worst day is also a busy day "because I wear so many hats that I can't accomplish anything." Many indicated that a majority of conflicts are related to being understaffed, the feeling that there's an uneven distribution of responsibility, or that every department is overly burdened with assigned tasks.

In this conflict of interests, the opposition was often between the real and versus the ideal. Ideally, employees want to take care of customers. Harsh reality dictates that task accomplishment will weigh heavily on the minds of employees. An experienced teller admitted, "We run things as smoothly as possible. We wait on customers promptly and happily. We're told to keep our heads and fall apart after the bank closes." In a new employee orientation meeting, one manager reminded staff to "project an 'all is smooth' attitude to customers."

Similar to the theme of community involvement, a sense of "customer orientation" was seen in the selection *of heroes* and the reasoning behind interviewees' choices. For example, one person named a hero as having "an amazing customer focus." Another said her hero possessed "great communication skills." These responses indicate that heroes are admired for their ability to connect with customers and model the dedication that is demanded of the entire staff.

Many organizational *rules* are related to a customer focus. Out of the 17 employees who responded to a question inquiring about unwritten rules, 6 indicated that pampering the customer is an unstated but very real expectation. A new employee said he'd already learned never to tell a customer "No." A seasoned veteran in the Bank added that you "don't make customers mad." Thus, expecting professionalism, as one manager put it, involves an understanding of "how to talk to customers." Values, heroes, and rules all underscore a focus on customers. This flows naturally out of a commitment to the community. The conflict between attention to customers and task accomplishment seems to be an issue for most employees. The organization's higher priority, of course, is taking care of the customer.

Theme 3: Conservative Ideals and Practices

Z Bank has built its reputation around and takes great pride in being conservative, viewing stability and responsibility as its obligations to the community.

Throughout its 92-year history, Z Bank has stood for stability and conservatism. The underlying theme is that conservative, responsible growth is the key to long-lasting success. In our interviews, we did not ask directly for *stories*.

In asking about the history of the bank, however, we discovered a legacy of personal sacrifice and dedication to community that exemplifies the kind of stability that Z Bank desires. During the Depression, James William, owner and president, put his personal assets on the line to save the Bank from financial ruin. Tradition was upheld when the Gregg family acquired the Bank. One employee said the Barnetts "have demonstrated the same care and understanding of community. They have displayed honesty and integrity." These character traits are closely tied to conservatism.

To understand Z's culture, it is crucial to know that the Bank has always valued conservative growth. Mike Barnett, one of Z Bank's principal shareholders, indicated that the bank has "a reputation for a conservative stand; stability and integrity are most important." Consistent with that philosophy is the fact that all of Z Bank's growth has come from within. Never in its history has Z grown through purchasing another banking institution. In contrast, its rival bank grows predominantly through acquiring the assets of other banks. The attitude we discerned could be stated as, "Let *them* be known for innovation and creativity. *We'll* stand for stability, being careful and conservative." As an outsider, Lara noticed immediately the discrepancy in the *physical setting* between public and private areas. She noted rich wood and plush leather furnishings in the lobby of the main bank. She saw expensive, ethnic artwork on the first and second floors. When she went to the third floor (where customers rarely need to go), she saw metal desks, cramped spaces, fluorescent lighting, and antiquated equipment. We immediately connected the public face of the Bank with Z's customer focus; the private face related to its conservative spending in areas where customers will never go. Even the elaborate decor of the Right Town branches enhances the image of Z Bank as a pillar in the community. The main Bank's massive atrium and elaborate tapestries and artwork speak to the stability that Z represents in the community. The nonverbal message that Lara got was, "We've made wise investment choices and can afford these types of luxuries." On the other hand, the Rose Bud convenience store location and the other out-of-town branches project a simpler, much friendlier, nonthreatening environment. This relates to Z's ability to target every clientele. One employee said, "There's a branch for everyone."

While investigating the atmosphere of the organization, we discovered a continuum of conservatism. In the main Bank, the *rules* are most restrictive and the environment most formal. One employee explained, "The main bank has upper society customers while the branches have the common people." Six people mentioned specifically that the branches are more relaxed. One teller compared working in the main Bank to "working in a morgue." Another teller said that the Rose Bud branch is fun because it "doesn't have a 'bank' atmosphere."

Related to atmosphere are unwritten rules dictating acceptable codes of conduct for various locations. For example, one branch manager said that at the main Bank, tellers are spread apart and are not permitted to talk to each other. In contrast, tellers converse freely in several of the branches. Two male employees mentioned that beards were unacceptable at the branches. One branch manager noted the difference in the dress code, specifically saying that the main bank was more formal while the branches "fudged" a little on dress-code policies.

When asked what they would change about the organization, a significant number mentioned the need to be more aggressive financially and more innovative in marketing. One respondent said, "We're basically on target, but we need to sell ourselves better." Another commented, "We don't take advantage of opportunities when they present themselves."

Through stories, physical setting, and unwritten rules, we saw conservative ideals and practices come to life. We found especially interesting the pride that management felt regarding this stance versus the embarrassment that many younger loan officers and staff expressed. A "generation gap" seems to exist between older management and younger management, where younger employees are questioning the wisdom of being so conservative.

Theme 4: Family—The Tie That Binds

A family metaphor exists that unifies employees and links nearly all of Z Bank's activities and programs.

Z Bank has operated for nearly a century under the metaphor of family. "We're one big, happy family" pervades everything management tries to do. The most obvious time period when this can be observed is the holidays. During our interviews, we asked people to comment on *ceremonies or rituals* in the organization. Almost without exception (18 out of 20 respondents), employees mentioned the Christmas season, including such traditions as the annual Christmas banquet, children's party (for the employees' kids), smaller get-togethers, and the open house, Although not explicitly addressed, we got the feeling that this bevy of seasonal activity ties the family atmosphere of the holidays to the familial image of the bank. Other activities that are commonly associated with family include the annual picnic at the president's farm and monthly birthday parties. As Trice and Beyer (1984) describe in their typology of rites, these can be classified as rites of integration because they remind people of their common bond and revive feelings of loyalty.

Like the rest of society, the Z Bank family may have become somewhat dysfunctional. When asking about *rules* related to decision making and management style, we found a discrepancy between management and staff responses. Management believes that decisions come from the bottom up, addressing issues at whatever level of management is appropriate. On the other hand, nonmanagement asserts that decisions come from the top, usually from the mouth of the president or one of the executive vice presidents.

Another way to analyze this information related to decision making is from an insider-outsider perspective. Lara (an outsider) was told by four out of nine respondents that decisions are made by committees. On the other hand, Amy (an insider) was told that even if committees were in place or branch managers were empowered, ultimate authority rested in the hands of the president or executive vice presidents.

The realities of the decision-making process relate directly to the *metaphor* of the traditional family. One employee said she had asked her male branch manager if he ever felt like "daddy taking care of his kids." In other words, the family metaphor sometimes comes across as paternalistic. In reality, true decision making lies in the hands of a few, and the goal of top management is to evaluate decisions or conflict situations in light of what's best for everyone.

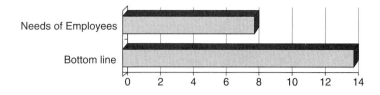

Appendix Figure 15.3 Management's Top Priority

A classic definition of paternalism[1] is that A (in this case, management) assumes it knows better than B (the staff as a whole or individual staff members) what's best for B. One example involves the story of an employee who had worked in the same teller window for more than 10 years. When she asked to do something else, she was "allowed to quit" because they wouldn't accommodate her request. After 12 years of service, she had not earned the right to suggest a different job for herself. Management would not entertain the possibility of a new position for her because they believed they knew better than she where her talents would be utilized best.

The overwhelming "evidence" for this attitude comes from the interview question asking how committed to employee satisfaction the organization is. The top *value* is profitability, sometimes to the detriment of employee satisfaction. Fourteen of the 22 respondents reported that management shows a greater concern for the bottom line than for the individual needs of employees. (See Appendix Figure 15.3.) One loan officer suggested, "One of our shortcomings is the tendency not to hear what is said." Another employee said, "They're committed, but it has to work for Z Bank. The priority is what's good for the bank before the individual." One member of top management explained, "I'm committed to a greater whole—running the organization." This lends further support to the paternalistic attitude that pervades Z Bank, because the individual's needs are subordinated to the greater good.

Looking at rituals, rules, and values reveals a family metaphor that may not be as well suited to defining the culture as it once was. Of course, we realize that in any organization, profitability must be a top concern of management. We sensed, however, a sentiment among employees that this focus may be detrimental to the atmosphere that constitutes Z Bank's culture.

Definition of Culture

The four themes we discovered center around community, customers, conservatism, and family. We believe that a root metaphor of family encompasses these four themes and defines Z Bank's culture. A family, by definition, shows care and concern for its members. It shares a common heritage as well as common interests and goals.

Care and Concern for Its Members

The most obvious theme is that of a family that unifies employees and links all activities. Elements related to this theme were ceremonies and rituals, rules, and values. The ceremonies associated with the Christmas season, especially, communicate care and concern between Z Bank's employees as gifts are exchanged and fellowship is encouraged through get-togethers and parties.

Rules related to decision making revealed two different points of view, each a way that families can make decisions. Some members of the organization believed decisions come from the top, where "Daddy" tells his children how things are going to be done. On the other hand were those who said decisions flow from committees, where all members of the family are consulted and feel free to make contributions.

Common Heritage

Families descend from a common ancestor, with a legacy of beliefs and values passed from generation to generation. Tied together through stories and ideals, they share a heritage that is unmistakable. The theme addressing a common heritage is the conservative ideals and practices evidenced through stories and rules. The legacy of sacrifice that began with James William started a tradition of valuing stability and integrity. Since only five men have served as president in 92 years, stability comes from the top and steadies the entire organization.

Families are characterized by informal codes of conduct defining acceptable behavior for each member. Z Bank's code of conduct includes attitudes about dress, topics of conversation, and a strong work ethic. Also, as in a family, Z's younger employees can be seen as questioning the wisdom of days gone by.

Common Interests and Goals

A family tends to share certain interests and goals. Especially important is the common desire to promote its own health and well-being. After those self-preservation interests are taken care of, the goals of a family turn outward toward making a difference in the lives of those around them. Z's commitment to the surrounding community parallels a family's interest in helping those outside its borders. The theme of community-centeredness was expressed through physical setting and heroes.

As was observed at the Raytown branch, the Z family is interested in its community. The bulletin boards, local newspapers, and conversations indicated a vested interest in local school, church, and civic activities. The heroes highlighted by employees also showed an admiration for leadership that extended to the community. The heroes, in turn, evidenced the value placed on community involvement and service.

Review of Process

Strengths

We believe our greatest strength was using a team approach that paired an organizational insider with an organizational outsider. The outsider brings a fresh perspective, coming into the organization with *no* expectations or preconceived notions. The insider has the advantage of knowing people and understanding both the structure of the organization and its jargon. Another advantage of a team approach is that there is opportunity to spend more time in observation and to interview a more representative number of employees. A related strength was our confidence that we did get a representative sample, observing in five locations and interviewing more than 25% of the entire staff. Finally, we believe we gained the support of management early on and benefited from their suggestions and influence while we completed our observations and interviews.

Limitations

We have pinpointed several areas where we know that experience will remedy many of our limitations in the future. First, we have seen how our inexperience in writing interview questions caused us to "waste" some questions. For example, we found no practical use for the question that asked what a typical day was like. Along those same lines, we realized we could have probed deeper in other areas; especially finding more ways to ask about stories.

Related to our team approach was the feeling that respondents weren't really honest with Lara as the outsider. In looking at interview responses, there is a definite discrepancy between some of the answers she was given compared with some of Amy's. Lara believes respondents "sugarcoated" out of a strong sense of company loyalty. On the other hand, Amy sensed that employees were honest with her, feeling free to express themselves to someone who is "part of the family."

Related to striving for a representative sample was our realization late in the process that we might have biased the data by talking with a large number of employees who had worked for Z Bank for 5 or more years. Since the average length of service is more than 7 years, it may have been statistically representative to speak to so many with long tenures, but we tended to get the same answers repeatedly whereas newer employees might have provided a different perspective. Furthermore, we now see the potential for a managerial bias because we interviewed *so many* in management but only a handful of employees. Only 7 of the 25 interviewed were not related to management in some way.

Conclusion

In this cultural audit, we have discussed the history of Z Bank as well as its heroes, rules, values, and rituals. In doing so, we believe we have painted an accurate portrait of Z Bank. We provided a rationale for our methods and division of labor. We have both explored and supported four themes that capture the essence of the Z Bank culture: community, customers, conservatism, and family. Ultimately, we have defined the culture as a root metaphor: "Z Bank is like a family," and we have explored several facets of family life that also describe the culture of Z Bank. Finally, we have enumerated our strengths and admitted our limitations, knowing that we have learned from each of our mistakes. Through examples, frequency counts, quotes, and paraphrases, it is our hope that we have brought Z Bank to life for all those who read this audit.

Note

1. *Communication Ethics* by Jaksa and Pritchard, p. 210.

Case Study References

Jaksa, J., & Pritchard, M. (1994). *Communication ethics: Methods of analysis.* Belmont, CA: Wadsworth.

Meyer, J. (1995). Tell me a story: Eliciting organizational values from narratives. *Communication Quarterly, 43,* 210–224.

Schall, M. (1983). A communication-rules approach to organizational culture. *Administration Science Quarterly, 28,* 557–581.

Trice, H., & Beyer, J. (1984). Studying organizational culture through rites and ceremonies. *Academy of Management Review, 1,* 653–669.

References

Adams, S. (1996). *The Dilbert principle*. New York: HarperCollins.

Allen, B. J. (1995). "Diversity" and organizational communication. *Journal of Applied Communication, 23*, 143–155.

Autry, J. (1991). *Love and profit: The art of caring leadership*. New York: Avon.

Axley, S. (1984). Managerial and organizational communication in terms of the conduit metaphor. *Academy of Management Review, 9*, 428–437.

Babbie, E. (2001). *The practice of social research* (9th ed.). Belmont, CA: Wadsworth.

Bantz, C., & Pepper, G. (1993). Organizational communication culture. In *Understanding organizations: Interpreting organizational communication cultures* (chap. 2, pp. 17–32). Columbia: University of South Carolina Press.

Barrett, W. (1979). *The illusion of technique*. Garden City, NY: Anchor.

Bellah, R., Madsen, R., Sullivan, W., Swidler, A., & Tipton, S. (1992). *The good society*. New York: Vintage.

Bennis, W. (1986). *Leaders and culture: Orchestrating the organizational culture*. New York: The Conference Board.

Benoit, W. L. (1995). *Accounts, excuses and apologies: A theory of image restoration strategies*. Albany: SUNY Press.

Bolman, L., & Deal, T. (1998). *Reframing organizations* (2nd ed.). San Francisco: Jossey-Bass.

Bormann, E. (1969). *Interpersonal communication in the modern organization*. Englewood Cliffs. NJ: Prentice Hall.

Brenton, A. (1993). Demystifying the magic of language: Critical linguistic case analysis of legitimization of authority. *Journal of Applied Communication Research, 21*, 227–244.

Brenton, A., & Driskill, G. (1991, November). *A pluralistic and critical analysis of organizational outcomes*. Paper presented to the annual meeting of the National Communication Association, Atlanta, GA.

Bridges, W. (1991). *Managing transitions: Making the most of change*. Reading, MA: Perseus.

Brown, M. H. (1990). Defining stories in organizations: Characteristics and functions. In J. A. Anderson (Ed.), *Communication yearbook 13* (pp. 162–190). Newbury Park, CA: Sage.

Chao, J. T., Waltz, P. M., & Gardner, P. H. (1992). Formal and informal mentorships: A comparison of mentoring functions and contrast with nonmentored counterparts. *Personnel Psychology, 45*, 619–636.

Clair, R. P. (1993). The use of framing devices to sequester organizational narratives: Hegemony and harassment. *Communication Monographs, 60*, 113–136.

Clair, R. P. (1998). *Organizing silence: A world of possibilities*. Albany: SUNY Press.

Clampitt, P., Lemke, S., & Hazen, M. (1992). *Thought patterns of effective organizational communicators*. Unpublished manuscript, University of Wisconsin, Green Bay.

Cleveland, J. N., Stockdale, M., & Murphy, K. R. (2000). *Women and men in organizations*. Mahwah, NJ: Lawrence Erlbaum.

Collins, J. (2001). *Good to great: Why some companies make the leap and others don't*. New York: HarperCollins.

Condon, J. (1997). *Good neighbors: Communicating with the Mexicans* (2nd ed.). Yarmouth, ME: Intercultural Press.

Conquergood, D. (1991). Rethinking ethnography: Towards a critical cultural politics. *Communication Monographs, 58*, 179–194.

Conrad, C., & Poole, S. M. (1998). *Strategic organizational communication: Into the twenty-first century* (4th ed.). Fort Worth, TX: Harcourt Brace College.

Cotton, J. L. (1995, May). *Protegee outcomes from formal and informal mentoring*. Paper presented at the annual meeting of the Society for Industrial and Organizational Psychology, Orlando, FL.

Cox, T. H. (1993). *Cultural diversity in organizations: Theory, research and practice*. San Francisco: Berret-Koehler.

Crandall, N., & Wooton, L. (1978). Development strategies of organizational productivity. *California Management Review, 21*, 37–46.

Davis, S. M. (1984). *Managing corporate culture*. Cambridge, MA: Ballinger.

Deal, T., & Kennedy, A. (1982). *Corporate cultures.* New York: Addison-Wesley.

Deal, T., & Kennedy, A. (2000). *Corporate cultures.* Cambridge, MA: Perseus.

Deetz, S. (1991). *Democracy in an age of corporate colonization.* Albany: SUNY Press.

Deetz, S., Tracy, S., & Simpson, J. (2000). *Leading organizations through transition: Communication and cultural change.* Thousand Oaks: CA: Sage.

DeWine, S. (1994). *The consultant's craft: Improving organizational communication.* New York: St. Martin's.

Dodd, C. (1997). *Intercultural communication.* Dubuque, IA: McGraw-Hill.

Driskill, G. (1995). Managing cultural differences: A rules analysis in a bi-cultural organization. *Howard Journal of Communications, 5*(4), 353–379.

Driskill, G., & Downs, C. (1995). Hidden differences in competent communication: A case study of Asian Indians in a bi-national organization. *International Journal of Intercultural Relations, 19*(4), 505–522.

Driskill, G., & Honey, M. (1994, April). *Think aloud interviews and problem solving strategies: A comparison of competent and non-competent co-worker communication.* Paper presented to the Central States Communication Association, Oklahoma City, OK.

Driskill, G., & Meyer, J. (1994, April). *Purple monsters eating water fountains: Action research and children's language games.* Paper presented at the meeting of the Central States Communication Association, Oklahoma City, OK.

Driskill, G., & Meyer, J. (1996, November). *Communication patterns in the day care organization: An application of the coordinated management of meaning.* Paper presented to the Speech Communication Association, San Diego, CA.

Eblen, A., & Eblen, J. (1987). *A sense of place: Setting as symbol in an organizational culture.* Paper presented at the annual meeting of the Speech Communication Association, Boston.

Eisenberg, E. (1984). Ambiguity as strategy in organizational communication. *Communication Monographs, 51,* 227–242.

Eisenberg, E., Andrews, L., Murphy, A., & Laine-Timmerman, L. (1999). Transforming organizations through communication. In P. Salem (Ed.), *Organizational communication and change* (pp. 125–147). Cresskill, NJ: Hampton Press.

Eisenberg, E., & Goodall, H. (2001). *Organizational communication: Balancing creativity and constraint* (2nd ed.). New York: St. Martin's.

Eisenberg, E., & Riley, P. (1988). Organizational symbols and sense-making. In G. M. Goldhaber & G. A. Barnett (Eds.), *Handbook of organizational communication* (pp. 131–158). Norwood, NJ: Ablex.

Eisenberg, E., & Riley, P. (2001). Organizational culture. In F. M. Jablin & L. L. Putnam (Eds.), *The new handbook of organizational communication* (pp. 291–322). Thousand Oaks, CA: Sage.

Fairhurst, G., & Sarr, R. (1996). *The art of framing: Managing the language of leadership.* San Francisco: Jossey-Bass.

Fisher, W. (1987). *Human communication as narration: Toward a philosophy of reason, value, and action.* Columbia: University of South Carolina Press.

Florida, R. (2002). *The rise of the creative class and how it's transforming work, leisure, community, and everyday life.* New York: Basic Books.

Fowler, R. (1986). *Linguistic criticism.* Oxford, UK: Oxford University Press.

Frederick, W. (1995). *Values, nature, and culture in the American corporation.* New York: Oxford University Press.

Frost, P., Moore, L., Louis, M., Lundberg, C., & Martin, J. (1985). *Organizational culture.* Beverly Hills, CA: Sage.

Gardner, J. (1990). *On leadership.* New York: Free Press.

Geertz, C. (1973). *The interpretation of cultures.* New York: Basic Books.

Giddens, A. (1979). *Central problems in social theory.* London: Macmillan.

Goodall, H. L. (1989). *Casing a promised land.* Carbondale: Southern Illinois University Press.

Harre, H., & Secord, P. F. (1973). *The explanation of social behavior.* Totowa, NJ: Littlefield, Adams.

Harris, L. (1979). *Communication competence: Empirical tests of a systematic model.* Unpublished doctoral dissertation, University of Massachusetts, Amherst.

Harris, P., & Moran, R. (2000). *Managing cultural differences: Global leadership strategies for the 21st century* (6th ed.). Houston, TX: Gulf Professional.

Hart, R. (2000). *Diction 5.0* [Computer software]. Thousand Oaks, CA: Sage.

Harter, L. M., Stephens, R. J., & Japp, P. M. (2000). President Clinton's apology for the Tuskegee syphilis experiment: A narrative of remembrance, redefinition, and reconciliation. *Howard Journal of Communications, 11,* 19–35.

Hofstede, G. (2003). *Culture's consequences: Comparing values, behaviors, institutions and organizations across nations.* Newbury Park, CA: Sage.

Holmes, M. (1988). *Depth-interpretation of organizational memorandum.* Paper presented at the annual meeting of the Speech Communication Association.

Jung, C. (1964). *Man and his symbols.* London: Aldus Books.

Kanter, R. M. (1977). *Men and women of the corporation.* New York: Basic Books.

Kirkwood, W. (1983). Story-telling and self confrontation: Parables as communication strategies. *Quarterly Journal of Speech, 69,* 56–74.

Kirkwood, W. (1985). Parables as metaphors and examples. *Quarterly Journal of Speech, 71,* 422–440.

Kirkwood, W. (1992). Narrative and the rhetoric of possibility. *Communication Monographs, 59,* 30–47.

Knoten, T. (1999). The Foreign Corrupt Practices Act: Practicable considerations for U.S. corporations. *Journal of the Missouri Bar, 55*(1). Retrieved January 21, 2004, from http://mobar.org/journal/1999/janfeb/knoten.htm

Kotter, J. P. (1995, March-April). Leading change: Why transformation efforts fail. *Harvard Business Review,* pp. 59–67.

Kotter, J., & Heskett, J. (1992). *Corporate culture and performance.* New York: Macmillan.

Kramer, M., & Noland, T. (1999). Communication during job promotions: A case of ongoing assimilation. *Journal of Application Communication Research, 27*(4), 335–355.

Kreps, G. I. (1983). Using interpretive research: Development of a socialization program at RCA. In L. Putnam & M. Pacanowsky (Eds.), *Communication and organizations: An interpretive approach* (pp. 243–254). Beverly Hills, CA: Sage.

Kunda, G. (1993). *Engineering culture: Control and commitment in a high-tech corporation.* Philadelphia: Temple University Press.

Laird, A. (1982). *An investigation of communication rules and productivity in three organizations.* Unpublished doctoral dissertation, University of Kansas.

Larkey, L. K. (1996). The development and validation of the workforce diversity questionnaire: An instrument to assess interactions in diverse workgroups. *Management Communication Quarterly, 9,* 296–337.

Levi-Strauss, C. (1967). *The scope of anthropology.* New York: Jonathan Cape.

Louis, M. R. (1985). Perspectives on organizational culture. In P. J. Frost, L. F. Moore, M. R. Louis, C. C. Lundbert, & J. Martin (Eds.), *Organizational culture.* Newbury Park, CA: Sage.

Mali, P. (1978). *Improving total productivity.* New York: John Wiley.

Marris, P. (1974). *Loss and change.* New York: Pantheon.

Martin, J. (1992). *Cultures in organizations: Three perspectives.* New York: Oxford University Press.

Meares, M., Oetzel, J., Torres, A., Derkacs, D., & Ginossar, T. (2004). Employee mistreatment and muted voices in the culturally diverse workplace. *Journal of Applied Communication Research, 32*(1), 4–27.

Meyer, J. (1992). *Values in narratives: A key to studying culture in organizations.* Paper presented at the Speech Communication Association, Chicago.

Meyer, J. (1994, April). *Childcare values: A look inside day care culture.* Paper presented at the Central States Communication Association, Oklahoma City, OK.

Meyer, J. (1995). Tell me a story: Eliciting organizational values from narratives. *Communication Quarterly, 43,* 210–224.

Meyer, J. (1997). Humor in member narratives: Uniting and dividing at work. *Western Journal of Communication, 61,* 188–208.

Meyer, J. (2000). Humor as a double-edged sword: Four functions of humor in communication. *Communication Theory, 10*(3), 310–331.

Meyerson, D., & Martin, J. (1987). Cultural change: An integration of three different views. *Journal of Management Studies, 24,* 625–647.

Miles, M., & Huberman, A. (1984). *Qualitative data analysis: A sourcebook of new methods.* Beverly Hills, CA: Sage.

Miller, V., & Jablin, F. (1991). Information seeking during organizational entry. *Academy of Management Review, 16,* 92–120.

Moran, R., & Harris, P. (1982). *Managing cultural synergy.* Houston, TX: Gulf.

Morgan, C. (2004). Corporate governance. Retrieved January 19, 2004, from http://www .acxiom.com/default.aspx?ID=2192&Country_Code=USA

Morgan, G. (1986). *Images of organization.* Newbury Park, CA: Sage.

Morgan, G. (1997). *Images of organization* (2nd ed.). Newbury Park, CA: Sage.

Mumby, D. (1993). *Narrative and social control.* Newbury Park, CA: Sage.

Mumby, D. (1997). The problem of hegemony: Rereading Gramsci for organizational studies. *Western Journal of Communication, 61,* 343–375.

Nicotera, A., & Cushman, D. (1992). Organizational ethics: A within-organization view. *Journal of Applied Communication Research, 20*(4), 437–462.

O'Brien, C. (1980). *A rule-based approach to communication within a formal organization: Theory and case study.* Unpublished doctoral dissertation, University of Massachusetts, Amherst.

Ouchi, W. (1981). *Theory Z*. Reading, MA: Addison-Wesley.

Pacanowsky, M., & O'Donnell-Trujillo, N. (1982). Communication and organizational cultures. *Western Journal of Speech Communication, 46,* 115–130.

Pacanowsky, M., & O'Donnell-Trujillo, N. (1983). Organizational communication as cultural performance. *Communication Monographs, 50,* 126–147.

Patel, A., & Reinsch, L. (2003). Companies can apologize: Corporate apologies and legal liability. *Business Communication Quarterly, 66,* 9–25.

Pearce, W. (1994). *Interpersonal communication: Making social worlds.* New York: HarperCollins.

Peters, T., & Waterman, R. (1982). *In search of excellence.* New York: Harper & Row.

Poole, M. S. (1992). Structuration and the group communication process. In L. Samovar & R. Cathcart (Eds.), *Small group communication: A reader* (6th ed.). Dubuque, IA: William C. Brown.

Poole, M., Seibold, D., & McPhee, R. (1986). A structurational approach to theory-building in group decision-making research. In R. Hirokawa & M. Poole (Eds.), *Communication and group decision making.* Newbury Park, CA: Sage.

Prato, L. (2000). Asking the tough questions: Debate over a controversial interview with Pete Rose puts the spotlight on sports journalism. *American Journalism Review, 22,* 78.

Rauschenberg, G. (1989). *Comparing official metaphors to myths and stories: Critical incidents as shared realities.* Paper presented at the annual meeting of the International Communication Association, San Francisco.

Rosenfeld, L. B., Richman, J. M., & May, S. K. (2004). Information adequacy, job satisfaction, and organizational culture in a dispersed-network organization. *Journal of Applied Communication Research, 32,* 28–54.

Saffold, G. (1998). Culture traits, strength, and organizational performance: Moving beyond "strong" culture. *Academy of Management Review, 13,* 546–558.

Schall, M. (1983). A communication-rules approach to organizational culture. *Administrative Science Quarterly, 28,* 557–581.

Schein, E. (1992). *Organizational culture and leadership* (2nd ed.). San Francisco: Jossey-Bass.

Scher, S. J., & Darley, J. M. (1997). How effective are things people say to apologize? Effects of the realization of the apology speech act. *Journal of Psycholinguistic Research, 26,* 127–141.

Seeger, M., & Ulmer, R. (2003). Explaining Enron: Communication and responsible leadership. *Management Communication Quarterly, 17*(1), 58–84.

Shafron, A. (2004). Aaron Feurstein: Bankrupt and wealthy. Retrieved January 19, 2004, from http://www.aish.com/societyWork/work/Aaron_Feuerstein_BankruptandWealthy.asp

Shakespeare, W. (1954). *As you like it* (S. Burchell, Ed.). New Haven, CT: Yale University Press.

Shockley-Zalabak, P., & Morley, D. D. (1994). Creating a culture: A longitudinal examination of the influence on management and employee values on communication rule stability and emergence. *Human Communication Research, 20,* 334–355.

Sigman, S. J. (1980). On communication rules from a social perspective. *Human Communication Research, 7,* 37–51.

Singe, P. (1990). *The fifth discipline: The art and practice of the learning organization.* Garden City, NY: Doubleday.

Smircich, L. (1983). Concepts of culture and organizational analysis. *Administrative Science Quarterly, 28,* 339–358.

Smith, P., & Peterson, M. (1989). *Leadership, organizations, and culture.* London: Sage.

Smith, R., & Eisenberg, E. (1987). Conflict at Disneyland: A root-metaphor analysis. *Communication Monographs, 54,* 365–380.

Spitzberg, B., & Hecht, M. (1984). A component model of relational competence. *Human Communication Research, 10*(4), 575–599.

Stablien, R., & Nord, W. (1985). Practical and emancipatory interests in organizational symbolism: A review and evaluation. *Journal of Management, 11,* 13–28.

Strasberg, L. (1987). *A dream of passion: The development of the method.* Boston: Little, Brown.

Steers, R. (1977). *Organizational effectiveness: A behavioral view.* Santa Monica, CA: Goodyear.

Sugimoto, N. (1997). A Japan-U.S. comparison of apology styles. *Communication Research, 24,* 349–370.

Tompkins, P. K., & Cheney, G. (1985). Communication and unobtrusive control in contemporary organizations. In R. D. McPhee & P. K. Tompkins (Eds.), *Organizational communication: Traditional themes and new directions.* Newbury Park, CA: Sage.

Trice, H., & Beyer, J. (1984). Studying organizational cultures through rites and ceremonials. *Academy of Management Review, 9,* 653–669.

Ulmer, R. (2001). Effective crises management through established stakeholder relationships. *Management Communication Quarterly, 14*(4), 590–615.

U.S. Census. (2004). *U.S. interim projection by age, sex, race, and Hispanic origin.* Retrieved August 27, 2004, from http://www.census.gov/ipc/www/usinterimproj

Varner, I., & Beamer, L. (1995). *Intercultural communication the global workplace.* Chicago: Irwin.

Vineberg, S. (1991). *Method actors: Three generations of an American acting style.* New York: Schirmer Books.

Weick, K. E. (1979). *The social psychology of organizing* (2nd ed.). Reading, MA: Addison-Wesley.

Weick, K. E. (1995). *Sensemaking in organizations.* Thousand Oaks, CA: Sage.

Zak, M. W. (1994). It's like a prison in there. *Journal of Business and Technical Communication, 8,* 282–298.

Index

Action plans
    for change, 195–196
    communication, 196–199
    organizational development, 200–203
    recommendations, 203–206
Adams, S., 18
African Americans, 133, 138–139
Alien cultures, 84–87
Allen, B. J., 136
Ambiguity, 53–54, 147–148
Amy, H. A., 207
Andrews, L., 195
Apprehension, 90
Asian Americans, 133, 139
Atom analogy, 6
Autry, J., 187
Axley, S., 44

Babbie, E., 17
Barrett, W., 186, 196
Beamer, L., 191
Bellah, R., 164
Bennis, W., 171
Benoit, W. L., 104
Beyer, J., 49, 56, 81, 82, 214
Bolman, L., 33, 39, 49, 151, 171, 172, 174, 179, 180
Bormann, E., 58, 174
Bracketing, 79
Brenton, A., 45, 54, 140, 188
Bridges, W., 146–147, 152, 153
Brown, M. H., 17, 38, 45
Bryant, Kobe, 104

Caucasians, 132–133
Change
    action plans, 195–196
    cultural approach, 149
    forces driving, 145
    initiating, 194–195
    messages, 155–156
    metaphor and, 151–154
    plan, 157
    reactions to, 145–147
    reframing and, 171–173
    scenario, 158–159
    suggestions for, 152–154
Chao, J. T., 138
Cheney, G., 42, 178
Clair, R. P., 138
Clampitt, P., 151
Cleveland, J. N., 134
Clinton, Bill, 104, 175
Cognition, 30
Collins, J., 29, 190, 191

Communication
    change messages, 155–156
    contextualized, 197
    development, 196–199
    ethics, 169
    nonverbal, 93
    patterns, 18
    specific behavior, 197
    style, 50–51, 56
Condon, J., 29
Conflict reduction, 82
Conquergood, D., 39
Conrad, C., 19
Conservatism, 212–213
Constructs, 17, 21
Content analysis
    application, 106–107
    definition, 104
    rehearsal, 110
Context, 51–53
Cooperation, 91
Cotton, J. L., 138
Cox, T. H., 132, 133
Crandall, N., 187
Creative class, 135–136
Critical linguistic analysis, 108, 110
Cultural analysis
    benefits, 19–20
    communication patterns, 18
    data interpretation, 21
    data synthesis, 21
    determining, 9
    examples, 129–130
    insights, 7–8
    introduction, 65–69
    meaning, 5–7
    multiply method approach, 69
    in practice, 21
    proposal, 36
    reflection, 11–12
    single method approach, 69–70
    student example. *See* Student cultural analysis.
    textual, 104–108
    value of, 20
    writing about, 22–23
Cultural elements
    ambiguity, 53–54
    communication style, 50–51
    context, 51–53
    definition, 38
    history, 52
    identifying, 21
    informal rules, 46, 49–50
    interactive, 48–51

language/nonverbal, 45
metaphors, 46, 60–61
place, 53
reliance on, 38–39
rituals, 48–49
roles, 46–48
stories, 44–45, 57–58
symbols, 43–44
understanding, 39–41
values, 42–43
web sites, 55–56
Cultures
adaptive, 190–192
appropriate, 190
change and, 152–154
concept of, 21, 28–30
as constructs, 17
definitions, 27–28, 30–34
interpreting, model for, 120
levels, 32–33
manipulating, 189
meaning, 5
as metaphors, 29–30, 33–34
multiple views, 179–180
perspectives, 147–150
root metaphors, 31
shared cognition, 30
strong, 41, 189
unconscious aspects, 30
as variable, 28–29
weak, 41
Cushman, D., 162
Customer focus, 212

Darley, J. M., 104
Data collection
categorization, 81
interviewers, 67
methods overview, 66t
multiple methods, 69, 109, 111–112
objectivity and, 69
observations, 65–67
Davis, S. M., 170
Deal, T., 17, 28, 29, 33, 39, 46, 49, 128, 151, 171,
    172, 174, 179, 180, 189
Deetz, S., 7, 88, 146, 153, 172–173, 188
Definition, function of, 30
Degradation, rite of, 81
Dell computers, 111–112
Derkacs, D., 17, 167
DeWine, S., 195
Differentiation perspective, 148
Disney, Walt, 52
Diversity
creating, 139t
defining, 132
dominate groups, 136–140
embracing, 132–135
integrating, 135–136
marginalized groups, 136–140
survey, 140–143
understanding, 136–140
Dodd, C., 39, 133
Dominant groups, 136–140
Downs, C., 30, 59, 134
Driskill, G., 30, 57, 59, 134, 151, 188

Eblen, A., 43
Eblen, J., 43
Ecologizing, 166
Economizing, 163–164

Effectiveness
adaptive cultures, 190–192
appropriate cultures, 189
cultural links to, 192t
definition, 187–188
drawbacks, 190
gauging, 193
measuring, 188–189
strong cultures and, 189
Eisenberg, E., 17, 45, 46, 54, 58, 77, 131, 146, 161, 195
Enhancement, rite of, 82
Ethics
communication, 169
guidance, 161–162
value tensions, 162–163
Evolution, 146
Exploration, 90–91

Fairhurst, G., 60, 151, 177
Feuerstein Aaron, 161
Fiorina, Carly, 107
Fisher, W., 57
Florida, R., 53, 134–135, 138
Focus groups, 94
Fonda, Jane, 88
Fowler, R., 108
Fraternities, 138–139
Frederick, W., 162–164
Frost, P., 17

Gardner, J., 163
Gardner, P. H., 138
Geertz, C., 27, 28, 30
Giddens, A., 6, 18
Ginossar, T., 17, 167
Goodall, H. L., 58, 65, 131, 161

Harre, H., 89
Harris, L., 30, 89
Harris, P., 29, 133
Hart, R., 107
Harter, L. M., 104
Hazen, M., 151
Hecht, M., 151
Heroes
analyzing, 108
definition, 56
examples, 47
identification, 56
Heskett, J., 17, 164, 189, 190–191
Hewlett-Packard computers, 111
Hispanic Americans, 133
History
continuity, 176
cultural, 52
definition, 56
student analysis, 207–208
Hofstede, G., 29, 165
Holmes, M., 44
Honey, M., 151
Hubermann, A., 69

Improvisation, 144–145
Information, candid, 89–90
Information, valid, 89–90
Informed consent form, 71–72
Integration, rite of, 82
Integration perspective, 147–148
Interpretation
defining culture, 119–121
elements, 115–116

finding themes, 116–119
plot defining, 119–121
process of, 120–121
skill definition, 121–123
subplots, 116–117
time, 114–115
validity check, 123–124
write-up guides, 124–125
Interviewees
motivating, 90
pauses, 93
rapport with, 89–90
Interviews. *See also* Questions
alien culture, 101–102
ethnographic, 97
focus groups, 94
insider, 95
observation link, 67, 96–97
outsiders, 95
partners, 94
principles, 89–94
qualitative, 100
recording, 93–94
samples, 97–99

Jablin, J., 69
Jaksa, J., 215
Japp, P. M., 104
Jigsaw puzzle analogy, 6
Jobs, Steve, 135
Jung, C., 30

Kanter, R. M., 136
Kennedy, A., 17, 28, 29, 46, 128, 189
Kirkwood, W., 57
Knoten, T., 162
Kotter, J., 17, 153, 164, 189, 190–191
Kramer, M., 67
Kreps, G. I., 138
Kunda, G., 189

Laine-Timmerman, L., 195
Laird, A., 137
Language
analyzing, 108
leadership use, 177–178
nonverbal, 45, 56
usage, 108
Lay, Kenneth, 104
Leaders
assessment, 182–184
case study, 184–185
political, 180
reframing techniques, 171–173
symbolic, 173–180
Lemke, S., 151
Levi-Strauss, C., 30
Loss, 146
Louis, M. R., 15, 17, 40
Lundberg, C., 17

Madsen, R., 164
Mali, P., 188
Marginalized groups, 136–140
Marris, P., 145, 146
Martin, J., 17, 40, 54, 119, 120, 147, 148, 150, 151
McPhee, R., 18, 19
Meares, M., 17, 167
Meetings, 64
Metaphors
change and, 151–154
culture, 32–33
definition, 46, 56

examples, 46
game of, 60–61
identification, 46
mutates, 77
in themes, 119–120
Method acting
core of, 13
improvisation, 144–145
interviews, 88–89
introduction to, 68
observations, 74
tactics, 65
Meyer, J., 30, 38, 43, 45, 49, 57, 70, 211
Miles, M., 69
Miller, V., 69
Mission statement, 208
Moore, L., 17
Moran, R., 29, 133
Morgan, C., 163
Morgan, G., 33, 119, 151
Morley, D. D., 172
Mumby, D., 138
Mundane, 77
Murphy, A., 195
Murphy, K. R., 134

Narratives. *See* Stories
National Pan-Hellenic Council, 138–140
Nicotera, A., 162
Noland, T., 67
Nord, W., 150

Objectivity, 69
O'Brien, C., 137
Observations
alien cultures, 84–87
conducting, 77–81
data collection, 65–67
importance, 74
interviews link, 96–97
methods, 74–77
organizational variety, 82–83
rites, 81–82
O'Donnell-Trujillo, N., 17, 39
Oetzel, H., 17
Oetzel, J., 167
Organizations
changing, 16–17
definition, 7
development, 200–203
identifying, 10
insider advantage, 10
privilege, 136–137
selecting, 8–10
typology, 17
Ouchi, W., 29
Outlaws
definition, 47, 56
examples, 47–48
identification, 48

Pacanowsky, M., 17, 39
Passage, rites of, 81
Patel, A., 104
Paternalism, 215
Performance reviews, 187
Perspectives, 147–148
Pervasiveness, 116
Peters, T., 29, 40, 189
Place, 53
Poole, M., 18, 19
Poole, M. S., 19
Power aggrandizement, 164–165

Prato, L., 104
Pritchard, M., 215
Privilege, 136–137
Pronoun use, 108
Proposals, 36

Qualitative surveys, 100
Questions. *See also* Interviews
    closed, 91
    confusing issues, 108
    follow-up, 92
    insider, 79
    leading, 92–93
    open, 91
    probes, 93
    qualitative interviews, 100
    what, 78
    why, 78
    wording, 91–92

Rapport, 89–90
Rauschenberg, G., 45
Reagan, Ronald, 174, 175
Recording techniques, 93–94
Reframing, 171–173
Reinsch, L., 104
Renewal, rite of, 82
Rhetorical analysis, 104
Riley, P., 17
Rites, 81–82
Rituals
    aspects, 56
    capitalizing on, 175
    definition, 48–49
    examples, 49
    identification, 49
Roosevelt, Franklin D., 171
Rose, Pete, 104
Rosenfel, L. B., 41
Rules, 49–50, 56

Saffold, G., 116
Salience, 117
Sarr, R., 60, 151, 177
Schall, M., 30, 38, 50, 211
Schein, E., 28, 30, 31, 40, 42, 173
Scher, S. J., 104
Schock-Keck, L., 207
Secord, P. F., 89
Seeger, M., 42, 163
Seibold, D., 18, 19
Shafron, A., 161
Shakespeare, William, 3, 12
Shockley-Zalabak, P., 172
Sigman, S., 49
Simpson, J., 7, 88, 146, 153, 172–173, 188
Singe, P., 187
Smircich, L., 28, 30
Smith, R., 45, 46, 54, 77, 146
Spin, 178
Spitzberg, B., 151
Stablien, R., 150
Steers, R., 187
Stephens, R. J., 104
Stockdale, M., 134
Stories
    definition, 44, 56
    examples, 44
    identification, 44–45
    role of, 57–58
    symbolic leaders and, 174–175

Strasberg, L., 13, 16, 38, 73, 74, 103, 194
Structuration, 18–19, 22
Student cultural analysis
    definition of culture, 215–216
    framing, 210–215
    historical perspective, 207–208
    institutional structure, 208
    limitations, 217
    methods, 208–209
    mission statement, 208
    strengths, 216–217
Substitution, 146
Sugimoto, N., 104
Sullivan, W., 164
Summary sheets, 115
Surveys, 100, 140–143
Swidler, A., 164
Symbols
    definition, 43, 56
    examples, 43
    identification, 44

Textual analysis
    approaches, 104–105
    definition, 104
    methods, selection, 106–109
    texts for, choosing, 105–106
    valid/credible, 105
Themes
    finding, 116–119
    interpretation, 120–121
    root metaphors, 120
    underlying, 120
Tipton, S., 164
Tompkins, P. K., 42, 178
Torres, A., 17, 167
Tracy, S., 7, 88, 146, 153, 172–173, 188
Trice, H., 49, 56, 81, 82, 214

Ulmer, R., 42, 52, 161, 163
U.S. Census, 132–133

Values
    analyzing, 108
    conflicts, 161–167
    definition, 42, 55–56
    diversity, 135–136
    equality, 164–165
    examples, 42
    hierarchy, 164–165
    human, 163–164
    identification, 42–43
    language and, 177–178
    macroenvironment, 166
    microenvironment, 166
    profit, 163–164
    symbolic elements, 43
    tensions, 162–163
Varner, I., 191
Verb use, 108
Vineberg, S., 13, 38, 65, 88, 161
Voight, Jon, 88

Walton, Sam, 47, 52
Waltz, P. M., 138
Waterman, R., 29, 40, 189
Weick, K. E., 67, 77, 115–116
Wooten, L., 187

Zak, M. W., 132

About the Authors

Angela Laird Brenton is Dean of the College of Professional Studies at the University of Arkansas at Little Rock. She has taught graduate classes in Organizational Culture since 1982 at UALR, Pepperdine University, Abilene Christian University, and Southwest Missouri State University. She has published a number of articles about using qualitative research methods to study organizational communication—from critical linguistic analysis of organizational texts to analysis of organizational identification. She collaborated on the workbook with Gerald Driskill using materials she has developed over the years of teaching and consulting in the areas of organizational culture.

With her current administrative duties as dean of an eight-department college, she teaches primarily in the area of conflict analysis and mediation and plans future writing projects in that field. She is particularly interested in conflict analysis in religious and nonprofit organizations, as well as developing consensus in public policy disputes. She has been appointed as a founding faculty member of the Clinton School of Public Service, associated with the Clinton Presidential Library in Little Rock, and is currently developing a course in Communication Process and Conflict Transformation for that innovative master's degree in public service.

Gerald W. Driskill is an Associate Professor of Speech Communication at the University of Arkansas at Little Rock. He has taught graduate classes in Organizational Culture, Intercultural Communication, and Organizational Development and Communication at UALR since 1993. He has taught Managerial Communication in Bangkok, Thailand, and has published a number of organizational communication articles based on observation and interview transcript analysis in a multinational firm to analysis of communication patterns in day-care cultures. He has served as president of the local chapter of ASTD (American Society for Training and Development). This workbook grew from his collaboration with Angi Brenton as he received positive feedback from mid-level managers and others in the ASTD network who used the course material in their own organizations.

He continues to teach in the areas of organizational and intercultural communication. On campus he takes a lead role in internationalizing the curriculum. His current participant observer research focuses on communication and unity among religious, nonprofit, and government organizations engaged in community building. This research provides a window into issues relevant to leaders creating a culture of community mindedness within their organizations.